History of the People of Israel

Volume 1

History
of the
People of Israel
Till the time
of
King David

**By
Ernest Renan**

© Ross & Perry, Inc. 2001 All rights reserved.

Protected under the Berne Convention. Published 2001

Printed in The United States of America

Ross & Perry, Inc. Publishers
717 Second St., N.E., Suite 200
Washington, D.C. 20002
Telephone (202) 675-8300
Facsimile (801) 459-7535
info@RossPerry.com

SAN 253-8555

Library of Congress Control Number: 2001096571
http://www.rossperry.com

ISBN 1-931641-97-8

Image on cover provided by Rev. John DeLancey, Tour Leader,
www.biblicalisraeltours.com

∞ The paper used in this publication meets the requirements for permanence
established by the American National Standard for Information Sciences
"Permanence of Paper for Printed Library Materials" (ANSI Z39.48-1984).

All rights reserved. No copyrighted part of this publication may be reproduced,
stored in a retrieval system, or transmitted, in any form or by any means,
electronic, photocopying, recording, or otherwise, without the prior written
permission of the publisher.

CONTENTS.

PREFACE vii

Book I.

THE BENI-ISRAEL IN THE NOMAD STATE DOWN TO THEIR SETTLEMENT IN THE LAND OF CANAAN.

CHAPTER I.
ARRIVAL OF THE SEMITES IN SYRIA.—CANAANITES . . . 1

CHAPTER II.
THE NOMAD SEMITES 11

CHAPTER III.
RELIGIOUS CALLING OF THE NOMAD SEMITES 22

CHAPTER IV.
MONOTHEISM, ABSENCE OF MYTHOLOGY 38

CHAPTER V.
ANCIENT BABYLONIAN INFLUENCE 54

CHAPTER VI.
THE NAME OF IAHVEH 69

CONTENTS.

CHAPTER VII.
THE HEBREW OR TERACHITE GROUP 76

CHAPTER VIII.
THE BENI-JACOB, OR BENI-ISRAEL 88

CHAPTER IX.
RELIGION OF THE BENI-ISRAEL 99

CHAPTER X.
THE BENI-ISRAEL IN EGYPT 113

CHAPTER XI.
INFLUENCE OF EGYPT UPON ISRAEL 121

CHAPTER XII.
EXODUS OF ISRAEL 131

CHAPTER XIII.
ISRAEL IN THE DESERT OF PHARAN 141

CHAPTER XIV.
SINAI 157

CHAPTER XV.
JOURNEYING TOWARDS CANAAN 171

Book II.

THE BENI-ISRAEL AS FIXED TRIBES, FROM THE OCCUPATION OF THE COUNTRY OF CANAAN TO THE DEFINITIVE ESTABLISHMENT OF THE KINGDOM OF DAVID.

CHAPTER I.

The Beni-Israel beyond the Dead Sea and the Jordan . 179

CHAPTER II.

The Conquest of the Region beyond Jordan . . . 188

CHAPTER III.

Judah and Benjamin 200

CHAPTER IV.

The Conquest of Mount Ephraim and the North . . 207

CHAPTER V.

Development of Materialist Iahvehism 218

CHAPTER VI.

The Oracle of Iahveh 228

CHAPTER VII.

The Judges 241

CHAPTER VIII.

Deborah 253

CHAPTER IX.

First Attempts at Royalty.—Gideon, Abimelech . . 259

CONTENTS.

CHAPTER X.
GILEADITE LEGENDS.—JEPHTHAH 273

CHAPTER XI.
THE DANITES.—MYTH OF SAMSON 281

CHAPTER XII.
THE CIVIL WARS OF THE TRIBES 289

CHAPTER XIII.
PROGRESS OF THE RELIGIOUS AND POLITICAL ORGANISATION OF SAMUEL 301

CHAPTER XIV.
INSTITUTION OF ROYALTY 314

CHAPTER XV.
REIGN OF SAUL 322

CHAPTER XVI.
DAVID'S EARLY LIFE.—DEATH OF SAUL 331

CHAPTER XVII.
ISH-BOSHETH SUCCEEDS SAUL.—DAVID KING OF HEBRON . 350

CHAPTER XVIII.
DAVID KING OF JERUSALEM 357

PREFACE.

For a philosophic mind, that is to say for one engrossed in the origin of things, there are not more than three histories of real interest in the past of humanity: Greek history, the history of Israel, and Roman history. These three histories combined constitute what may be called the history of civilisation, civilisation being the result of the alternate collaboration of Greece, Judea, and Rome. Greece in my opinion has an exceptional past, for she founded, in the fullest sense of the word, rational and progressive humanism. Our science, our arts, our literature, our philosophy, our moral code, our political code, our strategy, our diplomacy, our maritime and international law, are of Greek origin. The framework of human culture created by Greece is susceptible of indefinite enlargement, but it is complete in its several parts. Progress will consist in constantly developing what Greece has conceived, in executing the designs which she has, so to speak, traced out for us.

Greece had only one thing wanting in the circle of her moral and intellectual activity, but this was an important void; she despised the humble and did not feel the need of a just God. Her philosophers, while dreaming of the immortality of the soul, were tolerant towards the iniquities of this world. Her religions were merely elegant municipal playthings; the idea of a universal religion never occurred to her. The ardent genius of a small tribe established in an obscure corner of Syria seemed created to supply this void in the Hellenic intellect. Israel never stood quietly by to see the world so badly governed, under the authority of a God reputed to be just. Her sages burned with anger over the abuses of the world. A bad man, dying old, rich, and at ease, kindled their fury, and the prophets in the ninth century B.C. elevated this idea to the height of a dogma. The Israelitish prophets were heated declaimers, such as we of the present day should denounce as socialists and anarchists. They were fanatics in the cause of social justice, and loudly proclaimed that if the world was not just, or capable of becoming so, it had better be destroyed—a view which, if utterly wrong, was very fertile in results, for, like all the doctrines of despair, such as the Russian nihilism of the present day, it led to deeds of heroism and brought about a grand awakening of the forces of humanity. The founders of Christianity, who were the direct successors of the prophets, spent their strength in an incessant call for the end of the world, and, strange to say, did in reality transform the world. Through Jesus, the apostles, and the second generation of Christians, there was founded a religion evolved from Judaism, which three centuries later imposed itself upon the leading races of humanity, and took the place of the petty patriotic playthings of ancient cities. With the churches, which were merely synagogues opened to the uncircumcised, was born an idea of popular association which encroached deeply upon the democracy of the Greek cities. Christianity, in a word, becomes in history as important an element as the liberal rationalism of the Greeks, though in some respects less assured of perpetuity. The tendency which leads the nineteenth century to secularise everything, to make a host of things lay instead of ecclesiastical, is a reaction against Christianity; but even supposing that it attains its end, Christianity will leave an imperishable trace of its existence. Liberalism will no longer have the monopoly of the government of the world. England and America will long preserve the vestiges of Biblical influence; and with us in France, the socialists — who are, unknown to themselves, the disciples of the prophets — will always bring the practical politicians to terms.

The great creations of Greece and Judea would not have overcome the world all by themselves. The world, to make it ready to accept Hellenism and Christianity, had to be prepared and made smooth, so to speak, for centuries beforehand. A great humanitary force had to be created, — a force powerful enough to beat down the obstacles which local patriotism offered to the idealistic propaganda of Greece and Judea. Rome fulfilled this extraordinary function. Her prodigious heroism created the empire of force in the world, and this force in reality served to propagate the work of Greece and the work of Judea, that is to say, civilisation. Force is not a pleasant thing to contemplate, and the recollections of Rome will never have the powerful attraction of the affairs of Greece and of Israel; but Roman history is none the less part and parcel of these histories, which are the pivot of all the rest, and which we may call providential, inasmuch as they have their appointed place on a plan which is elevated above the chops and changes of daily life. I say providential, not miraculous. Everything, in the progress of humanity, issues from one single principle, at once natural and ideal. If there is such a thing as one miraculous history, there are at least three. The Jewish history, which claims to have the monopoly of miracles, is not a whit more extraordinary than Greek history. If supernatural intervention is the sole explanation of the one, so it must be of the other. I will even add that, in my opinion, the greatest miracle of history is Greece herself. The simultaneous apparition in the Greek race of all that which goes to compose the honour and the pride of the human intellect impresses me far more than the passage of the Red Sea or of the Jordan. Happy will be the man who shall, at the age of sixty, write this history *con amore*, after having spent his whole life in the study of the works which so many learned schools have devoted to it. He will have for his recompense the greatest joy which man can taste, that of following up the evolutions of life in the very centre of the divine egg within which life first began to palpitate. And yet does it follow that, because I envy the future historian of the genius of Greece, I regret the Nazarite's vow which attached me early in life to the Jewish and Christian problem? Assuredly not. The Jewish and Christian histories have been the delight of eighteen centuries, and although they are now half vanquished by Greek rationalism, they are extraordinarily effective in the amelioration of morals. The Bible in its various transformations is, whatever may be said, the great book of consolation for humanity. It is by no means impossible that the world, tired out by the constant bankruptcy of liberalism, will once more become Jewish and Christian. It will be then that a disinterested history of these two great creeds will be of value; for the period when impartial studies upon the past of humanity are possible to us may not last very long. The taste for history is the most aristocratic of tastes; so it runs some risks.

In order to be quite consistent in carrying out the plan which I formed forty years ago of writing the *History of the Origins of Christianity* I ought to have commenced with the present volume. The origin of Christianity dates from the major prophets, who introduced moral ethics into religion about 850 B.C.; the prophecies of the ninth century have themselves their root in the ancient ideal of patriarchal life—an ideal partly created by the imagination, but one which had been a reality in the distant past of the tribe of Israel. My reason for not observing this chronological order, and for first plunging into the middle of my subject with my *Life of Jesus* was that human life is uncertain, and that I was particularly desirous of writing about the first century and a half of Christianity. And then, as I am fain to admit, Jesus had a great attraction for me. The dream of a kingdom of God, which would be governed by the law of love and mutual self-sacrifice, had always possessed a great charm for me. As soon as I found that I should probably have ample time to deal with the history of Israel as I had dealt with the history of Jesus, of the Apostles, of St. Paul, and of the early Churches, I seemed to gain fresh strength. For the last six years I have given my whole attention to this great work, and at the present moment the history is brought down to the epoch of Ezra; that is to say, down to the definite constitution of Judaism. If anything happened to me, the whole of this would be ready for publication, making in all three volumes, though the two following would scarcely be so thoroughly matured as this one. If I live, the second volume will appear in a twelve-month, and the third in two years' time. If, when they have all appeared, I find that my strength admits of it, I propose to write, in one volume, the history of the time of the Asmoneans. This would bring me up in point of time to the *Life of Jesus*, and so I should have completed the cycle which it was my desire to embrace. This fourth volume is much easier to compose than the others. I may even go so far as to say that there is but one way of doing it, and should I not have time to write it I should ask my publishers to translate one of the many works on the subject which have been written in Germany, and so complete the work. But I confess that I am so buoyed up by the pleasure of seeing it making good progress that I hope to terminate it myself, when I shall be able to chant with joy the " Lord, now lettest thou thy servant " of the aged Simeon.

In this first volume, the great religious movement of Israel, which swept the world along with it, has scarcely begun. The vocation of Israel is not yet clearly marked. That people had not, as yet, any clear mark upon its forehead to distinguish it from its neighbours and congeners. At first it might have been taken for a small Syro-Arabian tribe like so many others. But the childhood of the elect is full of signs and prognostics, which are only recognised afterwards. The most important period in the life of great men is their youth, inasmuch as it is then that their future is mapped out, as it were, behind a veil. It was during the patriarchal age that the destiny of Israel began to be written—nothing in the history of Israel can be explained without reference to the patriarchal age. This epoch, like all childhood, is obscured by the night of time; but it is the duty of the historian, who is searching into the causes of things, to pierce this obscurity by the aid quite as much of psychology as of philology. It will be objected that the golden age of the Aryans has quite as many documents to back it up as the patriarchal age, and yet the former is only a dream. The two cases do not run on parallel lines. The patriarchal age existed; it exists still in those countries where the nomad life of the Arabs is preserved in its original purity.

Despite the efforts which I have made not to sacrifice admiration to critical examination, and at the same time to let doubt preserve its rights, I know that the history of Israel, written in this way, must be distasteful to two classes of persons: first of all, to the uncompromising Israelites, who insist on having all or nothing, and demand that the characteristics of the past played by Israel shall be spoken of in a strain of unbroken eulogy. By a curious ethnographical misapprehension, the majority of the Jews of our day regard as their ancestors the members of the tribe in the midst of which was formed, by the influence of an imperceptible minority, the religion which they profess.* A foreigner never satisfies the nation whose history he writes. Daru is regarded in Venice as an enemy; all those who make a distinction between ancient and modern Greece are regarded as malefactors. No matter what may be said to the contrary, it is true that one can never go far enough to satisfy national vanity. Speaking in January, 1883, at the Cercle St. Simon,† I said: "There is no such a

---

* See the lecture on "Le Judaïsme comme race et comme religion," in my *Discours et Conférences*, p. 341 and following.

† In the lecture above cited.

thing as an immaculate history. The history of the Jewish people is one of the most beautiful we have, and I do not regret having devoted my life to it. But I am far from asserting that it is a history absolutely without blemish, for if it were, it would be a history outside humanity. If I could live a second life, I should certainly devote it to Greek history, which is in some respects a finer history than that of the Jews. They are, in a way of speaking, the two dominant histories of the world. Now, were I to write the history of the Greek peoples, I should not refrain from pointing out what is blameworthy in it. We may admire Greece without feeling ourselves called upon to admire Cleon and the evil pages in the annals of Athenian demagogy."

The work of Israel was accomplished, like all human undertakings, by means of violence and perfidy, amidst a tempest of oppositions, of passions, and of crimes without number. The Jewish intellect derived its strength from its least sympathetic characteristics, from its fanaticism and from its exclusive tendencies. This is, after all, a mere platitude. The French royalty, the Catholic unity of the Middle Ages, Protestantism, and the Revolution were brought into being by all kinds of crimes and errors. A great man owes as much to his defects as to his good qualities. The hardness and the brutal abruptness which so intelligibly shock our friend M. Taine in Napoleon were a part and parcel of his force. Had he been as well-bred, as polite, and unassuming as we are, he would not have got on; he would have been as powerless as we are.

This history will also be displeasing to the narrow-minded persons who have the French defect of not allowing that it is possible to write the history of times concerning which one has not a series of material facts to relate. There are no facts of this kind in the history of Israel up to the time of David. In order to content historians of this school, I should have had to publish the present volume as so many blank pages. Such a method is, to my mind, the very negation of all criticism. It has a double disadvantage, leading either to gross credulity or to not less purblind scepticism; the one side swallowing the crudest fables, while the other side, in order not to take in any fables, rejects the most precious truths. The truth is that we can still learn a good deal with regard to the epochs which are anterior to history, strictly so-called. The Homeric poems are not historical books, and yet is there anywhere a single page more dazzling with light than the picture of Greek life a thousand years B.C. which these poems give us? The Arab tales of the ante-Islam period are not history, and yet they admit of the painting of pictures which are wonderfully true to the original. The Arthurian romances of the Middle Ages do not contain a word of truth, and yet they are storehouses of information as to the social life of the epoch in which they were written. The legends are not, for the most part, historical, and yet they are marvellously instructive as regards the colour of the periods to which they belong and the habits of the time.

Narrow-minded critics, who deny the existence of the obscure periods upon which we have no strictly historical documents, deprive themselves of the truest and most important part of history. A romance is, in its way, a document, when one knows in what relation it stands to the age in which it was written. The historic generalities which we derive from ancient texts are truths arrived at by induction, but they are none the less certain for all that. How many things there are of which the same may be said. The whole system of the world is arrived at by the inductive reasoning out of observations; not by direct observation.

As I have said elsewhere,* we do not need to know, in histories of this kind, how things happened; it is sufficient for us to know how they may have happened. What was not true in one case was so in another. I admit that any opinions as to individuals are, in these circumstances, full of possibilities of error. But this is not a difficulty peculiar to the ages of fable; judgments upon individuals are, save in exceptional cases, only possible within an historic period either very rich in documents or very near to our own. And even then how many gates are open for the entrance of illusion! In such a case, every phrase should be accompanied by a "perhaps." I believe that I have used it pretty freely, but if the reader thinks it does not occur often enough, he can fill it in

* *Life of Jesus*, Preface, pp. 73-75 (Am. ed.).

at his own discretion * If he does this, he will arrive exactly at what I think.

In reality, Dom Calmet and Voltaire are the one as incapable as the other of understanding anything about ancient history, the one admitting everything that is written, the other rejecting everything as soon as he can detect a single flaw in the ancient writings. The defect of each is the same, and may be summed up in their incapacity to understand the difference of the times, and their failure to seize what constitutes the essence of popular tradition. When popular tradition knows nothing, it none the less continues its babble; and then it takes shadows for giants, and words for men. The exuberant feeling of trust and confidence, ending, when it has been abused, in childish suspicions —the want of criticism, in a word, which is characteristic of the French mind, in war and in politics as well as in the appreciation of antiquity—proceeds as a rule from too great simplicity of conception. We cannot keep clear of pit-falls, and we reason about Romulus, Æneas, and Joshua, in the same way that we do about Napoleon, just as if we had newspapers or state documents dating from the time of Romulus—just as if we knew Æneas from contemporary evidence—just as if writing had been an every-day affair in these

* The most perfect method to adopt in a case of this kind would be that of polychromatic printing, in which each part of a page or even of a phrase would be printed in inks of different shades, from very black ink, to mark certainty, down to the lightest possible tints, to mark the various degrees of probability, plausibility, and possibility. [This has been done in Bissell's "Genesis."]

remote times—just as if the prehistoric imagery had not been floating for five or six centuries amid the mists of oral tradition, in which nothing is visible at a distance of half a century—just as if the heroes of an age in which rivers had sons, in which mountains begat children, did not require to be treated in accordance with some special rules!

The Abbé Barthélemy disposed of all these childish ideas a hundred years ago,* when he wrote: "In those days there lived a man called Æneas; he was of illegitimate birth, a bigot and a coward; these qualities won him the esteem of King Priam, who, not knowing what present to make him, gave him one of his daughters in marriage. His history begins upon the night that Troy was taken. He quitted the city, lost his wife on the way, took ship, had an intrigue with Dido, Queen of Carthage, who survived him for four centuries, got up some very amusing sports near the tomb of his father, Anchises, who had died in Sicily, and eventually landed in Italy, near the mouth of the Tiber, where the first object which met his gaze was a sow which had just given birth to thirty white pigs."

I agree with Barthélemy that history does not lose much by being deprived of such stuff as this. If, when what is legendary has been eliminated or treated as legendary, there remains but an indistinct contour of figures which were once striking, no doubt, but which the hand of time has effaced, there is no help

* The *Mercure de France*, 1792, No. 13.

for it. History must perforce extract as much truth as possible from the indications which it has at command; it is doing a very sorry work when it relates a number of childish stories in a tone of the utmost seriousness. To depict the great men of a remote antiquity in the dimness of their distant past is not equivalent to diminishing their proportions. A giant placed in the furthest horizon of a picture is not the less a giant; but it would be contrary to all reason to give the giant the position of a figure in the foreground. Thus, for instance, it is no fault of mine if Moses, at the distance at which he stands, has the appearance of a shapeless column, like the pillar of salt which represents Lot's wife. Moses, if he ever existed, which there is every reason to suppose that he did, is fourteen or fifteen centuries anterior to Jesus. Jesus is known to us by at least one contemporary piece of evidence, that of St. Paul. His legend is the work of the second and third generation of Christians. The oldest legends relating to Moses are at least four or five centuries posterior to the age in which he lived, perhaps more. No one ever blamed Raphael for having, in his picture of the Transfiguration, painted Christ in heaven smaller than the apostles and the multitude of people upon the ground.

It has only been through the energetic efforts of modern criticism and philology that an insight has been obtained into the truth of these ancient texts, which seemed expressly designed to lead us astray.

The old epic tales, related in good faith, the theocratic after-touches, and the sacerdotal revisions are now and then piled one upon the other, in the same paragraph, and it needs a very practised eye to detect them. The problem is analogous to that presented by the Herculaneum rolls, where the eye can at first see nothing but hundreds of letters, without being able to say to what pages they belong, all the sheets sticking together and forming one carbonised mass. In the same way, in the historical parts of the Bible, the different wordings so run into one another, the scissors of the compilers have been plied so capriciously, that it is often impossible to make any attempt to sort them out.* The art of the critic, nevertheless, sometimes answers with wonderful success the challenges cast down to our sagacity. During the last twenty years, more especially, the problems relating to the history of Israel have been dissected with rare penetration by Reuss, Graf, Kuenen, Nœldeke, Wellhausen, and Stade. I assume that my readers are familiar with the works of these eminent men. They will find in them the explanation of a number of points which I could not treat in detail without repeating what has already been said very well.

The requirements of chronological order, which must be observed in history, will explain why a number of

* As regards the Hexateuch, I would advise those who are desirous of keeping themselves well informed to read the Perpetual Commentary of M. Dillmann, who exhibits the systems in a very complete form, and admits of a free and unbiassed opinion being formed.

questions, which are in connexity with those treated in this volume, will only be completely elucidated in the second, this being especially the case with the questions relating to the age and authority of the texts, I have been compelled to make use in this volume of texts the composition and remodelling of which will only be set forth in the second volume. In order that my readers may be able forthwith to see by what principles of criticism I have been guided, I have put together in four articles, which appeared in the *Revue des Deux Mondes* (March 1 and 15, Dec. 1 and 15, 1886), the principal passages of the second and of the third volume which relate to the compilation of the historical books of the Bible. Those who may think it worth while to read these four articles will be able to form an idea of the system of literary history which will be developed in the following volumes.

This system only differs, moreover, in one respect from that which is followed in the great German and Dutch schools. Side by side with the so-called Jehovist version of the Hexateuch, which appears to have been composed in the kingdom of Israel about 800 B.C., I admit an *ancient Elohist*, which I imagine to have been composed at Jerusalem rather later, about the time of Hezekiah. I thus avoid ascribing to a modern period the Elohist parts, such as the beginning of Genesis, which are so different from what the Jews have done since the Captivity. My views as to the *Iasar*, the *Book of the Wars of Iahveh*, and, speaking generally, all the old books of an epic, idyllic, and

PREFACE. xxiii

almost secular character, which preceded any compilation of the Pentateuch, are foreshadowed in advance in the present volume. Regarded from a documentary point of view, these books, written in the kingdom of the North and anterior to the great prophetic era, constitute very nearly the series which the German critics designate by the letter B.

With regard to the proper names which are known, I have adhered to the transcriptions in general use, even when these transcriptions are more or less defective, as in the case of *Salomon*, *Moïse* (Solomon, Moses), &c. In the case of names which have no recognised modern equivalent, I have created French transcriptions in conformity with our habits, following the ancient versions and not omitting the massoretic vowels, though without any servile adhesion to them. I have done my best to make all the names easy of pronunciation, without any special sign or notation. As a general rule, it will be found that each Hebrew consonant has been represented by a single letter. The only real difficulty was in the case of the Hebrew *schin*, answering to the English *sh*, the German *sch*, to the French *ch* in *chose*. These different transcriptions give rise to all kinds of misapprehensions. The Greek and Latin translators, who have found themselves face to face with the same difficulty, have rendered the Hebraic *chuintante* by the simple sibilant. I have followed their example in order to avoid the accumulation of letters, which are a cause of perpetual embarrassment for the French reader.

c

The corrections which I have been led to suggest in the Hebrew texts are indicated in the notes. The great advances made during the last thirty years by Semitic paleography—advances which are the result of the vast progress of Semitic epigraphy—now enable us to apply, without fear of error, to the text of the Bible the method of verbal criticism inaugurated in the eighteenth century by Père Houbigant. The insufficient data which were to be had with regard to the history of the Semitic writings made it impossible for this study to be founded upon any solid basis at that time. But in the present state of science the future of Hebraic philology lies in this direction. Formerly, the traditional Hebrew text was received with a sort of superstitious reverence, people forgetting that the ancient versions have often followed a better text. Since we have been able to reconstitute century by century the way in which the Hebrew writings were copied, the mistakes have become evident, and it has been found possible to lay down rules for correcting them. These rules, based upon paleography, are the principal subject of my lectures at the Collège de France. They will be found very faithfully summarised in the preface of M. Grätz's Commentary upon the Psalms. Those who are desirous of making themselves acquainted with these interesting researches must, in the first place, have before them the excellent tables of Semitic paleography drawn up by M. Euting.

The portion of Hebraic history dealt with in this

volume derives valuable light from Assyriology and Egyptology, those two great scientific creations of our century. In regard to the former, in his connection with the Bible, a very useful manual is M. Schrader's book, each edition of which keeps the reader well posted up in the condition of that science. In respect to Egyptology I have found the best and safest of guides in my learned colleague, M. Maspero, who has been kind enough to read all the chapters in this volume which touch upon Egypt, and to supply me with some very lucid notes which I have reprinted as they came from him.

Since I first began to address myself to the public upon religious history, now forty years ago, great changes have taken place. People no longer argue with one another as to the very foundation of religion, and that, to my mind, is a distinct step in advance. It is equivalent to admitting that there is room, in the infinite, for every one to fashion his own romance. Liberty, as understood in America, is the consequence of such a condition of things, and my belief is that, in the course of another century, nearly all the civilised nations will reach this point. We can afford to wait in patience, for, even at the present time, in nearly all civilised countries, no one is compelled to act in any way contrary to his conscience, everybody being free to contract marriage, bring up his children, and arrange for his funeral in the way that seems best to him. This is an immense result to have obtained. Once it is allowed that all the Churches, if not of equal value, are a matter of tradition and not of absolute truth, there is no reason why people should be at variance as to what is but a material fact of history. The interminable polemics to which the struggles of Catholicism, Protestantism, and Judaism have given rise, have ceased to be of any consequence outside the historical movement which they have brought about.

This historical interest, at all events, is in no way impaired. For a long time to come people will concern themselves about religions, after they have ceased to believe in them. The downfall of theology does not imply the downfall of the history of theology, any more than the small interest which now attaches to the study of metaphysical philosophy deprives the history of ancient philosophy of its interest. To see the past as it really was is the first delight of man, and the noblest—I may add the most useful—of his curiosities. It is always good to know the truth. If we could know the truth as to the past and the present of humanity, we should be perfect in our wisdom. Every fault has its origin in an error. If Louis XIV had learned the history of Protestantism from a better source than that of his Gallican theologians, he would not have revoked the Edict of Nantes. If St. Louis had possessed a better knowledge of the history of the Church, he would not have allowed his subjects to be decimated by the Inquisition. If Marcus-Aurelius had been better versed in the history of Christianity, the atrocious scenes of the amphitheatre at Lyons would never have been witnessed. If the legislators of the Revolution had known more of the essence of Catholicism from the time of the Council of Trent, they would never have dreamed of creating a French National Church. If the Radical party in France at the present day was not so ignorant of religious history, it would know that religions are like women, who can be got to do anything if they are taken in the right way, but of whom you can obtain nothing if you attempt to use force.

And is this sceptical or negative result the only one which comes out of the study of this long series of errors? Is it, after all, a matter of much importance to know what weary stages poor humanity has travelled to find that the summits of Olympus and Mount Sinai are deserts, that the heavens are void and the earth very small, that thunder is a phenomenon of more apparent than real amplitude, that the rainbow is but a play of light refracted in the raindrops? Not so. The reasoning of Kant remains as true as ever it was; moral affirmation creates its object. Religions, like philosophies, are all of them vain; but religion is no more vain than philosophy is. Without the hope of any recompense, man devotes himself to his duty even unto death. A victim of the injustice of his fellow-men, he lifts his eyes to heaven. A generous cause, in which his own interests are in no way concerned, often makes his heart beat. The *elohim* are not hidden aloft in the eternal snows, they are not to be met with, as in the time of Moses, in the mountain defiles; they dwell in the heart of man. You will never drive them out of that. Justice, truth, and goodness are willed by a higher power. The progress of reason was fatal only to the false gods. The true God of the universe, the one God, He whom men adore when they do a good deed, or when they seek the truth, or when they advise their fellow-men aright, is established for all eternity. It is the certain knowledge of having served, after my own fashion, despite all manner of defects, this good cause which inspires me with absolute confidence in the divine goodness. It is the conviction that this book will be of service to religious progress which has made me love it. As in the case of the *Life of Jesus*, I demand for the present volume, dealing as it does with very obscure times, a little of that indulgence which it is usual to grant to seers, and of which seers stand in need. Moreover, supposing that I have conjectured wrongly upon certain points, I am certain that I have rightly understood as a whole the unique work which the Spirit of God, that is to say the soul of the world, has realised through Israel.

HISTORY OF
THE PEOPLE OF ISRAEL.

BOOK I.

THE BENI-ISRAEL IN THE NOMAD STATE DOWN TO THEIR SETTLEMENT IN THE LAND OF CANAAN.

CHAPTER I.

ARRIVAL OF THE SEMITES IN SYRIA.—CANAANITES.

THE passage from the animal state to humanity did not take place upon a single part of the globe, nor by a single spontaneous effort. From several directions, either simultaneously or successively, the human conscience unravelled itself, elevated itself, purified itself, conceived the idea of justice, asserted the principles of right and duty. Language then came in to define and establish these conquests of mind over matter. The capitalisation of results, the solidarity of different generations, which are the essential conditions of progress, were henceforth rendered certain.

Language, like morality itself, was not the result of one single creation. The different tongues were formed separately, in diverse centres; they constituted irreducible families, types which, once formed, ran on side by side for centuries, without undergoing any material modification. There then ensued an element of grouping and separation of more capital importance than the question of race. For the point which it is necessary to bring into prominent notice is that the appearance of what may be called the different human species upon the one hand, and the appearance of the different families of languages upon the other, were facts separated from each other by many centuries, so much so that the division of human species and the division of the families of languages do not at all coincide.*

In each centre of linguistic creation, there were already individuals of very different species. It may well have been, moreover, that families very nearly related from the physiological point of view, but already separated from one another, created their language upon quite different types.

In this way, languages represent not ethnographical divisions of humanity, but constitutional facts of great antiquity and of incalculable importance; for language, being for any one race the very form and fashion of thought, the use of the same tongue, continued for centuries, becomes, for the family which confines itself to the same, a mould, a corset so to speak, more binding than even religion, legislation, manners, and

* I have dilated upon this point in *Les Langues et les Races*, a lecture delivered at the Sorbonne, March, 2, 1878 (*Bulletin de l'Association scientifique de France*, No. 540).

customs. Race of itself without the institutions appertaining to it is of trifling importance; the institutions are like the barrel-hoops by which the internal capacity of a durable recipient is determined. Of all institutions, the most long-lived is language. Thus language took almost entirely the place of race in the division of humanity into groups; or, to put it in another way, the word "race" assumed a different meaning. Language, religion, laws, and customs, came to constitute the race far more than blood. The blood itself, by means of the hereditary qualities which it transmitted, perpetuated institutions and habits of education far more than it did a genius inherent in the germs of life.

We must assume primitive humanity to have been very malevolent. The chief characteristics of man for many centuries were craft, a refinement of cunning, and a degree of lubricity, which, like that of the monkey, knew neither times nor seasons. But amid this mass of shameless satyrs, there were some groups which had the germs of better things in them. Love was in the course of time idealized in dreams. Slowly but surely a principle of authority was established. The need for order created the hierarchy. Force was met by imposture, and sacerdotal offices were founded by working upon the superstitious fears of men. Certain men persuaded others that they were the necessary intermediaries between them and the divinity. All this led to the creation of societies analogous to the Negro societies of Dahomey, of considerable strength, complicated, tyrannical, superstitious, devoid of morality, swift to shed blood. There was scarcely such a thing as family. The child, in those early ages, knew only his mother, women being the common property of the tribe.

The progress effected for centuries together within the fold of families comparatively well endowed with intelligence derived from these primitive groupings, resulted not in liberty, nor yet morality, but a fairly well-regulated state of things, in which much that was valuable was gained. In the distance of six or seven thousand years from the age in which we live, we can still catch a glimpse of three or four civilisations, or, to put it better, three or four great human hives, having their regular rules, their mode of life, their language, and their religious rites. They resembled republics of bees or of ants. The alluvial basins of the great rivers appear to have been very favourable to this early type of civilisation, of which China, now a wizened, old-fashioned-looking child, has handed down the pattern to the present day. The Yellow River, at the eastern extremity of Asia, the Ganges, to the south of the Himalayas, the Tigris and the Euphrates in Hither Asia, and the Nile in Africa witnessed the expansion of societies which were very perfect from the point of view of their general mechanism, but in which individual liberty and genius appear to have had no place. They were so many human flocks governed by a king, who was the son of Heaven, amid which one would look in vain for the principle which formed the Greek city, the Jewish church, the Germanic league, feudalism, chivalry, constitutional monarchy, a republic of reason. In such societies as these order is secured administratively by mandarins, by heads of departments, by an organised police. There is no such thing as a great statesman, a great orator, a great citizen. There is no more trace of a revolution or of a protest against the established order of things than in an ant-hill. It must not be forgotten, however, that it was these ancient societies which laid the first bases of the human edifice and made nearly all the material inventions. Chaldea and Egypt, in particular, supplied the Greeks and the Hebrews, not with their genius assuredly, but with the essential elements of their extraordinary work; they inoculated the Greeks and Hebrews with a host of ideas which these latter made fruitful and beneficial for humanity.

About the year 2000 B.C. we find an entirely new element making its appearance in history. The Aryans and the Semites make their presence felt in the world. Far from first becoming civilised in great agglomerations at a time, these races began, apparently, with the idea of the individual defending his rights against those around him. Their starting-point was the family. Like all great things the family was founded by the most atrocious means; millions of women stoned to death paved the way to conjugal fidelity. Jealousy, though not based upon a very noble principle, became an essential condition of progress. The male kept guard over his female. Armed with a club and aided by his dog, the honest satyr kept watch in front of the small fortification he had built; at the slightest suspicion he put the adulterous female to death by stoning her. These groups, noble in their conceptions by comparison with the others, closed their ranks and formed camps strong enough to isolate them amid the night of anarchy by which they were surrounded.

Thus there emerged from the savage state what may be called barbarian morality, which we catch a glimpse of in remote antiquity under two types, the Aryan and the Semitic. Material civilisation may, when these two types of relative probity appeared, have seemed to be already old; but true morality in reality was born with them. Chaldea was in possession of those singular institutions which were destined to become in some respects so favourable to the awakening of the human intellect. Egypt had reached its utmost expansion, and even in its maturity the first symptoms of its decrepitude were apparent. China was at once young and decrepit, almost as well administered as ever she had been. The new-comers, upon the contrary, were rugged, very inferior to the Egyptians and the ancient Babylonians of the ante-Semitic period in all that related to the material comforts of life; but they had the inward fire, poesy, passion, melancholy, the craving for another life, the secret of the future. The family principle, which implies womanly modesty, had with the Aryans all the strength of a band of iron. The tribe was, among the

Semites, a school of pride, respect, and mutual self-devotion. Out of this common ground there arose very marked moral and intellectual differences. Strict monogamy was the law of primitive Aryanism.* Woman had, at first, to share fully the duties and the dangers of the family, and this conferred certain manly and determined characteristics upon her. The child was brought up in common by his father and mother; he received the impress of his parents with extraordinary force. With the Semites the spirit of race was manifested in a not less marked degree; but monogamy was not strictly observed.† A respectable man was at liberty to possess several wives at the same time. In religion the contrast was not less marked. The primitive religion of the Aryan was unbridled polytheism. From the most ancient times the Semite patriarch had a secret tendency towards monotheism, or at least towards a simple and comparatively reasonable worship.

The languages, in particular, offered a marked contrast. The languages of the Aryans and the Semites differed essentially, though there were points of connexity between them. The Aryan language was immensely superior, especially in regard to the conjugation of verbs. This marvellous instrument, created

* The Aryan marriages may be judged from the model of the Roman marriages, the Romans offering the oldest type of Aryan society.

† See, for further details, *Hist. des langues sémitiques*, b. i. ch. i., and b. v. ch. ii.; also *Observations sur le monothéisme des peuples sémitiques*, in the *Journal asiatique*, Feb.-March, April-May, 1859.

by the instinct of primitive man, contained in the germ all the metaphysics which were afterwards to be developed through the Hindoo genius, the Greek genius, the German genius. The Semitic language, upon the contrary, started by making a capital fault in regard to the verb. The greatest blunder which this race has made (for it was the most irreparable), was to adopt, in treating the verb, a mechanism so faulty that the expression of the tenses and moods has always been imperfect and cumbersome. Even at the present time the Arab has to struggle in vain against the linguistic blunder which his ancestors made ten or fifteen thousand years ago.

The Aryan race, about the year 2000 B.C., had its centre in ancient Arya (now Afghanistan), and thence it had already thrown out eastward and northward branches which were in time to become Celts, Scythians (Germans and Sclavs), Pelasgi (Greeks and Italiots). About the same time the heart of the Semitic race appears to have been in Arabia, which was less arid than it is now;* and from Arabia seems to have started the conquest which made of Babylonia, hitherto Turanian, Cushite or Cephenian, a Semitic country. The Arameans† probably followed the same course. Finally, according to ancient

* In our time, Arabia, especially the southern part, is still drying up. Water is disappearing from places where it used to exist, and the inhabitants are emigrating towards Persia.

† The intimate connection between the ancient Aramaic and the ancient Arabic is one of the most striking outcomes of the progress of Semitic epigraphy. See *Revue de archéologie orientale*,

ARRIVAL OF THE SEMITES IN SYRIA.

traditions, it is from Arabia also that came into the basin of the Mediterranean the peoples who called themselves *Kenaani*, and whom the Greeks named *Phœnicians**. These peoples spread along the sea-shore, from the small island of Ruad to Jaffa. They spoke a language very analogous to what we call Hebrew.†
There is nothing to show that they were ever nomad. From the very first they entered upon trade and navigation, founding the great commercial and industrial cities of Sidon, Aradus, and the more hieratic city of Gebal (Byblos). Although they never formed any real continental empire, there were Canaanite tribes in the interior, and the whole of Palestine, especially to the west of the river Jordan, was peopled with them.

Syria thus became an entirely Semitic country. The lists of the names of the Syrian towns referred to in

---

year 1, No. II. (1885), and the inscriptions discovered by M. Doughty, published in the *Notices et Extraits* of the Académie des Inscriptions et Belles-Lettres, vol. xviii. part i.; *Revue de études juives*, July-Sept., 1884, p. 1 and following. All inscriptions proceeding from Arabic are Aramaic. The 'Ερεμβοί of Homer (Odyssey, iv. 84) vacillate curiously between ארמי and ערבי. Strabo, xvi. iv. 27.

* Herodotus, i. i. 1. Herr Budde's system (*Bibl. Urgeschichte*, p. 343 and following) as to the non-identity of the *Kenaani* and Phœnicians is refuted by the coinage of Laodicea (אם בכנען), by the tenth chapter of Genesis, by the acceptation of the term כנעני, merchant, by the Book of Judges, ch. xviii. v. 7, in which the Sidonian mode is assuredly the Phœnician mode, &c. Isaiah, ch. xix. v. 18.

† See *Corpus. inscr. semit.*, part i., the names of the Canaanite towns and kings are almost Hebrew.

the conquests of the Tothmes and the Rameses are full of Semitic words.* The Khétas, whom the Egyptian annals so often mention as detested neighbours, are probably the Canaanite *Hittim*, whose centre was at Hebron, but whose name seems to have been often used to designate the Canaanite populations† and even Syria.‡ The name of *Rotenu*, which is also used by the Egyptians to designate the populations of Syria, is probably the name of *Lotn*, or *Lot*, which is connected with the country about the Dead Sea.§ The primitive races of *Emim*, *Zomzommim*, and *Enakim*, were reduced to mere insignificant handfuls.‖

Egypt exercised a kind of suzerainty over the country. But, beyond the boundaries of the rich Phœnician cities, this suzerainty was nominal, being confined to expeditions, which were renewed from reign to reign, and which always resulted in an easy triumph. What little art there was in the country bore an Egyptian imprint of the most marked character.¶

* Mariette, *Karnak*, pl. 17—26 ; *Les Listes géogr. des pylones de Karnak*, quarto, 1875, with folio atlas ; Maspero in the *Zeitschrift für Ægypt. Sprache*, 1881, pp. 119—131 ; and in the *Memoirs of the Victoria Institute*, 1886, 1887; Chabas, *Le voyage d'un Egyptien*, quarto, Paris, 1866.   † See Gesenius, *Thes.*, word חת.

‡ This would be an abuse of terms, just as it is to employ the word "Allemand" to designate all the Germans, or the word "Anglais" to designate all British subjects.

§ See Gesenius, words לוט and לוטן. These two names appear to be of equivalent value.

‖ The establishment of the Philistines is posterior to this. See pp. 133, 134.

¶ See *Missions de Phénicie*, conclusions.

CHAPTER II.

THE NOMAD SEMITES.

The Semitic invasion of Syria was not confined to the Phœnicians, the Khetas, and the Rotenu. For centuries the region of the Jordan and of the Dead Sea was invaded by new comers, who spoke nearly the same language as the Canaanites. The settlement of the Semitic hordes and their transformation to town life were gradual processes, and did not affect the nomad life which most of the tribes continued to lead. Arabia and Syria were full of wandering families, who lived in tents and who carried about with them the secret of the fine language and of the fundamental ideas of their race. Tent life is that which gives the most opportunity and spare time for reflection and passion. Amid a life of this kind, austere and stately, there emerged one of the spirits of humanity, one of the forms through which the genius, which assumes bodily shape by our nerves and muscles, developed into expression and life. Judaism (of which Christianity is but a development) and Islamism have their roots in this ancient soil. They were, indeed, fathers of the faith, these chiefs of nomad clans, wandering through the desert, staid, honest in their own fashion, narrow-minded no doubt, but puritanic, full of horror for pagan impurities, believing in justice, and with their eyes lifted to heaven.*

Philosophy and science, which are the capital creations of humanity, could not spring from this source; but among the human agglomerations which were the first to conceive sentiments of order and the pride which is born of self-respect, that of the Semite herders must undoubtedly rank among the very first. The Hebrew encampment was, to the same extent as the Aryan *gard*, a sort of asylum of refuge, a virtuous selection amidst a world of violence, like the Turan, or of moral degradation, as were Egypt, and probably Assyria. Religion had, even at that period, a very real bearing upon honest living, and contributed in a certain measure to morality.

* The main document upon this primitive age is the Book of Genesis, regarded not as an historical work, but as the idealistic description of an age which really existed. A book which is not historical may very well supply a perfect historical picture: as, for instance, the *Kitâb-el-Aghâni*, the Homeric poems. The confirmation of the truthful colouring of the narratives of Genesis is to be found in the Book of Job, in the paintings in the Beni-Hassan grottoes in Egypt, and especially in the Arab life as it exists at the present time. The life which the Arabs lead now enables us to study the patriarchal society of antiquity as if it were still in existence. The type of this society is so unchangeable that we are justified in drawing conclusions from to-day back to a period of four or five thousand years. Islam has nothing to do with the characteristics of Arab life, having exercised very little influence upon the life of the nomads. The tribes who roam about in the neighbourhood of Mecca are scarcely Mussulman at all. The *Kitâb-el-Aghâni*, which is the exact image of Arab life before Mahomet, depicts scenes quite analogous to those of the ancient Hebrew narratives, and to what may be seen in our own day among the Bedouins of the desert.

THE NOMAD SEMITES.

This morality was obtained at the cost of a startling simplicity of ideas. The liberty of the individual, which in our eyes is the most highly prized result of civilisation, did not exist. Man then belonged not to himself but to his anthropological, linguistic, and religious group. None of those great emancipating facts which, by breaking up the too narrow framework of the nation, render the individual independent, no great fact like the Greek Civilisation, the Roman Empire, Christianity, Islamism, the Renaissance, the Reformation, Philosophy, or the Revolution had yet burst upon the world. The solidarity of the tribe was unbroken. What was justice for one was justice for the other; the crime of the one was visited upon his neighbour,* for the lot of the individual was bound up with the morality of the whole of which he formed part. Generations existed in their father; a tribe was a man; all the genealogies which were preserved by memory were conceived in this style, which was later the cause of such frequent mistakes.

With us responsibility is personal, and there can be no crime without a criminal intention. A crime committed unwittingly is an accident according to our ideas. Abimelech, King of Gerar, would not have been more to blame if he had not discovered Isaac's stratagem.† But to him there appeared to be all the difference in the world. He would have committed

* Genesis, ch. xviii., v. 23, and following. Ezekiel was the first of the Hebrews to refute this grave error.
† Genesis, ch. xxvi.

adultery without being aware of it, and adultery was an inward fire, a disorder which, of itself, led to the ruin and extermination of families.* Abimelech, therefore, might well say to Isaac, "What is this that thou wouldst have had me do?"

These nomad tribes would form groups, numbering as many as four or five hundred souls; when they became more numerous than that they interfered with each other in their grazing, and a subdivision took place;† but the recollection of the primitive relationship was preserved for centuries. It was a rare thing for the tribe to be reinforced by strangers. Great store was set by purity of blood, and the prouder of the chiefs sent sometimes to fetch wives from very remote regions, whence they believed their family had sprung at a remote date.‡ The chief of the family, or patriarch,§ embodied in himself all the social institutions of the time. His authority was absolute and unquestioned; he had no need of agents to cause himself to be respected. Power was vested, in reality, in the tribe as a whole. The only primitive measures known were death or expulsion from the tribe, which amounted to pretty much the same thing.|| Justice

* Job, ch. xxxi., v. 11, 28.
† Genesis, ch. xxxvi., v. 6, 7.
‡ Genesis, chs. xxiv., xxvii., xxviii.
§ This word is not met with before the first century of our era; but it is a very suitable one, so I have employed it.
|| The penalty of *hikkaret*, or separation from the tribe, soon ended in death, as the person who was outlawed had no longer any protection. See for a curious illustration of this practice among the Bedouins of our day Saulcy's *Voyages*, vol. i. pp.

was administered by the assembly of elders. The code consisted simply in the application of the *lex talionis*. The vengeance of blood, which was exacted as a family duty, sufficed to render murder almost as rare as it has become in our modern societies by the working of institutions far more complicated. It is the same still in Arabia, where, without any established government, the number of offences against the person is not greater than it is with us.

There were not, moreover, any external signs of power, the pivot upon which the society of that day moved being respect. The road to supreme power lay neither through violence, nor the popular vote, nor the hereditary principle, nor an established constitution. Authority was a self-evident fact, which carried the proof of it upon its face. Without any sort of military organisation, without priests or prophets, some of these nomad groups thus succeeded in realising very perfect societies or associations. There was no national existence, but thanks to the solidarity of the tribe life and property were fairly secure.

The head of the family had not, as a rule, more than one regular wife. In certain cases, nevertheless, the patriarch had two wives of equal status and of noble blood; often two sisters.* This *régime* had the usual bad results, that is to say, unpleasantness between

291, 292. The *hikkaret* is in force among the republic of ants. The ant which deviates from the rules of the community is expelled, and soon dies.

* Rachel and Leah.

brothers. The sons of the same mother were alone brothers (*amadelphi* or *adelphi*, having sucked at the same breast).* The patriarch had, besides, for concubines all the female slaves in his tent, especially those of his wife, and they bore him children, to the knowledge and often at the request of his wife.† These concubines' children had not rights equal to those of the sons of well-born wives, though they at the same time formed part and parcel of the family.

The privileges of primogeniture as between the sons of the well-born wife were considerable.‡ In case of twins being born, the midwife took care to tie a bit of red string round the arm of the first-born.§ The eldest born was the head of the family; the father as a rule allotted each son his share. His blessing carried its own weight with it, like one of the sacraments so to speak, even when there was a mistake as to the identity of the person blessed.|| There were no illegitimate children; all the prostitutes were foreigners; the guilty woman was burnt or stoned,¶ and the fruit of her womb destroyed with her; if the child was born it was stoned to death. Upon the other hand, the wife had, to a certain extent, a right to bear children.**

---

* Genesis, ch. xliii., v. 29, 30.
† History of Abraham and Sarah.
‡ Genesis, ch. xxvii.
§ Genesis, ch. xxxviii., v. 27, 28.
|| Esau, Genesis, ch. xlviii.
¶ Genesis, ch. xxxviii., v. 25.
** Genesis, ch. xxxviii., v. 8 and the following; the Book of Ruth.

If her husband died, it was her duty to appeal to her brother-in-law or to some member of her husband's family; any attempt to evade this duty was looked upon as a gross offence.*

Slavery was, and has remained, one of the necessities of the life which these tribes led, and it was recruited by inter-tribal wars or by purchase. The slave formed part of the family, and as the material labour entailed by the life his master led was inconsiderable, the lot of the male slave was not at all a hard one. The male slave enjoyed his master's confidence, and he shared all the sentiments of his tribe. With his master's protection overshadowing him, he was almost as much respected as the latter. The female slave, upon the contrary, was set the hardest tasks, such, for instance, as the grinding at the mill and the drawing of water.†

Although they did not inhabit any regularly-built towns, the nomad Semites did not pass their whole lives wandering from one pasturage to another. The tribe often remained for a long time at the same place, and even ran up hastily built houses, such as may be seen in the present day in the poor little Syrian villages. Houses were regarded as a gift of God, who built them for those with whom He was well pleased.‡ There is an abundance of broken stones over all the

---

* Genesis, ch. xxxviii., v. 9. The explanation generally given distorts the nature of the offence here referred to.

† Exodus, ch. xi., v. 5; Isaiah, ch. xlii., v. 2; Job, ch. xxi., v. 10.

‡ Exodus, ch. i., v. 21.

surface of the soil of Syria. By putting these together as closely as they will go, and by filling up the interstices with branches, a shelter is obtained which those who have occupied it can abandon without scruple when the tribe moves off to some other place. The camels'-hair tents, secured by ropes, must have been very like the Arab tents of the present day. Of course the furniture needed in a life of this kind was very scanty, being confined to earthenware vessels and clothing, while almost the sole luxury consisted of bracelets, and rings for the noses and ears of the women. A chased dish was reserved for strangers of distinction.*

The food consisted of milk and meat. In the course of the sojourn, often extending over several years, which was made in the same place, there was time to sow wheat and plant vineyards. As a rule, however, the corn and wine were purchased from the sedentary populations, for the nomad tribe frequently traversed regions in which there were towns and resident inhabitants. Contracts and bargains were then made between the two.† These wealthy tribes, among whom a principle of order and of justice prevailed, were by no means displeasing to the resident inhabitants, and from their intercommunications often arose alliances, and even marriage proposals.‡ The herds were

* Judges, ch. v., v. 25.
† Genesis, ch. xxxiv.
‡ Genesis, ch. xxxiv., noting at the same time the difference between the two combined narratives. According to the Jehovist, Dinah was not done violence to ; she was merely eloped with.

formed of oxen, ewes, and goats, and the beast of burden was the camel; the animal used for riding, the ass. The horse appears to have been very rarely found among these tribes.* It was held in no esteem as a beast of burden, being regarded merely as an animal to be employed for purposes of amusement, or as a charger, for the use of kings and warriors. There were no wheeled vehicles of any kind.

Intellectual culture did not exist, not at least as we understand it; writing was unknown,† and the requirements of these simple souls were very few. But tent life, bringing as it does individuals into perpetual communication with one another, and affording them abundant leisure, is a school of its kind, especially as regards elegant diction and poetry. The poetry of the nomad Semites consisted in a symmetrical partition of the phrase into parallel fractions and in the use of picked words. Even at this early period, assuredly, the tribes possessed small *divans*, composed of melodies of eight or ten verses relating to the incidents of their nomad life, analogous to the *Jasher* of the Israelites and to the *Kitáb-el-Agháni* of the Arabs.

The real monuments of the period were, as is the case with all people who cannot write, the stones which they reared, the columns erected in memory of

* There is no mention of the horse in the enumeration of the animals which constituted the fortune of Job.

† The signet referred to (Genesis, ch. xxxviii., v. 18) must be an anachronism on the part of the Jehovist compiler.

some event, and upon which was often represented a hand, whence the name of *iad*,* or heaps of stones, *gal*, or *galgal*,† the "heaps of witness" (*galeëd*),‡ according to a custom which still exists in the East. The name of these heaps was a memorial to future generations.§ Sometimes large trees of very ancient growth were chosen as memorials.

This type of society, which has survived to our own day among the Arab tribes which have escaped any contamination from without, is too incomplete to have made much advance in the way of civilisation; but at first it contributed materially to the foundation of that which humanity most needed: honesty and the family instinct. In a society of this kind young men were of much less importance than with the Greeks; the dominant figure was the elder, the sheik, who was the depository of wisdom and power. The type of perfection, as is still the case with the Arabs, was the staid, well-born, well-bred,|| very courteous¶ aristocrat, who took a very serious view of life, and avoided all contact with rough and coarse

---

* Gesenius, *Thes.*, p. 568. Synonyms of יד and of שם, Samuel, book i., ch. xv., v. 12; ch. xviii., v. 18; Isaiah, ch. lvi., v. 5.

† *Galgal*, or *gilgal*, is only met with as the name of a place; but this word is always accompanied by the definite article and associated with the idea of ancient and idolatrous worship.

‡ Genesis, ch. xxxi., v. 45, and following.

§ The same usage prevailed among the Touaregs, down almost to our own day.

|| Genesis, ch. xxiv.

¶ Many anecdotes as to the politeness of the Arabs will occur to the reader.

people. The outcome of all this was an essentially pacific disposition, something which was at once generous, proud, and loyal, a condition of mind denoting persons who were at peace with themselves, who were prepared to defend their own rights and respect those of others. The gradation from this to a carping, litigious, and selfish disposition was easy, and craft was, as a matter of fact, esteemed rather highly in this ancient world.* Prudence was the first of virtues; untruthfulness was thought little of; but the fear of a higher power, which certain crimes (murder and adultery) irritated, had already some effect. Religion implied a rudimentary moral code; mysterious forces recompensed good deeds in a languid and intermittent way; but these same forces in some cases visited ill-deeds with punishment.

It was in this way of viewing religion that those pastoral tribes were superior to all the peoples of their day; and it is on this account that they occupy the foremost place in the history of humanity.

* Read the whole history of Jacob, a masterpiece of ethnographical psychology. Jacob is the very type of the *Arammi obed* (Deuteronomy, ch. xxvi., v. 5), or nomad Semite.

CHAPTER III.

RELIGIOUS CALLING OF THE NOMAD SEMITES.

WHAT Greece was as regards intellectual culture and Rome as regards politics, the nomad Semites were as regards religion. It was by means of religion that these worthy pastoral tribes of Syria reached an exceptional position in the world. The promises made to Abraham are mythical only in form. Abraham, the imaginary ancestor of these tribes, was in reality the father in religion of all peoples.

Man at the outset of his progressive life was in complete ignorance, and almost of necessity steeped in error. He was for thousands of years crazy after having been for thousands of years an animal. He has scarcely even now emerged from childhood. Primitive astronomy, based merely upon observation, was but a tissue of deceptions. Thanks to a scientific development continued for centuries, man has succeeded in detecting the errors into which the aspect of the firmament had caused him to fall, notably the greatest of all, viz. that the earth was motionless. In regard to the moral order of things, the truth was much more difficult to discover, and a great many human brains are still refractory to it. At first man imagined space to be peopled with free and passionate forces, open to be invoked and moved from their purposes. He created a divine world in his own image, and treated the gods of it as he liked to be treated by his inferiors. There was an exchange of politeness between trembling man and the potent forces by which he believed himself to be surrounded. A constant course of experience, confirmed by exact science, has proved to us that this primitive hypothesis of free causes quite independent of us is altogether erroneous. No signs have been discovered in nature of any intelligent agent superior to man. Nature is inexorable; its laws are blind. Prayer never encounters any being that it can turn from its purpose. No prayer or aspiration has ever healed a disease or won a battle. But, in order to reach this truth, of which the learned men of Babylon perhaps caught a glimpse, and which the Greek philosophers saw to perfection as far back as 500 B.C., it was necessary that whole generations of learned men should combine their efforts. What sort of idea could they form of wind who had no notion as to the real existence of the air? The nature of thunder was only discovered about a century ago; how, then, could primitive man see in it aught else but the explosion of the wrath of an all-powerful being, dwelling in the clouds and on the summits of the mountains? The sea, the watercourses, and the springs, having an individuality of their own, and acting as persons (we still speak of the sea as being angry, a spring as being beneficent, and water as asleep), almost necessarily became personified. Birth, disease, death, delirium, a trance, sleep and dreams made a deep effect upon the popular mind, as they still do, and there are but a few who see that these phenomena have their rise in our own organisation. The course of human affairs gave rise to even more erroneous judgments. Accidents, good or bad luck, the bearing of children or sterility, wealth, success, ascendancy, and authority, were interpreted as favours accorded to man by superior beings, or as humiliations more or less capable of being warded off.

Terror, panic, and lack of self-possession were the consequences of this very erroneous system of nature, and the adage, "Primus in orbe deos fecit timor," is true to the letter. Man believed himself to be surrounded by enemies whom he endeavoured to appease. As his senses were scarcely at all developed, he was the dupe of constant hallucinations. An unexpected breath of wind, a sudden sound, were regarded by him as tokens. An exaggerated spiritualism led him to look for spirits everywhere, invisible beings, shadows or doubles of real things,* which pursued him wherever he went and became confounded in his mind with the subjective phenomena he was conscious of. The type of such an existence as this is to be seen, or at any rate might have been studied a few years ago, in the Maldive Islands for one place. The natives of these poverty-stricken islets barricaded themselves in

* Réville's *Religion des peuples non civilisés*, vol. i. pp. 67 and following, pp. 228 and following; vol. ii. pp. 89 and following.

their huts of a night, believing that in the darkness the air was full of evil spirits whom they could hear fluttering about. The dread of darkness and other unreasoning fears, which are still very great among certain races of men, as, for instance, in Brittany, are the reduced remnants of what was originally a fact of the first importance.

Like all the ancient peoples in history, the nomad Semite believed that he was living amid a supernatural environment. The world, as he imagined, was surrounded, penetrated, and governed by the *Elohim*, by myriads of active beings very analogous to the "spirits" of the savages, full of life, translucid, inseparable in a way from one another, with no distinct proper names like the Aryan gods, so that it was difficult not to regard them as a whole and confound them all together. The old Greek polytheism or that of our time is not proved by the use of the plural *dii*, but by the separate names of Zeus, Hermes, &c. One *Eloh* has no name to distinguish him from another *Eloh*, so that all of them united act as one single being, and that the word *Elohim* is construed with the verb in the singular.*

Elohim is everywhere; his breath is universal life; through Elohim everything lives. Whatever happens is his (or their) work. He brings children into existence; he causes women to be fruitful; † he slays; he

* It was the same with אלם, with the Phœnicians. *Corpus inscr. semit.*, 1st part, pp. 6, 146. For other facts of a similar kind see *Journal asiatique*, Feb.-March, 1859, pp. 218, and following.

† Genesis, ch. xxx., v. 2, 22; ch. xxxiii., v. 5.

(or they) is heard in the sounds which cannot be explained; he (or they) breathes forth terror.* The atmospheric phenomena, more especially, are his (or their) work. He is the subject of verbs which are as a rule impersonal: "He thunders, he rains." † The crash of the thunder is his voice, the lightning is his light; whatever is great or extraordinary is ascribed to him.

A very characteristic usage of Semitic monotheism is derived from this, — namely, the habit of designating Elohim merely by the pronoun of the third person. When this was done it was usual to pronounce the pronoun very emphatically, accompanied by a gesture heavenwards. The name of God thus became a kind of grammatical element of the Semitic languages, the perpetual subject, which there was no need to express in speech. ‡

The proper names bore evidence of this pious custom, names such as *Abihou* (He is my father), *Elihou* (He is my God), *Abdo* (the servant of Him), *Davdo* (the favourite of Him), *Hanno* (the grace of Him); names which became by abbreviation *Abd* or *Obed*, *David*, *Hanan*, &c.§ Man, as well as nature, was under

* Genesis, ch. xxxv., v. 5; Joshua, ch. x., v. 10.

† Comp. [Ζεὺς] ὔει.

‡ This occurs very frequently in the Book of Job, where God is frequently spoken of without any direct reference. See, for an instance of this, ch. xii., v. 13 and following; ch. xxiii., v. 3; and particularly the last speech of Bildad (ch. xxv., v. 2 and following).

§ See *Mém.* upon the abbreviated theophoric names, in the *Revue des études juives*, Oct.-Dec., 1882.

the immediate dependence of Elohim or of the elohim. Whatever befell him in the way of good or evil, unexpected catastrophes, or sudden death, came from on high. Heaven killed the wicked man, and was the general upholder of order in the universe. No doubt this Elohim of doubtful identity is still far removed from the just and moral God of the prophets; but one can see that he will in due course become so, whereas Varouna, Zeus, and Diespiter will never succeed in becoming honest and just, and will eventually be abandoned by those who worship them.

It would be a great exaggeration to trace back to a very remote antiquity the purified and clear beliefs of philosophical spiritualism. The unity of causes was, to these perplexed consciences, no more than the indivisibility of causes. When we have unravelled as far as possible the confusion of ideas which were mixed up in primitive psychology, we find that the prayer of the terrified human being of those times found utterance in two forms of theology differing the one from the other. The Aryan when in peril addressed himself to the element which threatened danger or to the god which ruled this element. When at sea he invoked Poseidon or Neptune; when sick he made his vows to Asclepios; while he prayed to Demeter or Ceres for an abundant harvest. The Gauls had almost as many minor gods as there were medical or veterinary specialities. The number of these gods consequently became enormous, and each of them had a distinct name of his own. The Semite, upon the contrary, always invokes one and the same Being; whether at sea, or in battle, or in dread of a storm, or smitten with disease, his prayer goes up to the same God. One sovereign ruled over all things, but this sovereign bore different names in different tribes. In some cases he was called *El*, or *Alon*, or *Eloah;* in other cases *Elion*, *Saddaï*, *Baal*, *Adonaï*, *Ram*, *Milik* or *Moloch*.* But all these names in reality have the same meaning; they are nearly all of them synonymous; they all signify "the Lord," or "the Most High," or "the Almighty;" they mark some special excellence. They no more imply distinct individualities than do the different names of the Virgin Mary, *Notre Dame de Carmel*, *Notre Dame de Bon Secours*, *Notre Dame du Pilier* in Catholic countries. They are different words, not different gods.† Everywhere we find that it is the supreme master of the universe who is adored under these names in appearance so different. No doubt this notion of a supreme God was very vague, and in no wise resembled the symbols of the Jew and the Mussulman. The usages of scholastic theology which we have had inculcated on us by the catechism had no existence for brains which were incapable of seizing any dogma. The elohim, which were generally bound together, sometimes exercised an isolated action.

---

* See my essay on the primitive monotheism of the Semitic peoples, in the *Journal asiatique*, Feb.-March., March-April, 1859.

† Compare the names of the temples at Sidon, Malta, Carthage, *Corpus inscr. semit.*, part i., Nos. 8, 132, 247, 248, 249, 250, 255.

They never were in opposition with one another; but, like the angels of a much more modern mythology, they often exercised different functions. Thus each tribe had its protecting god, whose function it was to watch over it, direct it, and promote its success in every one of its enterprises. We shall find the Beni-Israel attaching themselves, like all the ancient tribes, to this narrow idea, and their god becoming, in order to protect the tribe of his choice, the most unjust and jealous of gods. The god of the tribe followed the individual even when he left his tribe, and continued to be his god when he was upon the territory of strange gods.* There was some analogy between this and the personified Fortuna of the Roman families,† and, as a matter of fact, the protecting gods were often called by the name of *Gad* (Fortune).‡ In this way the god was identified with the tribe, and the victories and defeats of the tribe were his own defeats and victories. If defeated, he was subjected to the insults of the conqueror, and no distinction was made between his name and that of the tribe.§

---

* Teïma Inscription in the Louvre, Nœldeke, *Altaram. Inschriften*, Berlin, 1884. *Revue d'arch. orientale*, 1885, pp. 41 and following.

† Orelli-Henzen, No. 1769. Cf. No. 5787 and *Corpus inscr. gr.*, No. 2693 *b*.

‡ Such as the Fortuna of Taym, at Palmyra. *Comptes rendus de l'Académie des Inscriptions et Belles-Lettres*, April 2, 1869.

§ Inscription of Mesa, lines 12, 13, 18. The title of book מלחמות יהוה; the song of Heshbon, Numbers, ch. xxi., v. 29.

The god of the tribe was followed by the local god presiding over a province, having his fixed dwelling-place and often his sanctuary (a column, an altar, a high place) at a given spot;* very powerful in his own region, so much so that those who were passing through it deemed it necessary to render him homage, if only to deter him from doing them a bad turn.† A very common expression among the nomads at a certain epoch—the Salm, or the Baal, or the Moloch of such and such a place‡—to designate the central point of a worship—was not perhaps as yet employed, but the people were coming to it. Jacob saw in his dream " the God of Bethel."§ He did homage to the place where he had his dream by erecting a pillar there, and pouring oil upon the top of it.‖ Thus the holy place dates from the utmost antiquity of Semitic worship.

The consequence of all this was a certain religious eclecticism, of which we have the type in the priceless inscription discovered at Teïma, in the centre of Arabia.¶ Salmsezab, the author of this inscription,

---

* Teïma Inscription (see the preceding page).

† Second Book of Kings, ch. xvii., v. 25 and following.

‡ Teïma Inscription. This form is very common in Aramaic epigraphy. See *Corpus inscr. semit.*, part i., 183, 365, 366; Constantine, Costa, 12; Inscription d'Altiburos (*Journal asiatique*, April-June, 1887); de Vogüé, *Syrie Centrale. Inscriptions sémitiques*, pp. 107—111. Compare Jeremiah, ch. li., v. 44.

§ Genesis, ch. xxxi., v. 13, האל ביראל. For the grammatical question see Gesenius, *Lehrg.*, pp. 657, 658.

‖ Genesis, ch. xxviii., v. 18, and following.

¶ *Revue d'arch. orient.*, *l.c.* Compare the curious Sabean inscrip-

not only stipulates for his right to sacrifice in foreign
lands to his own god, whose priest he is, and whose
name is embodied in his own; but he desires that the
gods of these foreign countries, whose power he ac-
knowledges, shall find pleasure in the sacrifices which he
is about to offer to his own god, and shall regard these
sacrifices as being offered to themselves. More than
that, he desires that the holy place consecrated to his
god may be under the protection of the gods of Teïma,
and he founds upon foreign soil the worship of his own
personal god, and sets apart, out of what we may call
the public worship fund of the country where he is, a
fixed sum (in palm-trees) for the worship of his
personal god. The gods of Teïma accept this singular
bargain, become guarantors for it, and grant their protection to Salmsezab. Jacob is not less simple in what
he did at Bethel, for we read in Genesis (ch. xxviii.,
v. 20-22), "If Iahveh will be with me, and will
keep me in this way that I go, and will give me bread
to eat, and raiment to put on, so that I come again to
my father's house in peace: then shall Iahveh be my
God; and this stone, which I have set for a pillar,
shall be God's house; and of all that thou shalt give
me, I will surely give the tenth unto thee."

Facts of this kind must have been common at the
time when the Semitic nomad tribes were divided
between the worship of the family gods and the worship of the provincial gods, having a more or less

tion of Medaïn-Salih, No. 29 (D. H. Müller, *Œst. Monatsschrift
für den Orient*, November, 1884, p. 279).

territorial jurisdiction. Ruth, the Moabite, upon reaching Israelitish soil, adopted outright the god of Israel; but heads of families and persons of importance were doubtless more particular, and this must often have given rise to rather complicated bargains. It is very possible that during the reign of Solomon several conventions of this kind were made at Jerusalem, and it may be that in the very temple of Solomon Tyrians sacrificed to Baal, upon the assumption that these sacrifices were not displeasing to Iahveh.

These individual selections, this particularising of the divine nation, so contrary to the idea which the Semites ultimately propagated through Judaism and Islamism, did not prevent the *Elohim* who were grouped in *dii consentes* from forming a superior power which inspired universal dread. The men of every tribe recognised their supreme authority, and stood in awe of them. They were supposed to be capable of punishing crimes which would never be known to men;[*] so much so that the fear of elohim (or of Elohim) prevented many evil deeds. They saw everything, being scattered over all the earth, and they therefore had knowledge of and traced out a host of misdeeds, which escaped human justice. They thus constituted a sort of secret tribunal. The accidents without any apparent cause, the maladies, the sudden deaths and other disasters, were regarded as the acts of justice done by the Elohim. The word

[*] Genesis, ch. xx., v. 11.

yirea, "fear," inferring as it did an unknown world behind it, was synonymous with "piety."* The commission of a crime entailed a constant apprehension of what the elohim might do.† To fear God was to believe in the reality of the moral sense; a man who feared God was a conscientious man.

Sometimes the elohim were called *Beni-Elohim*, "the sons of the gods, the divine race." When the elohim became a single being, of definite individuality, the *Beni-Elohim* became his host, a great body of angels, in perfect communion with him, coming now and then before him to do him worship.‡ Some of them had personal duties assigned to them, especially Satan, or the detractor, who was engaged in finding fault with the universe, while the true children of God could see only its harmonies. But it took centuries to establish any sort of order or hierarchy in this divine chaos.

Such a conception, to which our formularies have as a matter of course given a consistency which it did not before possess, was very superior to that which there are good grounds for attributing to the Aryans, not but what Semitic theology is infinitely removed from that which positive science has caused to prevail. If science has driven from the world the special and the local gods, it has not in any way given a helping hand to the hypothesis of a single providence, concerning itself in

---

* Job, ch. iv., v. 6 ; ch. xv., v. 4.
† Genesis, ch. xlii., v. 28.
‡ Job, ch. i., v. 6 ; compare Genesis, ch. vi., v. 1 and following.

detail with the particular occurrences of this universe.
It has never been discovered that a superior being
concerns himself with events either of the physical
or moral order. But this simplicity constituted, to
begin with at all events, a yoke less heavy than that of
the Aryan religion. The nomad Semites were, of all
the ancient peoples about whom we know anything,
the least given to idolatry, or to the gross superstitions
of sorcery. The Aryan race did not display any of the
superiority in religion which it was destined to exhibit
later in other ways. In its infancy we find it half
demented with terror. The absurd *tantra*, the all-
potent formula, took strong hold on it.* The various
manifestations of nature are forces which have to be
overcome. The Greeks alone succeeded in correcting
themselves of a defect of which they were at first no
freer than others. The Latins and the Italiots practised even up to our era the most childishly materialist
religion. The Gauls were the most superstitious of
peoples. The horrible ferocity of the Scythians was in
a great measure due to their exaggerated belief in the
survival of the individual after death.

The belief in the spirituality of the soul and in
immortality, far from being the outcome of refined
reflection, are in reality childish conceptions of men
incapable of making a serious analysis of their ideas.
The fundamental error of the savage, as I have already
said, is spiritism, that is to say the stupidly realistic

* Take, as a proof of this, the Vedas, the Gallic, Italiot, Scan-
danavian, and other religions.

opinion which leads him to believe that in everything complex there is a spirit which forms its unity. A house, a tree, a ship, each has its spirit. It is the principle of form opposed to matter, the base of the Greek as of every other philosophy, which, wrongly conceived by rude intellects, produces these abberrations. It appears quite clear that the primitive Aryan was much more given to spiritism than the primitive Semite; and that he personified far better the natural unities. For him everything had a soul, and he distinguished between the body and the soul in man, admitting that the one could exist without the other. The Semite soon formed a sounder theory. In his view that which did not breathe did not live. Life was the breath of God pervading the universe.* So long as it is in the nostrils of man, this latter lives.† When the breath mounts up again to God, all that remains is a little clay. The spiritistic tendency of the early ages reasserted itself in the belief in the *refaïm*, the empty shadows of the dead which dwell under the earth; but none of these things became a principle giving birth to mythology or fables. A rough outline of primitive common-sense preserved this race of men from the chimeras in which other human families found at times their greatness, at other times their ruin.

In these great and complex questions of the origin of things, it is nearly always impossible to distinguish

* Compare the passages in which the *Rouah Elohim* is spoken of.

† Job, ch. xxvii., v. 8.

between that which was due to the primitive gifts of the race and that which the incidents of history have grafted on to them. The causes of Semitic monotheism were more compound than simple, and it will probably be safe to attribute a larger share to the habits of a nomad life than to the influence of blood. For, upon the one hand, peoples who have nothing Semitic about them, but who lead a life analogous to that of the nomad Semites, such as the Kirghiz, or the present inhabitants of the upper basin of the White Nile, resemble very closely the ancient patriarchs of the desert. Upon the other hand, the Himyarites and Assyrians of the second age, who, at all events so far as language is concerned, are thoroughly Semitic, do not exhibit the religious puritanism found in the nomad Semites. It appears then that tent life was the main factor in the selection of the religious aristocracy which destroyed paganism and converted the world to monotheism. The roots of this great fact go deep down into the soil of ancient history. The tent of the Semite patriarch was the starting point of the religious progress of humanity.

It may be said of the nomad that he is at once the most and the least religious of men. His faith is the firmest that there is; twice it has conquered the world, and yet, to judge from externals, it would seem as if his religion was a sort of *minimum*, a quintessence, a residue, a congeries of negative precautions. Worship holds but a very small place in the life of the nomad; a superficial observer is tempted to regard this proud

vagrant as being indifferent, not to say sceptical.*
His mode of life made it impossible for him to have
statues and temples. His gallant bearing and instincts
inspired him with a horror of superstition and abject
practices. His philosophic reflection, pursued with
intensity in a narrow circle of observation, imparted to
him very simple ideas, and as it is the nature of religious progress always to simplify, the immediate result
was that the religion of the nomad became more intense
than that of peoples more civilised than himself. The
nomad Semite was a Protestant, and many of the
populations which adopted Protestantism about the
sixteenth century were far from equalling in intellectual culture the Italy of the time of Leo X. Religious
servility was repulsive to them; and this fine feeling
afterwards brought its reward, and has been placed to
their credit.

* Such is essentially the character of the nomad Arab. I have dwelt upon this in detail in my *Mélanges d'histoires et de voyages*, pp. 305 and following.

CHAPTER IV.

MONOTHEISM, ABSENCE OF MYTHOLOGY.

WITH a certain type of language of its own, the Semitic, like the Aryan, seems, as we see, to have at first had for its common share a certain type of religion. The fundamental idea of this religion was the supremacy of one common master in heaven and earth. All this remained very vague and confused up to the ninth century B.C., but it was, none the less, in the germ from the very first, and was due mainly, as I have said, to the character of the nomad life which impresses upon all races without distinction so deep a mark. One very decisive proof of this was the little liking which nomads as a rule have for figures in painting or sculpture. A nation which has figured presentments before it almost infallibly becomes idolatrous. The interdict placed upon them by the Hebrew legislators may be said to have been imposed upon the nomads by the very laws of their existence. Nomad life made impossible the paraphernalia necessary for an idolatrous worship; the pantheon must be as portable as the *douar*, and the Bedouin's habits limited him to a few insignificant *teraphim*, and a portable ark in which the sacred objects were enclosed.

MONOTHEISM, ABSENCE OF MYTHOLOGY.

What was wanting in the Semite far more even than a taste for the plastic arts was mythology,* which, quite as much as painting and sculpture, is the mother of polytheism. The principle of mythology is the investing of words with life; whereas the Semitic languages do not readily lend themselves to personifications of this kind. A feature in the peoples who speak them is a want of fertility both of imagination and language. Each word was to the primitive Aryan pregnant, if I may so speak, and comprised within itself a potential myth. The subject of such phrases as, "Death struck him down," "a malady carried him off," "the thunder roars," "it rains," &c., was, in his eyes, a being doing in reality the deed expressed by the verb. In the eyes of the Semite, upon the contrary, all the facts the cause of which is unknown have one same cause. All phenomena, more especially those of meteorology, which had so deep an interest for primitive peoples, were ascribed to the same being. In regard to life, the same breath animated all things. The thunder was the voice of God; the lightning was his light; the storm cloud his veil; hail the missiles of his wrath. Rain, in all the primitive mythologies of the Indo-European race, is represented as the fruit of the union of heaven and earth. In the Book of Job, which is the expression of a very ancient theology, it is God who opens the windows of heaven, who has "divided the water-courses for the overflowing of waters," and

* See *Journal asiatique*, April-May, 1859, pp. 426 and following.

"hath begotten the drops of dew."* Aurora, in the Aryan mythologies, is the object of an extraordinary number of myths, in which she is assigned a personal part and assumes many different names. She is the daughter of Night; she is espoused by the Sun; she begets Tithonus, or the Day; she loves Kephalos (the large head, the Sun); she has for her rival Procris (the Dew); she flies from the pursuit of the Sun, and is destroyed by his embrace. In the Book of Job, upon the contrary, God commands the morning, makes the stars rise or set, and appoints to light and darkness their respective bounds.†

Nearly all the roots of the Aryan languages thus contained a concealed divinity, whereas the Semitic roots are dry, inorganic, and quite incapable of giving birth to a mythology. When one fully realises the power of the root *div*, designating the brightness of the clear sky, one can readily understand how from this root have come *dies*, *divum* (sub dio), *Deva*, *Zeus*, *Jupiter*, *Diespiter*, *and Diauspiter*. The words *Agni* (ignis), *Varuna* (Οὐρανός); *Gê* or *Dê* (Δημήτηρ), also contained the germ of individualities which, becoming further and still further removed from their primitive naturalist meaning, in time, and after the lapse of centuries, got to be no more than mere characters in romance.‡ It would be idle to attempt to derive a

---

* Job, ch. xxxvi., xxxvii., xxxviii.

† Job, ch. xi., v. 7; ch. xxxviii., v. 12-15, 19-20.

‡ *Nomina numina*, to employ the expression used by Eugène Burnouf.

theology of the same order from the most essential words of Semitic languages, such as *or*, "light;" *samâ*, "the heavens;" *ars*, "the earth;" *nâr*, "fire." None of the names of the Semitic gods is connected with any such words as these. The roots in this family of languages are, if I may say so, realistic and non-transparent; they did not lend themselves to metaphysics or mythology. The difficulty of explaining in Hebrew the simplest philosophical notions in the Book of Job and in Ecclesiastes is something quite astonishing. The physical imagery which, in the Semitic languages, is still almost on the surface, obscures abstract deduction and prevents anything like a delicate background in speech.

The incapacity of the Semitic languages to express the mythological and epic conceptions of the Aryan peoples is not less striking. One fails to realise what Homer or Hesiod would be like if translated into Hebrew. This is because, with the Semites, it is not merely the expression, but the train of thought itself, which is profoundly monotheistic. The foreign mythologies become transformed under Semite treatment into dull historical narratives. Euhemerism is their sole system of interpretation, as we see in Berosus, Sanchoniathon, and all the other writers who have transmitted details upon the Syrian and Babylonian myths, in the Arab historians and polygraphers, and in the first pages of Genesis itself.* This singular

* See my memoir on Sanchoniathon in the *Mémoires de l'Académie des Inscriptions*, vol. xxiii., part 2, 1858.

system is due to the most deep-rooted laws of their intellectual constitution. For monotheism is of necessity euhemerist in its estimates of the mythological religions. Understanding nothing of the primitive divinisation of the forces of nature, which was the source of all mythology, it had only one way of giving a meaning to these great constructions of ancient genius, and that was to look upon them as so much embellished history, and as so many series of deified men.

This callow philosophy contained, it should be added, only one error; it exaggerated beyond measure the notion of the intentional intervention of superior forces in the current of human affairs. The nomad Semitic race was the religious race *par excellence*, because it was, taking it altogether, the least superstitious of the human families, less of a dupe than any other to the dream of the hereafter, of that phantasmagoria of a double or of a shadow which survives in the regions below. It rigorously put away from it those human sacrifices which the city-dwelling Semites indulged in quite as much as the Aryans. It regarded as of quite secondary importance amulets and idols; it suppressed the chimeras of complete survival after death, chimeras which were homicidal in those days, as they deprived man of the true notion of death and caused him to be very indifferent to how many murders he committed.* Yes, even at this remote epoch of which I am now speaking, the Semite shepherd

---

* See Herodotus's account of the royal Scythians. Book iv., lx.—lxxiii.

MONOTHEISM, ABSENCE OF MYTHOLOGY.

bore upon his forehead the seal of the absolute God, upon which was written, "This race will rid the earth of superstition."

The simplicity in worship of these ancient pastors has never been equalled. In the way of material images, the nomad Semite had only the *nesb* or *masséba*,* columns placed in the ground, which were consecrated by pouring oil upon the summit of them.† These *ansab* covered the whole of ancient Arabia, especially the region of Mecca; previous to the time of Mahomet‡ they were looked upon as gods. When the tribe decamped it left these gods of stone behind it, and those who came after it treated them with the same respect. Sacrifice is the oldest and most serious error, as it is the one most difficult to eradicate, among those bequeathed to us by the state of unreason which man passed through in his infancy. Primitive man (without distinction of race) believed that the way to calm the unknown forces which surrounded him was to win them over as men are won over, by making them some present. This was not unnatural, for these gods whom he wanted to make favourable to him were evil-disposed and selfish. The idea that it was a cruel insult to try and corrupt them, as one might to corrupt a judge, would

* See *Corpus inscr. semit.*, part i., Nos. 44, 122, and 122 *bis*, 123 and 123 *bis*, 139, 147, 194, 195, 380; 9th of Hadrumetes, Euting, *Pun. Steine*, 26, 27.

† Genesis, ch. xxviii., v. 18; ch. xxxi., v. 13; ch. xxxv., v. 1, 7; ch. xliii., v. 4.

‡ Koran, v., 4, 92; Freytag, *Lex.*, iv., p. 286; *Corpus inscr. semit.*, part i., p. 154.

never suggest itself to beings of such low morality and so devoid of reasoning power. If a man was eaten out by cancer, it was a god who was eating his flesh; what more natural, then, than to offer him fresh meat of a better kind? The object offered in sacrifice is always that which the man himself would like to have offered him. The *Söma* is, in the Hindoo language, something exquisite. The animal killed upon the altar is always excellent, without spot; the parts which are burnt are those which are esteemed the most highly. This revolting absurdity, which the first apparition of religious common sense should have swept away, had become an act of subjection, a feudal service (as it were) due to the Divinity, which the patriarchal faith did not succeed in shaking itself free of. The prophets of the eighth century B.C. were the first to protest against this aberration, and even then they could not suppress it.

In most cases, moreover, the sacrifice was only the preliminary of a repast to which it was desired that a special solemnity should be given.* The animal offered to the Divinity, or rather what remained of it after the choice morsels had been burnt, was eaten either by the family alone or by any guests who might be present. It was the same with the peoples described by Homer,† and in nearly the whole of antiquity. To eat in common was a sacramental act. Thus, for

* Genesis, ch. xxvi., v. 30, 31; ch. xxxii., v. 54; Exodus, ch. xviii., v. 12.

† *Iliad*, i., 464—469; *Odyssey*, iii., 461—463, 470—472; xiv., 425—453; Euripides, *Electra*, 835 and following.

MONOTHEISM, ABSENCE OF MYTHOLOGY.

instance, in order to consecrate "a heap of witness," bread was eaten upon the top of the stones so piled up.* The compacts and alliances made were celebrated to the accompaniment of solemn sacrifices, during which the animals offered up were cut into two parts, the one being placed opposite to the other, while the contracting parties passed between them.† In very special circumstances, it was believed that a mysterious fire, equivalent to the acceptance of the sacrifice by the divinity, passed between the pieces of the animal slain.‡

The tribe had no priests or professional sacrificers. The patriarch sacrificed for himself, his sons, and all the tribe. Preparation was made for the sacrifice by a state of saintliness ($qods$) or of purification, resulting from certain acts of external cleanliness, and certain acts of abstinence, notably from sexual indulgence.§ Cleanliness was, in the primitive faith, one of the essential conditions for drawing near to God, and one of the first measures of the legislators was, by preventing people from eating what was unclean, to wean them from habits which encouraged what was gross.‖ It is probable that the more respectable of the tribe had, at

---

* Genesis, ch. xxxi., v. 46.

† Genesis, ch. xv., v. 10—17; Exodus, ch. xxiv., v. 8. Ὅρκια πιστὰ ταμόντες. *Iliad*, ii. 124; iii. 105; Jeremiah, ch. xxxiv., v. 18; Demosthenes, *Adv. Aristocr.*, 68; Pausanias, IV., xv., 4.

‡ Genesis, ch. xv., v. 17; a very ancient legend. Compare the sacrifices of Balaam, Numbers, ch. xxii. and xxiii.

§ Exodus, ch. xix., v. 10 and following; see the example of Laocoon in Greek history.

‖ *Cædibus et victu fœdo.*

that early period, given up drinking blood.* Upon holy days no leavened bread was eaten, fermentation and mixtures being regarded as more or less impure.†

The nomad had few festivals; the festival (*hag*) implying a fixed religious centre. The idea of *hag* is closely connected with that of pilgrimage, of processions around a sanctuary, and of dancing in a circle. This word, common to all the Semitic languages without exception, unquestionably dates from the ancient epoch in which the common ancestors of the Hebrews, the Arabs, and the Arameans all lived within a very limited area.

Together with the word *hag* all the Semitic peoples use the word *som* or *soum*, signifying the fast, the presentation of one's self to the divinity, who is supposed to see everything, with an air of contrition and with mourning garments. The Elohim were supposed to be in some measure jealous of the happiness of mortals, so that a certain satisfaction was accorded to their *nemesis* by appearing before them with contrition and self-imposed humiliation. The garments of the afflicted (the *saq*)‡ and the heaping of ashes on

---

* A prescription earlier than any written code. First book of Samuel, ch. xiv., v. 31, and Genesis, ch. ix., v. 4.

† The *Book of Covenants* (9th century) contains the germ of these prescriptions. The Levitical version is much more modern, but it merely registers the existence of ancient usages.

‡ This word, which has been adopted by all the Mediterranean people, in consequence of their trade with the Phœnicians, was applied to very coarse cloth of a dark colour. They were afterwards named *Cilicium*, being principally made in Cilicia.

MONOTHEISM, ABSENCE OF MYTHOLOGY. 47

the head, or the shaving of the head,* were the forced accompaniment of the fast. The prayer of the man wearing the *saq* was regarded as being very efficacious; for Elohim would surely have pity upon one reduced to so sad a state, who could not in any way give him umbrage. In public calamities, more especially, the *som* and the *saq* were invariably resorted to.† In very ancient times the *som* was observed at certain periods of the year. The institution of the month of fasting among the Arabs was very anterior to Islamism. Thus the *som* appears as a monotheistic practice. The only being to whom fasting can be acceptable is the supreme God. It is a general rite, and no one particular god would have any means of distinguishing that the homage was addressed to him more than to any other deity.

The oldest cycle of the Semitic festivals was governed by agriculture, and even the nomads were guided by this habit. The *paskh*, or spring festival,‡ characterised by the use of unleavened bread, may perhaps have just begun to dawn. The shearing of the ewes, in David's time,§ may almost be regarded as a festival. The vintage was celebrated by dancing.‖ The custom of sounding the trumpet at each new moon, and of posting sentinels to observe the first

* Amos, ch. viii., v. 10.
† Judges, ch. xx., v. 26; First Book of Samuel, ch. vii., v. 6; ch. xxxi., v. 13; Joel, ch. i. and ii.
‡ Leviticus, ch. xxiii., v. 9—22; ancient fragment.
§ Second Book of Samuel, ch. xiii., v. 23, &c.
‖ Judges, ch. ix., v. 27; ch. xxi., v. 20 and following.

appearance of the "sickle"—a very useful custom among a people knowing nothing of scientific astronomy—may have already been in existence. In any event, the appearance of the new moon was made the occasion for sacrifices and festivals.* The Sabbath was so useless to the nomads, whose labour was essentially of an intermittent kind,† that the ancient nomad Semites probably did not observe it, although they saw this wholesome practice observed in Assyria.

Some other rites, common to all Semitic creeds, seem to attest the unity of these religions and their patriarchal origin. Such are the Sakæa of the Phœnicians, and of the Babylonians,‡ festivals which were annually celebrated under the tent, and which remind one of the feast of tabernacles of the Hebrews. Leviticus speaks of this festival as being a memorial of the ancient nomad life of the Hebrews.§ This explanation has been met by the objection that the booths made of boughs would be a very inaccurate representation of a sojourn in Arabia Petræa. But at a period much earlier than the compiling of the Book of Leviticus, in the book of Hosea,‖ the same comparison is made, and instead of huts made of boughs, tabernacles are

---

* First Book of Samuel, ch. xx., v. 5, 18, 24.
† The nomad Arabs of the East are scarcely at all acquainted with the Mussulman Friday.
‡ Ἑορτὴ Σακαιῶν = חג הסכות. See Movers, *Die Rel. der Phœn.*, pp. 480 and following.
§ Leviticus, ch. xxiii, v. 42, and following.
‖ Hosea, ch. xii., v. 10.

spoken of.* There is therefore good reason for regarding this feast of tabernacles as a souvenir of the primitive life common to all the Semitic peoples, being preserved even among those who had travelled the farthest away from it.

The *nabi*, or man inspired by God (sorcerer, diviner of the future, or prophet), had no place in a society where the father of the family had absolute power. The patriarch would assuredly have prevented the *nabi*, as he did the *cohen*, from acquiring an important position or endangering his own supremacy. Prophecy does not appear to have developed except among the tribes already established. The belief in revelations through dreams was universal, and the gift of explaining them was also a revelation.† Man protected by a god did all his acts under the inspiration of this familiar demon. It was in dreams for the most part that the voice of his god spoke to him.‡ Certain trees, such as the turpentine tree, were regarded as oracular, because they had deep roots in the ground and seemed to be old.§

A sort of deism without metaphysics was what the fathers of Judaism and Islamism inaugurated at that early period, with a very sure and unerring instinct.

* אהלים.

† Genesis, ch. xl., v. 8; ch. xli., v. 28, 32, 38, 39.

‡ Job, ch. xxxiii., v. 15. It was doubtless in dreams that Camos spoke to Mesa: ויאמר לי כמש. Inscr., Daibon, lines 14, 32.

§ *Elon Moré, Elon Mamré, Elon Meonenim*, Judges, ch. ix., v. 37.

This god of theirs, formed by a fusion of the nameless divinities, became the absolute God who loves what is good and hates what is evil, the God whose worship is prompted by an honest heart. The inroad of the scientific mind within the last century has made a great change in the relation of things. What was an advantage has become a drawback. The Semitic mind and intellect have appeared as hostile to experimental science and to research into the mechanical causes of the world. In appearance nearer than Paganism to the rational conception of the universe, the theology of the nomad Semite, transported into scholastic minds, has been in reality more injurious to positive science than polytheism. Paganism persecuted science less bitterly than the monotheistic religions originating with the Semites. Islam was the destruction of positive philosophy, which attempted to struggle into being among some of the peoples which it had subjected.* Christian theology, with its Bible, has, for the last three centuries, been the worst enemy of science. Nothing can be more dangerous, in one sense, than what is half absurd and half true; for humanity is but of middling force; it throws up too strong a poison; it drags life on with the dose of stupidity which is not sufficient to kill it. It is all a question of time and age. Islam represents progress to the negro who adopts it. Eliphaz of Théman,

---

* I have dwelt in detail upon this point in my *Conférences et Discours*, pp. 375 and following.

though holding with regard to the universe ideas the most opposite to the truth, was very superior, for the time in which he lived, to the superstitious Gaul or to the Italiot, as he is described to us in the *Eugubine* tablets and the hymns of the Arvales Fratres. And yet, for all that, the positive science of nature will be found to proceed far more readily from the genius of Gaul or of Italy than from that of Théman. A Breton peasant is far more of an unconscious Pagan than a Mussulman; and yet a very little schooling will make the Breton peasant into a man of good sound reasoning, readily understanding positivist naturalism, whereas the Mussulman can only be brought to a conception of this sort with the utmost difficulty, and rejects it as an abomination.

And yet these ancient patriarchs of the Syrian deserts were in reality corner-stones for humanity. They are the "trismegists" of religious history. Judaism, Christianity, and Islamism all proceed from them. The essential point, for a nation as well as for an individual, is to have an ideal behind it. The branches of the Semitic family which had gone through the nomad life retained their recollection of it after they had emerged from it, and carried their minds back to it as to an ideal. The descendants of these ancient puritans of the desert could not tear away their thoughts from the paradise inhabited by their forefathers. We are all of us beset by the thought of what we sprung from. The charm of patriarchal life had an invincible spell over the imagination of the succeeding centuries.* This mode of existence stood out as being essentially noble and pure—purer, no doubt, than it was in reality, and the more ardent minds were constantly yearning to go back to it. The march towards monotheism, which was the whole *circulus* of the life of these peoples, is in reality nothing more than a return to the intuition of their early history. Henceforth the tendency of the Semitic peoples, who are the most richly endowed with the spirit of the race, will be to rejuvenate the visions of this distant past.

The branch whose history I am relating will more particularly be found from age to age impelled by the desire to reconstitute this patriarchal state in which superstition, social complications, and the violence of the wealthy will effect a sweeping change. The author of the Book of Job finds his conception of religious perfection in the practices of the desert. The Rechabites set themselves up for carrying on the traditions of the ancient mode of life, and were very highly esteemed on that account. The schism of the northern tribes, after Solomon's reign, was due to the instinctive repugnance which they felt for straying away from the path which their forefathers trod. We shall find the school of Elijah or Elisha founding the whole movement of the following centuries upon a reaction towards the

* We came one day, while travelling in Syria, upon a Bedouin encampment. My men, who were not any of them nomads, were seized with sudden enthusiasm, and greeted these vagrants as brethren of more noble status than themselves.

past. The greater prophets, who were the purest representatives of the spirit of race, made this their programme; the Mosaic *Torah,* in its different ages, was a utopian reversion toward the patriarchal ideal, to a society in which there should be neither rich nor poor, neither sovereigns nor subjects; in a word, to the ancient tribal system, founded solely upon the family and upon the association of affiliated families. It is certain that the primitive nomad was more advanced in religious matters than David and Omri: he knew nothing of the cruel Iahveh; human sacrifices, in which the national deity delighted, did not exist at all, or at all events had not the character of sheer extermination.

It often happens that the ideal of a people is an aim conceived in advance, which that people puts before it in order to stimulate itself to reach its end. For the peoples who descended from the tent of the patriarchs, on the contrary, their ideal was behind them; and it was one which they saw in actual existence among the tribes that had retained their nomad mode of life. They did not, therefore, create a myth when they joyed in the stories of the oldest patriarchal life, — they were rather recalling a memory; and this memory of a lost purity and happiness was ever tempting them to revert to a state, the perfection of which had assuredly been exaggerated, but which had left an indelible trace upon the character of the nation.

CHAPTER V.

ANCIENT BABYLONIAN INFLUENCE.

As a rule, a powerfully organised civilisation, girt by barbarians or nomads, exercises two opposing influences upon these populations. It at once attracts and repels them. It attracts them by the thousand and one advantages which an active form of civilisation offers to poor persons in a state of dire distress. It repels them by an air of hardness and immorality. This is the feeling of the Arabs in Algeria, who, while recognising the material superiority of French society, regard it with nothing but disgust, deeming it to be devoid of any high principle and to be a reflection upon the liberty of action of an honourable man, who should not allow himself to be thus ticketed and numbered. Ever since civilisation has gained the mastery in the world, this view can but lead to the ruin of the human families which make it the limit of their vision. But, in the early ages, such a sentiment was often of a preservative tendency. Through it the Semitic tent succeeded in keeping itself pure from many abominations, the remains of primitive bestiality, and from the aberrations which accompanied the first delirious ideas of a dawning conscience. Probity was of more value than it is at the present time for the general work of progress. It was a delicate little plant, not acclimatised anywhere, menaced with destruction wherever it grew, without which the human culture could not flourish. Whatever protected it served to forward the progress of true civilisation.

As a rule, the nomad hordes which, as we have seen, bore within them, simple shepherds as they were, a lofty moral principle, lived side by side with societies already established that did not in any way become mixed with them. These small groups of simple creatures had a sort of horror for what they did not understand. Egypt, and Assyria more especially, were to them unfathomable depths. The enormous number of slaves and functionaries must have been revolting to them, while the gigantic buildings struck them as sheer acts of folly and of undue pride. But in most cases the attraction proved too strong. The tribe assented to certain conditions of authority, and sought its sustenance in the interstices of a greater society than itself. It must be remarked that these ancient civilisations were not as compact as our own; they had internal gaps in which the nomad could find room, and which seemed as it were to invite him to occupy them. It was in this way that Egypt has always attracted the Arabs, and has found room for them in its administrative system, apparently so closely filled in. The population of Babylonia does not appear to have been at all dense;* shepherd bands could easily occupy a place in the country analogous to that of the Bedouins of the present day in Syria and Egypt, or of the Gypsies in those countries where they are the most numerous.

Among the nomad Semites who migrated from Arabia into the more favoured countries bordering upon the Mediterranean, some arrived direct from Arabia, while others, stopped by the great desert, made a circuit along the Euphrates and reached Syria at Mabug and Aleppo, after having made a more or less lengthened sojourn upon Babylonian soil. This sojourn made a deep mark upon them. The prevalent language of Babylonia had for a long time been the Semitic idiom known as Assyrian. It is doubtful whether the tribes speaking the Hebrew or Aramaic languages were able to understand it. But the civilisation which these tribes had before their eyes while wandering over the vast marshes of the Euphrates was, if I may so express myself, a speaking one, even for those who could not unravel the complicated mystery of its sacred writings.

Babylon was for centuries a still more brilliant beacon-light than Egypt, shining out amid profound darkness. It cannot be said with certainty to what race belonged the creators of this civilisation as ancient as that of Egypt, and not less original in its character. They were neither Semites nor Aryans. The name of Turanians is vague and doubtful. The application to

* This seems proved by the way in which the kings of Assyria and of Chaldæa transplanted the inhabitants.

ANCIENT BABYLONIAN INFLUENCE.

them of the names of Cushites and Cephenes is quite arbitrary. The language which they spoke has not been unveiled to us, and we are in ignorance as to whether it remains concealed beneath the still undeciphered Accadian or Sumerian inscriptions. It appears, however, that the first impression of the Assyriologists was the correct one.* The Assyrian hieroglyphicism, the origin of what is called cuneiform writing, was neither Semitic nor Aryan, and it was only later that it was used to write Semitic and Aryan idioms.

In close connexion with the creation of Assyrian hieroglyphicism was the creation of a whole school which plays a leading part in the history of human genius. Assyria had, from the very first, her castes of savants and priests. She created arithmetic, geometry, the calendar, and astronomy; she organised human existence, and, by establishing the week, brought into existence the Sabbath. So rational science was formed. A number of meteorological data, which still hold good, and which even the great innovations of the French Revolution were powerless to affect, were established. The seven planets gave their names to the seven days of the week, and the seventh day had special characteristics which marked it as a day of rest.† The divisions of the circle and of time were the same as they are at the present day for

---

* Oppert, *Expéd. scientif. en Mésopotamie*, vol. ii. (Paris, 1859). See *Journal des Savants*, March, 1859, pp. 181 and following

† Schrader, *Die Keilinschriften und das A. T.*, vol. ii. pp. 18, &c.; G. Smith, *The Assyrian Eponym Canon*, pp. 19 and following.

all nations. There was an abundance of literature, half mythical, half scientific, which claimed to relate the origin of the world and of humanity. The popular imagination was charmed by interminable tales of gods and giants.* But all this literature was pervaded by a most remarkable current of ideas. It was not a mere simple mythology, sporting amid the endless play of words, and following into the dim distance the capricious flight of metaphor; it betrayed a glimmering of scientific hypotheses, starting from accurate and correct observations, generalising in some cases with singular good sense, and expressing the first perceptions of reasoning in a form which may seem to us overstrained, now that we have come to proceed only by the analytical method in the research after causes.

In a word, the human intellect at this advanced post of its development tentatively claimed to explain the origin of the world without the intervention of the gods. Spontaneous generation, too hastily concluded, was the fundamental dogma of Babylonian science.† The world ‡ came out of chaos,§ from a

* F. Lenormant, *Les Origines de l'Histoire*, vol. i. (1880).

† Berosus, Damascius, Nabathean Agriculture, fragment discovered by Smith (allowing for the rectifications of Abbé Quentin). See Chwolson, *Die Ssabier* (St. Petersburg, 1859); Lenormant, *Origines de l'Histoire*, vol. i., appendix. *Comment. sur Bérose* (Paris, 1871); my essays upon Sanchoniathon and upon Nabathean Agriculture (*Mém de l'Acad. des Insc. et Belles-Lettres*, vol. xxiii. part ii., and vol. xxiv., part i.

‡ See Lenormant and Schrader's works quoted above.

§ תהו = تِيهٌ • בהו = βααύ de Sanchoniathon, *Ialdebaoth* of the Gnostics.

ANCIENT BABYLONIAN INFLUENCE.

profound abyss (Tiamat),* from a fruitful mudbank, after the model of the great alluvions which the Euphrates and Tigris form where their waters unite. From this moist chaos, vivified by an amorous wind,† emerged one after another creations more or less discordant, which disappeared to make room for beings more in harmony with one another, and lastly for man.

The dwelling-place of this primitive humanity was Lower Chaldæa, conceived as being a paradise, the source of all the rivers,‡ with the sacred tree in the middle of it.§ Ten great mythical reigns, each lasting about a thousand years, made up the duration of this primordial age, during which deified men built the first towns, invented arts, and laid the foundations of civilised life.‖

A deluge, from which only one man, taking refuge on a ship with those of the animal species intended to reproduce their race, escaped, separated the mythical from an heroic age teeming with the stories of giants born of the connection between demons and women. The origin of Babylon and of Nineveh was ascribed to

* תהום = Mummu Tiamat (תהומת) = ταυθὲ of Damascius = ταυατθ (for θαλατθ) of Berosus.

† רוח = Πνεῦμα of Sanchoniathon. 'Απασών of Damascius = חפצון = Πόθος.

‡ Fr. Delitzsch, *Wo lag das Paradies?* (Leipsic, 1881).

§ Menant. *Cylindres de l'Assyrie*, pp. 61 and following; *Cylindres de la Chaldée*, pp. 189 and following; Lenormant, *Origines de l'Histoire*, vol. i. pp. 74 and following.

‖ Compare with the Phœnician fables handed down by Sanchoniathon, fables the Assyrian original of which scarcely admits of a doubt.

this race of giants, the most celebrated of whom was the hunter Merodak or Nimrod, who strangled a lion by squeezing it against his belt.* The hillocks of bricks which served as foundations to the Babylonian temples, and especially the gigantic Borsippa, the tower of tongues, became the subject of innumerable legends, which each generation has moulded into accordance with its bent of thought.

Another centre of legends, to the south of Babylon, was the ancient land of Ur,† with its mythical king, Father Orham, looked upon as a founder, a pacific legislator, and a saint.‡ It is the oldest locality of Babylonia; and the texts taken from it represent the still lineal form of the so-called cuneiform writing.§ The kings of Ur are the oldest known Babylonian dynasty. A brick elevation marks the site of the principal temple. Ur, or Our-Casdim, as the Hebrews

* See Musée du Louvre, Assyrian room, Nos. 4 and 5. See Schrader's work quoted above, pp. 92, 93.

† Now Moqayyar, or, as erroneously written, Moghayr. See Schrader, pp. 129 and following; Loftus, *Chald. and Sus.*, pp. 127 and following; Menant, *Bab. et la Chald.*, p. 71 and following; George Smith, *Chald. Gen.*, p. 246; Delitzsch, pp. 226, 227; Maspero, *Hist. Anc.*, 4th edition, pp. 154 and following.

‡ Rawlinson, *Cuneiform Inscriptions of Western Asia*, vol. i., plates 1 and following; Oppert, *Expéd. de Mésop.*, vol. i., pp. 264—266; *Hist. des Empires de Chald. et d'Assyrie*, pp. 16 and following; Menant, *Cyl. de la Chald.*, pp. 127—158; *Collection de Clercq*, pp. 14 and following, pp. 31, 67 and following. There is a doubt as to all these combinations, the reading Ourkhammou not being certain. The Assyriologists take it to be the name of a real king.

§ British Museum, *Cuneiform Inscriptions*, vol. i., plates 1 and following.

ANCIENT BABYLONIAN INFLUENCE.

called it, may be regarded as the first centre of Babylonian or Chaldean civilisation.

All the large towns in this marshy region where the Euphrates and Tigris meet had in the same way their divine legends, dating from the most remote antiquity. Erech* equalled Ur in nobility and religious importance.† The recently discovered sculptures of Tello‡ show us the dwellers in the primitive Lower Chaldæa under the most original and striking aspect. These strange cities of Ur, Erech, Babel, and Tello made the very strongest impression upon the nomad Semites who had migrated from Arabia. Those enormous pyramids, the object in creating which was quite beyond their comprehension, gave rise to no end of fables.§ The nomad, like the barbarian, does not understand large buildings; he has the most childish tales to explain the existence of all colossal ruins.∥ The wonderful tower of Borsippa, more especially, must have suggested the

---

* Now Warka.

† Loftus, pp. 139 and following, 160 and following; Delitzsch, p. 94.

‡ *Découvertes en Chaldée*, by M. de Sarzec (Paris, Leroux), originals in the Louvre.

§ Genesis, ch. xi., v. 1 and following; Herodotus, book i., p. 181. We know of at least three towers of Babel: Birs-Nemroud, Babil, and Akerkouf.

∥ Tales about Palmyra, Balbeck, the monuments in the Hauran, Petra, the alleged Themoudite fortresses, which are merely tombs. *Notices et Extraits de l'Acad. des Inscr. et Belles-Lettres*, vol. xviii., part ii., pp. 4, 5. Compare with the *Mirabilia urbis Romæ* of the Middle Ages.

most singular ideas, as, for instance, whether the power of man carried so far is not an insult to God.

The wanderings of the nomads did not lead them much in the direction of the Tigris or Nineveh. They generally halted in that part of Mesopotamia known as Padan-Aram, the principal centres of which were Harran, Sarug, Edessa. From the point of view of its civilisation this country was an annex of Assyria, a sort of Aramaic Babylon. Aramaic was spoken in it, and this alone would have been sufficient to make many important changes in the traditions of Babel and Ur. Harran, moreover, appears to have been even then, what it remained up to the thirteenth century, a city of syncretism, in which the myths of Babylonian origin underwent all kinds of transformations. The great seer of the Israelite legends, Balaam, is supposed to have come from there.* Harran, in the course of its long and singular history, stands out at every epoch as a sort of colony and emporium of Babylonian ideas.†

The pastors found here the cycle of Chaldean ideas under a form more acceptable to them, gilded over as they were by a sort of Semitic varnish. The names of characteristic personages, for instance that of the first woman (*Hava*, "she who gives life"), possibly the name of the god Iahveh,‡ stood out as Aramaic words easily

* Numbers, ch. xxii., v. 5; ch. xxiii., v. 7; Schrader, pp. 155, 156.

† Chwolson, *Die Ssabier und der Ssabismus* (St. Petersburg, 1856).

‡ See the following chapter.

understood. The hero of the deluge became a man well pleasing to heaven, called sometimes Hanok, at other times Noah. The ark rested upon the mountains of the land of Ararat (Armenia), whereas in the Assyrian text there is no allusion to this northern country. The inhabitants of Padan-Aram were particularly attached to the legend of the fabled Orham, king of Ur, and called him Aborham (Abraham),* the Father-Orham, a name which was destined to go down into the deepest strata of mythological history, pater Orchamus.† These kings of Ur were more or less patriarchs, at once kings and fathers of their peoples.‡ The Assyrians often depicted them, and always in a way which harmonises with the Abraham of tradition, as seated in an arm-chair, with a benevolent aspect and without any sort of military pomp or circumstance. The chief title of Father-Orham to the veneration of his pacific admirers was that he had substituted the sacrifice of a ram for that of human beings, as in the case of his son Isaac.§ I am inclined to think that this Orham is the real or imaginary person who has lent his name

* In very early times the letters ה and ח were used indifferently in Semitic etymology.

 † Rexit Achæmenias urbes pater Orchamus, isque
  Septimus a prisco numeratur origine Belo.

Ovid, *Metam.*, iv., p. 212. *Pater* no doubt had in Ovid's text a more limited meaning (*pater ejus*, scil. *Leucothoes*); but the expression *Pater Orchamus* seems none the less to have forced itself upon Ovid by tradition.

‡ Menant, *Cyl. de la Chaldée*, pp. 129—136, 137—143; *Catal. de la coll. De Clercq*, pp. 17 and following.

§ Menant, *Cyl. de la Chaldée*, pp. 144 and following, 146, 147, 151. *Catal. De Clercq*, pp. 17 and following.

and several of the most characteristic traits to the history of Abraham. This may be all the more readily admitted because these myths of Orham were generally represented on small cylinders of very little value, which were passed about among the nomads as talismans, and which must have given a great impetus to their imagination.*

The myth of Nimrod also figures in the Biblical narratives under a form peculiarly typical of Harran. He remained right into the Middle Ages one of the gods of the city of Harran.† Most of the incidents borrowed from Babylonia which are to be found in the early chapters of Genesis are not taken at first hand; they have come through Padan, and represent Babylonia as seen through Harran memories. The names of the antediluvian patriarchs,‡ answering to the mythical kings of Babylon, also appear to be Harranian combinations.

The Semite herders who led their flocks in this region understood all this§ and were much struck by it. Their situation was like that of Mahomet, unable either to read or write, in the presence of Judaism and

* Menant, see previous note.

† Assemani, *Bibl. Orient.*, vol. i. p. 327; Wellhausen, *Prolegomena*, p. x.

‡ See the two identical lists, one Jehovist, the other Elohist, Genesis, ch. iv. and v.

§ The influence of the Babylonian cosmogonies also crops up again among the Phœnicians (Sanchoniathon, Damascius). But that perhaps is due to more recent adaptations. See *Mémoires de l'Acad. des Inscript. et Belles-Lettres*, vol. xxiii., part ii., pp. 241 and following.

Christianity, overloaded with writings. Everything was done by word of mouth, by popular narrative. The resemblance between the Hebrew narratives and the ancient Babylonian narratives was of the same kind as that between the Koran and the Old Testament and the Gospels. In accordance with their Euhemerist intellect, opposed as it was to mythology, the nomad Semites simplified these ancient fables, flattened them down, so to speak, and reduced them to dimensions which admitted of their being carried about with the baggage of the nomad. By the mere process of passing into the hands of the Aramaic populations or wandering pastors, who knew nothing of writing, these theogonic epics came to have a childish and almost puerile aspect. The story of the creation became toned down; Paradise was materialised, and its topography, the farther one got from Lower Chaldea, became vague and contradictory; the mythical kings, who, according to the Assyrian narratives, reigned for three or four thousand years, became patriarchs, who lived eight or nine hundred years. This seemed less difficult to believe. At the same time the deluge assumed a moral meaning; it was a punishment. The myths as to the origin of Babel assume a hostile physiognomy: Babel is a proud city; an insult against God. Ur, upon the contrary, is a primitive cradle of holiness.

In this way an element of capital importance was introduced into the Semitic tradition. The basis of the religion which was adopted by the world is the simple and moral elohism of the Semite pastor. But it was an insufficient basis. What was wanted, especially in view of the disgust of mythology induced by the result of many centuries, was a seeming explanation of the origin of things, a cosmogony with an air of being reasonable, positive, and historical. The strange mixture of real science and of fable contained in the Chaldean-Hebraic system marked it out to fill this void. Boiled down, strapped tight, if I may so express myself, upon the back of the nomad's beast of burden, dilūted for centuries in memoirs without any sort of precision and mercilessly condensed, the proto-Chaldean narratives have given us the first twelve chapters of Genesis, and there is not, perhaps, any part of the Bible which has had more important consequences. Humanity has supposed that it possessed in them an historical narrative of the things about which it was most anxious to know, I mean its infancy and early progress. The very real good sense which is to be found at the root of these symbols would make us forget what there is defective about them. Their mythological side was to serve as a passport to what is superficially reasonable about them. Originally given by the Hebrew pundits in two parallel versions, but afterwards fused into one single text, the narratives in question have become the necessary preliminary to all sacred history.

Owing to the narrowness of Christian dogmatism, these semi-scientific pages were in the Middle Ages a serious obstacle to the awakening of the human intellect.

The whole theory of the universe was thought to be contained in the six days' work. Even in our time, the lack of criticism, both in France and England, general among savants who concern themselves solely with physical and mathematical sciences, has caused a great deal of nonsense to be written upon this subject. It must not be forgotten, however, that the chapter *Bereshith* was science for the day in which it was written. The old Babylonian spirit breathes in it still. The succession of the creations and ages of the world, the idea that the world has a growth, a history, in which each state proceeds from the previous state by an organic development, was an immense advance upon a level theory of the universe, conceived as a material and lifeless aggregate. The factitious simplicity of the Bible narrative, the exaggerated aversion which its pages exhibit for big figures and lengthy periods, have masked the powerful evolutionary spirit which lies at the bottom of it; but the genius of the unknown Darwins whom Babylon possessed 4,000 years ago is always found in it. The eloquent words, "In the beginning God created the heaven and the earth," was like the cold mistral which cleared the sky, like the sweep of the broom which drove away beyond our horizon the chimeras which darkened it. A free will, as implied by the words "He created," substituted for ten thousand capricious fancies, is a progress of its kind. The great truth of the unity of the world and of the absolute solidarity of all its various parts, which polytheism failed to appreciate, is at least clearly perceived in these narratives, in which all parts of nature bring forth by the action of the same thought and the effect of the same creative Word.

The nomad herder would not have invented these strange stories; but he has caused them to live. Chaldean cosmogony would never have conquered the world in the exuberant form which it assumed in the Assyrian texts; its simplification by the Semitic genius was effected just at the very time when the human intellect was craving clear ideas upon a subject of which nothing clear can be known.

Everything repeats itself in the history of the human intellect. In this instance, the dried herbarium was more fruitful than the verdant field. Monstrosities which would have remained buried in the heap of Oriental balderdash, have become palpable realities. The clear and sober imagination of Israel has effected this miracle. What reads as grotesque in Berosus appears in the Bible narrative so true and so natural, that we, with our Western credulity, have treated it as history, and have imagined, when we adopted these fables, that we have been discarding mythology.

CHAPTER VI.

THE NAME OF IAHVEH.

It is very possible that the long history of religion, which, starting from the nomad's tent, has resulted in Christianity or Islamism, derives from primitive Assyria, or from Accadian Assyria, as it is called, another element of capital importance; that is, the name of *Iahoué* or *Iahveh*.* This proper name is, in the theology of the nomad Semites, a strange misuse of terms. Why should a proper name be given to one who

---

* The pronunciation *Jehovah* has only been used since the seventeenth century. It constitutes a regular impossibility, inasmuch as the vowels יְהֹוָה are taken from the word אֲדֹנָי. There would, if we are guided by the Massoretic text, be as good reason for saying *Jehovih*, as the Massoretes punctuate יֱהֹוִה wherever the text runs אדני יהוה. This is what is called a perpetual keri; this presents no difficulty when we remember that in the first half of the Middle Ages there was no compound sheva. Let us imagine that it was compulsory to substitute the name of Lutèce for Paris; would that legitimise the form of Purèse? The real vowels of יהוה are unknown. The ancients transcribed ΙΕΥΩ, ΙΑΟΥ, ΙΑΩ; Clement of Alexandria gives 'Ιαουέ; Theodoretus tells us that the Samaritans pronounced ΙΑΒΕ. St. Epiphany adopts the same form. St. Jerome gives *Iaho* (see the texts collected by Gesenius, *Thes.*, p. 577). We find also ΙΕΥΕ (Stade, *Z.*, 1881, p. 346; 1882, pp. 173, 174). The form *Iahveh* or *Iahweh* seems therefore accurately to represent the pronunciation of at least the fourth century of our era.

has no congener, who is alone of his kind? The name was in all probability borrowed by these peoples from abroad. Nothing goes to show that *Iahveh* was indigenous to Egypt. In Assyria, upon the contrary, and especially in the Chaldean countries bordering upon Padan-Aram, the word *Iahou* or *Iahveh* seems to have been employed to designate God.* The root hawa, written with a soft *h* or a hard *h*,† signifies in the Aramaic tongue, the being, the breath, or the life, something analogous to *rouah*. The mother of life, the first woman, was called Hawwa; the master of life, the supreme being, may have been called *Iahwa*. This name was more especially used when speaking of the god who presided over the greatest of nature's phenomena, the thunder. The Semite herdsmen, it seems, were much struck by this, and came to regard *Iahoua* as synonymous with *El* or *Elohim*. The Canaanites, or at all events the Hamathites, adopted the same synonym. We find the Jews having a king called *Io-iaqim* and *El-iaqim*, while in Hamath we find a king named *Iahubid* and *Ilubid*.‡

The holy name became contracted into *Iahou* or *Io*, and was shortened to *Iah*. But the Mesa inscrip-

* Schrader, pp. 23 and following. The classic IAΩ is always considered by the Greeks to be of Assyrian origin.

† The distinction between those two articulations scarcely existed before the invention of writing. Even after the introduction of the alphabet, the ה and the ח were often confounded in sound and in the way in which they were formed. See above, note *, p. 68.

‡ Schrader.

THE NAME OF IAHVEH.

tion,* which dates from about 875 B.C., gives the name יהוה written in four letters as in classic Hebrew. Even from this epoch, moreover, the tetragrammaton was explained by the verb *haïa*, which is the Hebraic form of *hawa*: "I am he that I am," and "I am" became a regular substantive.† In this way a metaphysical meaning was arrived at, without much departure, perhaps, from the primitive meaning.

Let me hasten to add that all these points are surrounded by the gravest doubts. We shall see, as we proceed, that it is also very possible that Iahveh was the local god of Sinai or the provincial god of Palestine.‡ Of all the obscure questions in these ancient histories, this assuredly is the most hopeless. These proper names of Iahveh, of Chemosh, which the Syro-Arabian peoples gave to their supreme god, are quite an insoluble problem. My opinion is that the patriarchal elohism is to be regarded as anterior and superior to Iahveism, to Camosism, &c. It was an immense advantage that the gods had only a generic name, removing all idea of personality. It may be regarded as a step in advance, too, when these *elohim*, unified in one single Elohim, acted as one single being. But it was a step backward when they had a proper name, such as *Camos*, *Iahveh*, *Rimmon*, and constituted for each people a jealous, egoistical, and per-

* Line 18.
† Exodus, ch. iii., v. 14, Jehovist; Exodus, ch. vi., v. 2, 3, Elohist.
‡ See pp. 101, 102, 158 and following, 194.

sonal god. The people of Israel alone corrected the defects of its national god, suppressed his proper name, and brought it to be only a synonym of Elohim.

The story of this slow transformation, which was a reversion to the primitive patriarchal state, will be the subject of this history. For the present it will be sufficient to point out that *Iahveh* plays no important part in the history of Israel until Israel has become a nation attached to one soil. The religious progress of Israel will be found to consist in reverting from Iahveh to Elohim, in modifying Iahveh, and in stripping him of his personal attributes and leaving him only the abstract existence of Elohim. Iahveh is a special god, the god of a human family and of a country; as such he is neither better nor worse than the other protecting deities. Elohim is the universal God, the God of the human race. In reality it is to Elohim and not to Iahveh that the world has been converted. The world has become deist, that is to say elohist, and not iahveist. It has forgotten how the name of Iahveh is pronounced; each people will continue to place the vowels in its own way. Neither Christianity nor Islamism know Iahveh. It is a word entirely eliminated from pious use; it is the name of a barbarian and foreign god.

The pantheon of these wandering peoples, reduced to preserving ancient words in default of ancient images, contained in this way a host of uncomprehended vocables which were in turn used or cast aside

THE NAME OF IAHVEH.

by the religious mode of the day, and which came like spectres upon the imagination. *Sebaoth* is assuredly one of the most peculiar of these ancient divine names which have become enigmas. The expression "*Sebaoth*" to denote the Divinity appears to proceed from the same order of ideas as *elohim*. The word *sebaoth* signifies "the armies, the series, the orders" of creatures, and especially of celestial creatures, of stars, of angels. It corresponds to the word *álamin* ("the worlds") of the Koran, which is itself the Hebrew *olam* (the Phœnician *oulom*), translated in the Gnostic and Jewish Greek by Αἰών.* All this, it will be observed, does not differ much from the Babylonian ideas. *Sebaoth* means "the worlds," as *Elohim* means "the forces." *Sebaoth*, like *Elohim*, becomes a collective singular, or rather a plural reduced to the signification of a singular, designating the Supreme Being, after having designated the series of beings. *Sebaoth*, used by itself, was synonymous with God; *Sebaoth* was equivalent to *Elohim*, and when Iahveh took to himself all the divine names, he also took that of *Sebaoth*,† without any fresh shade of meaning entering into the Hebrew conception of Providence, to so great an extent was this

* Hebrews, ch. i., v. 2.

† The expression יהוה צבאות is familiar to the prophets of the eighth century B.C., Amos, Hosea, Isaiah, and Micah. In other parts of the Prophets and in the Psalms it seems to have become so by force of imitation. It is a poetic expression which the very ancient narratives do not contain. The expression יהוה אלהי צבאות belongs to a period in which the ancient meaning was not understood, and in which it was considered grammatically correct to say, Iahveh (God of the) Sebaoth.

conception the very base, the limit, and the expression of the genius of these peoples.

The religious institutions of Babylon were hardly of a character to be imitated by nomads. The Sabbath, or the seventh day's rest, was perhaps the Chaldean institution which astonished the Semites more than any other. For the Bedouin, with no regular hours of work, life was a perpetual Sabbath. In a land where public works, executed by forced labour, had been carried very far, a period of rest seemed necessary, in the interests both of the master and the slave. The number seven played a very important part in Babylonian ideas, and the period of seven days, recurring four times in a lunar month, marked divisions of time corresponding very closely with human strength. Let me add that the number six was the basis of Babylonian numeration, so that 6×1 represented very much what 12×1 does to us. The seventh was something supererogatory and unclassed, like the thirteenth with us. The Sabbath is thus an institution of a very advanced stage of civilisation, not a patriarchal usage. It doubtless formed part of the first relay of customs brought from Chaldæa by the patriarchs. The nomads only adopted it at first so far as it suited them, and it was not until much later, and in a social condition of quite a different kind, that they made further progress upon this point.

A very characteristic fact it is that the nomads, who adopted so many Chaldean institutions, did not take the division of the day into twenty-four hours. Up to the

Græco-Roman period, the Jews divided the day just like the Arabs, that is to say into characteristic periods.* The word *saa*, "hour," does not exist in ancient Hebrew. With regard to the measures of weight, length, and capacity, the nomad Semites, like the whole of the old world, knew of no others but those established by Babylon.†

* Nehemiah, ch. vii., v. 8.
† Researches of Bœckh, Brandis, and Six.

CHAPTER VII.

THE HEBREW OR TERACHITE GROUP.

THE Euphrates may be regarded as the high road of the nomad Semites who came in contact with Assyria. Ascending its course in a north-westerly direction, they reached the city of Harran, which was, as it were, their rallying point. From there a great number of them came back to the Euphrates, which they crossed at Thapsacus or Beredjik, then entering upon the Syrian deserts, to the east of the Antilibanus, regions singularly bare in the eye of the dweller in cities, but very suitable for the rearing of flocks and herds. They were particularly fond of the land of Us or Aus, now the dwelling-place of the Anezis, the land of Terach (the Trachonitides), the region of Damascus, and the south of Palestine, to which the Canaanites had not penetrated. They never went near the coast, and probably had, like the Arabs, an aversion for the sea, regarding it as so much abstracted from creation.*

These tribes, first of all trans-Euphratian, which had become, by crossing the stream, cis-Euphratian, took

* In the Apocalypse (ch. xxi., v. 1), one of the characteristics of the world made perfect is to be the disappearance of the sea

THE HEBREW OR TERACHITE GROUP. 77

the generic name of *Hebrew* (*Ibrim*, "those of the other side"), though we do not know whether they took it when they placed the Euphrates between themselves and their brethren who remained in the Paddan-Aram, or whether it was the Canaanites who called them "those from beyond," or, to be more accurate, "those who had crossed the river."* These *Ibrim*, in any event, appear to have been closely allied to the Arphaxadites (people of the mountainous province to the north of Nineveh), to the town of Paliga, near Circesium, to the towns of Ragho, Sarug, and Nahor, not far from the Euphrates.† Then we find them, by a sudden bound, transported to the Trachonitides,‡ to the south-east of Damascus, and in the region of the Hauran. Great as may be the distance which separates them from the Paddan-Aram, their eyes are never removed from their ancient country, and more especially from Harran.§

The Terachite family was destined to be still further deeply divided, but it never lost the sense of its unity. It was this family above all others which jealously preserved the religion of Ur-Casdim, and stoutly adhered to its claim of Ab-Orham as its supreme father. The unvarying tradition was that Terach, the father of the

* Genesis, ch. xiv., v. 13; Septuagint, ὁ περάτης; Aquila, ὁ περαΐτης. Mythic eponym; Eber.

† Genesis, ch. xi.

‡ תרח = Τραχών. I think that חרן stands for חורן, the Hauran.

§ The life of Jacob is still half-way between the Padan-Aram and Syria properly so called. Genesis, ch. xxiv., xxvii., xxviii.

race, was a native of Ur-Casdim, and that Ab-Orham was his son. This Ab-Orham was represented sometimes as a man, sometimes as a god. The tribes originally ascribed to him the part of supreme ancestor and divine patriarch. The Hebrews pronounced his name *Abraham*, which they interpreted "Father of many nations;"* but they often changed this name to *Ab-Ram*, "the mighty Father," to obtain a meaning more in conformity with the past which was ascribed to him. He was a pacific and humane father. It was related how, when it was his duty to sacrifice his first-born son, he substituted for him a ram.† It was an honour to have for one's ancestor so great a civiliser, a man who had been in communion with El or Iahou. Damascus also reckoned Abraham among its fabled kings,‡ and if that is borrowed from the Biblical traditions, it is probably a plagiarism of very ancient date.

To be of Ur-Casdim descent became, in the eyes of all Hebrews, a title of high nobility. The Israelite Hebrews have reached so great a celebrity in history that they have absorbed altogether the name of Hebrews; but, originally, this name applied to many other peoples. The Ammonites, the Edomites, and the Moabites claimed Abraham as their common ancestor. They felt themselves still to be brethren in the

* Genesis, ch. xvii., v. 5 (Elohist).
† See above, pp. 63, 64.
‡ Nicholas of Damascus, in Jos., *Ant.* I., vii., 2; Justin, xxxvi., v. 2. Berosus does not mention Abraham by name; but according to Josephus he designates him without naming him.

strictest sense of the word. This fraternity was at times irksome to the Israelites, who were so often disdainful of their congeners. Ammon, Edom, Moab, and Ishmael are connected with the Father of the peoples by insulting not to say obscene legends.*
But a thousand historical incidents treasured up in the memory of Israel spoke more loudly than hatred, and proved that all these peoples were connected with one another by the tie of a close relationship.

The religious resemblance between them was particularly striking. The religion of the Moabites and that of the Edomites unquestionably differed but little at first from that of the Israelites.† Edom, more particularly, had from the very first a school of sages; that of Theman,‡ in which the problem of man's destiny was discussed from the standpoint of the monotheistic philosophy of the Hebrews, and in which it was sought to give a meaning to life by admitting only two fundamental principles: an eternal God and fleeting man.§ The numerous Arab tribes devoted to the worship of El, Ishmaelites, Adabelites, Bethuelites, Raguelites, Jeramelites, Malkielites, Iahlelites, Iah-

---

* Genesis, ch. xvi., xvii., xix., xxv., xxxvi.

† Ruth and the episode of Balaam do not denote any religious difference between the Moabites and the Israelites.

‡ Somewhere about Petra.

§ The Book of Job, composed by an Israelite, but with the intention of presenting a Themanite ideal. The attention of the author to local colour does not admit of the supposition that he would have attributed the monotheistic philosophy to these peoples, if such had not been the doctrine of the wise men of the country.

selites, Iemuelites,* Midianites,† Kenites,‡ Calebites or Calbelites,§ Kenizzites,|| Ausites,¶ Beni-Qedem or Saracens,** who roamed or trafficked in these Syrian deserts and in the North of Arabia, then far more busy with life than they are to-day, had probably no other theology. Lastly, the episodes of Melchisedech, priest of *El-Elion*, and of Abimelech of Geraar, though not possessing a clearly historical character, demonstrate the existence of a wide zone of comparatively pure worship at the junction of the Arabian and Syrian deserts.

The Hebrews, as they spread through the eastern parts of Syria, encountered therefore, wherever they went, populations having a strong analogy with them-

* Note these forms: יחצאלי, יחלאלי, מלכיאלי, ישמעאלי, ירחמאלי, parallel to ישראלי, and which would seem to infer יוספאלי, יצחקאלי, יעקבאלי. See *Revue des études juives*, Oct.-Dec., 1882, pp. 162 and following. רעואל, בתואל, אדבאל are certainly also the names of tribes. It is the same with ימואל, son of Simeon. Magdiel and Mehetabel are probably names of the same kind. Note קין, the imaginary eponym of the Kenites, Numbers, ch. xxvi., v. 22; Judges, ch. iv., v. 11. Comp. *Œst. Monatsschrift*, Nov., 1884, p. 279.

† Relations of Moses with Jethro and Midian (Exodus, ch. xviii., v. 1 to 12), a very ancient fragment. Jethro is probably an Arab form with a final vowel.

‡ The Kenites (which stood perhaps for Kenielites, קיניאל) are Arabs, not Canaanites. They were always on very good terms with Israel.

§ See pp. 89 and 90 below.

|| קנז stands perhaps for קנזאל.

¶ Compatriots of Job, supposed to be monotheist.

** Orientals, generic name of the nomad Arabs to the east of Palestine (land of the Anezis).

THE HEBREW OR TERACHITE GROUP.

selves. The Ishmaelites, the Midianites, and a whole series of Arab tribes grouped under the names of Cethura and Agar,* were classed as Abrahamites. All these peoples belonged to different branches of one and the same genealogical tree; they understood each other's dialects; their manners and customs were much the same. They formed one vast brotherhood, from Harran to the Negeb (Southern Palestine); all these scattered groups treated one another as brethren, and aided one another like members of one dispersed family.†

The relations of the Terachites with the Canaanites were, upon the contrary, very unfriendly, though they spoke a similar language, and doubtless belonged to the same race. In after years the Hebrews, out of their great hatred, denied this latter fact, ‡ but the community of language, § without any conquest of the country to explain it, is a consideration which must take precedence of any other. The Canaanites and the Terachites were closely related, and there were times

---

* Hagar is the Arabia Petræa (هجر, Koran, xv.), by the primitive equivalence of ה and ח. Cf. הגרים, Psalm, lxxxiii., v. 7; 1 Chronicles, ch. v., v. 10, 19, 20; Paul to the Galatians, ch. iv., v. 24, 25; 'Αγραῖοι of Eratosthenes (Strabo, XVI., iv., 2).

† See the exquisite idyls in ch. xxiv. and xxix. of Genesis.

‡ Genesis, ch. x., where the Canaanites are traced back to Ham, doubtless because, at the time this ethnographical table was compiled, the Canaanites were already Egyptianised in habits and civilisation.

§ The Phœnician language only differed from the Hebrew in slight dialectic respects. See *Corpus inscr. semit.*, part i.

when the enlightened Israelites would admit this;*
but the Hebrew character and mode of life differed
totally from those of the Canaanites.† The Hebrews
remained for a long time nomads and pastors, and even
when established they always preserved the patriarchal
type of life and their aversion for large towns with
regular buildings and organised states.

There is no doubt one hypothesis which cannot be
rejected as impossible. The ancient critics clung to it,
and the recent epigraphic discoveries have lent a certain air of probability to it. It is that according to
which the Abrahamites, before entering the land of
Canaan, spoke Aramaic, and upon entering that land
adopted the language of the country, that is to say,
Hebrew.‡ When we find the Arabian desert furnishing only Aramaic inscriptions,§ some of which date
from the most remote antiquity, we are led to imagine
that the Abrahamites at first spoke the same dialect,
which we find upon these ancient stelæ left by nomads
who appear to have resembled them very closely.∥

---

* Isaiah, ch. xix., v. 18, speaks of the Hebrew as "the language of Canaan."

† Judges, ch. xviii., v. 7.

‡ Isaiah, see above.

§ *Notices et Extraits*, vol. xviii., part i.; *Revue d'archæologie, orientale*, 1st year, pp. 41 and following. Compare with the epigraphic collection of Sinaï, Safa, the Nabatheans, and Palmyra, which will be found in the second part of the *Corpus inscr. semit.*

∥ Note the very striking expression ארמי אבד (Deut., ch. xxvi., v. 5). "Wandering Aramean" applied to the ancestors of the Hebrew people. *Salm Sézab* of the Teïma inscription is in reality an *Arammi obed*, a nomad patriarch, speaking Aramaic.

Seductive as such a theory may be, it is one which cannot be accepted; for the change of language which in that case must have occurred among the Beni-Israel must also be imagined to have taken place, and for the same reason, among the Moabites and Edomites. The Moabites unquestionably spoke the same language as the Israelites.* It would have to be supposed, too, that Moab and Israel came to an agreement to change their language at the same moment. If it is admissible that the Beni-Israel, in their close contact with the Canaanites, came to adopt the latter's language, that could not have been the case with Moab, Edom, and Ammon, who did not appear to have taken the place of any previous Canaanite populations. Moab, Edom, Ammon, Israel, Canaan spoke then the same language from a community of origin, which constituted a somewhat close relationship, and not as the outcome of changes resulting from emigration or conquest.

With regard to the Aramaic-speaking populations, if we were to go by grammar alone, we should imagine them to be separated from the Hebrews by a deep gulf, dating from thousands of years. But the race sympathy is also a factor which has to be taken into account. Laban, the father of the pastors who spoke Aramaic, is in the closest relationship with the Isaakites and the Israelites. Marriages between these two are constantly taking place. They all of them inhabit the same

* The Mesa inscription, not to speak of many other Biblical proofs.

grazing ground, from Euphrates to the sea, the coast only excepted; they play each other all sorts of ill-natured tricks, which do not lead to an absolute rupture. When the separation made further progress, Galeed is the limit of Aramean and of Hebrew.* A *gal* or *men-hir* indicated the line of demarcation, being called *Galeed* by the Hebrew-speaking populations of the south and west, and *Iegar Sahadouta* by the Arameans of Damascus. Laban and Jacob swear according to the same rite, erecting a tumulus and eating bread upon it. The "heap of witness" is to remind the Hebrews and the Arameans that they have given their daughters to each other in marriage, that they have the same ancestors and the same God, and that this God is the God of Abraham, the "fear of Isaac."

The difference, then, between the Hebrews and the Canaanites was much more marked than between the various nomad families compared with one another. Nevertheless, among these populations vaguely confounded under the name Canaan, several had great analogy with the Hebrews, and especially with the Israelites. Thus, for instance, the Giblites (inhabitants of Byblus and Berytus), who formed in Phœnicia a settlement apart,† adored *El*, and had, in a

---

* Genesis, ch. xxxi., v. 43 and following, a beautiful ethnographical myth, written with the clear purpose of its double meaning.

† See the systematic and exaggerated but nevertheless true demonstration of Movers, *Die phœn. Alt.*, I., pp. 103 and following. Also *Miss. de Phén.*, pp. 214, 215. It is worthy of remark that Gebal is not included, in Genesis x., among the sons of Canaan.

religious sense, the closest analogy with the Israelites. Their dialect resembled Hebrew far more than that of the Canaanites properly so called. The stela of Iehaumelek, King of Byblus,* might be, except for the divine names on it, the stela of a king of Jerusalem.

The linguistic geography of Syria was from this date forward settled for a long time to come. The language which we call Hebrew, characterised by the article *h*, the *status constructus*, the plural in *im*, the absence of emphatic terminations, the interior passives, was spoken all along the coast from Aradus to Jaffa, &c., in the whole of Palestine and Celesyria as far as Hamath. Aramaic was spoken at Damascus, upon the slopes of Antilibanus, in the region of Aleppo, in the Paddan-Aram, and in the deserts of Northern Arabia. Arabic existed, no doubt, with all its grammatical refinements, in the centre of Arabia, near Mecca; but it was quite unknown in the countries of which I am speaking. Probably the Ishmaelites and the Cethurian tribes spoke a Hebrew or Aramaic dialect, and not Arabic in the sense applied to that word since Islamism came into existence.†

Phœnician Hebrew no doubt had its own dialects. The Terachite peoples must all have used nearly identical idioms,‡ but between Hebrew and Phœnician the differences were very real.§ It is more than

* *Corpus inscr. semit.*, p. i., No. 1.
† Teïma inscription. *Rev. d'Archéol. orient.* See above.
‡ Mesa inscription.
§ Relative pronouns and suffix pronouns slightly different; usage of vowels entirely distinct.

probable, nevertheless, that a *Kanaan* and an *Ibri* understood each other, whereas an *Ibri* and an *Arammi* would not have done so, owing to the difficulty which the unlettered man has to make allowance for varieties of dialect. Though not equalling the infinite delicacy of the Arabic spoken in the centre of Arabia, Hebrew-Phœnician possessed a high degree of suppleness and perfection, and was very superior to Aramaic, the heaviness of which prevented it from ever being suitable for the conveyance of original eloquence and poetry.

A quiver full of steel arrows, a cable with strong coils, a trumpet of brass, crashing through the air with two or three sharp notes, such is Hebrew. A language of this kind is not adapted to the expression of philosophic thought, or scientific result, or doubt, or the sentiment of the infinite. The letters of its books are not to be many; but they are to be letters of fire. This language is not destined to say much, but what it does is beaten out upon an anvil. It is to pour out floods of anger, and utter cries of rage against the abuses of the world, calling the four winds of heaven to the assault of the citadels of evil. Like the jubilee horn of the sanctuary, it will be put to no profane use; it will never express the innate joy of the conscience or the serenity of nature; but it will sound the note of the holy war against injustice and the call to the great assemblies; it will have accents of rejoicing and accents of terror; it will become the clarion of the new-moon festival, or the trumpet of judgment.

Fortunately, the Hellenic genius will in its turn compose for the expression of the joys and sorrows of the soul a seven-stringed lute, which will vibrate in unison with what is human; a great organ with a thousand pipes, equal to the harmonies of life. For Greece there were in store the most ravishing of joys, from the dance in chorus upon the summits of the Taygetus to the banquet of Aspasia, from the smile of Alcibiades to the austerity of the Portico, from the song of Anacreon to the philosophical drama of Æschylus and to the dreams put into dialogue by Plato.

CHAPTER VIII.

THE BENI-JACOB, OR BENI-ISRAEL.

AMONG these nomad tribes, speaking all the same language and professing nearly all the same creeds, alliances and compacts were constantly being made and unmade.* It was not an uncommon thing for new groups to be formed bearing names which had not been heard of before. Religion was generally the cause of these schisms. A profound instinct led the Hebrew to the most purified form of religion, but the masses were not capable of so much elevation, yielding constantly to the demoralising influences from outside. The human sacrifices, in particular, must have led to frequent secessions. When the masses, terrified by some imaginary sign of divine wrath, committed their first-born to the flames, the puritans withdrew rather than be responsible for any such horrible proceeding. The idolatrous practices also provoked severe struggles. To raise the hand to the mouth when the sun or moon were shining brightly was regarded as sacrilegious.† The truly pious men swore that they would recognise only El, and look only to him for protection, direction,

* Teima inscription, *Revue d'archéol. orientale*, first year, pp. 48 and following.
† Job, ch. xxxi., v. 26 and following.

THE BENI-JACOB, OR BENI-ISRAEL.

and reward. This explains why there are so many Hebrew or Arab tribes whose name marks a special connection with El : * *Ishmael,* "he who in El answers favourably ; " *Raguel,* "he of whom El is the shepherd or friend; " *Irhamel,* "him on whom El has pity; " *Bethuel,* and *Adabel,* the meaning of which is obscure ; with the ethnical derivations of Ishmaeli, Irhameli,† &c. Often with names of this kind, *El* was omitted, *Irham* being used instead of *Irhamel*; *Caleb* instead of *Calbel*.‡ This last name, singular as it is, need not create any surprise, for "Dog of El" was an energetic way of expressing the faithful attachment of a tribe to the God to which it had devoted itself.§

Among the tribes thus devoted to the worship of El, and which were connected with the mythical Abraham of Ur-Casdim, there was one which distinguished itself by a sort of religious gravity and scrupulous attachment to the supreme God. Its name was Israel, the meaning of which word was doubtful,‖

---

* See above, pp. 79, 80.

† The Jerahmelites were an Arab tribe dwelling to the south of the desert of Judah, towards the Dead Sea. First Book of Samuel, ch. xxvii., v. 10 ; ch. xxx. v. 29. They are, I believe, the *Nabathean Geremelienses* of Pozzuolo. *Corpus inscr. lat.*, vol. x., part i., No. 1578 ; *Journal asiat.*, Oct., 1873, p. 384.

‡ The form כלבאלם exists in Phœnician. See *Corpus inscr. semit.*, part i., Nos. 49, 52 ; cf. 86. Note the form כלובי, First Book of Chronicles, ch. ii., v. 9, and the intimate connection of the Calebites and the Jerahmelites.

§ Compare with the Χόλαιϐος or Arabic *Coleib*. *Journ. asiat.*, Jan., 1882, p. 11. The title "dog of God" is sometimes taken as an honourable one by certain Mussulmans.

‖ The etymology in Genesis, ch. xxxii., v. 28, is quite fictitious.

though it unquestionably indicated the submission under which this family was towards El.*

A kind of synonym of Israel was *Iakobel*,† "He whom El rewards," or "He who follows El, who marches step by step in the ways that He has traced."‡ This name was abridged to Jacob,§ as that of *Irhamel* was to *Irham*|| or Calbel to Caleb. *Beni-Jacob*, or *Beni-Israel* was the name of the tribe; and in course of time Jacob was taken to be a living person, grandson of Abraham. The name of his father Isaak is probably also an abbreviation for *Isaakel*, "He upon whom God smiles." ¶

* The distinction of שׂ and שׁ did not exist in ancient times. It may be, therefore, that the root is ישר. The meaning would be "He whom El directs in the right path," or "Rectitude of El." It is certain that the analogy of the forms ירחם, יעקב, יוסף, כלב, for כלבאל, יוספאל, יעקבאל, ירחמאל, leads one to suppose a form ישר for ישראל. This form crops up again, perhaps, in the title of the celebrated book ספר הישר, and especially in the caritative ישרון of the ancient canticles, wrongly written ישרים in one of the *masal* of Baalam (Numbers, ch. xxiii., v. 10). Compare 1 Chronicles, ch. xxv., v. 14 and the variants. Compare Stade, *Zeitschrift*, 1885, pp. 162, 163. An objection to the explanation, "He whom El directs," is that, according to the analogy of יעקב, of יצחק, of יוסף, the י should be a prefix.

† This name appears in the list of the campaigns of Tothmes III. (No. 102). See Groff in the *Rev. égyptol.*, vol. iv., pp. 95 and following, 146 and following; Stade, *Zeitsch. für die altt. Wiss.*, 1886, pp. 1 and following.

‡ Compare with יעקביה, a very plausible correction.

§ See Mem. upon the abbreviated theophoric names, in the *Revue des études juives*, Oct.-Dec., 1882. With regard to יוסף for יוספאל, see p. 94 below. We find, too, in the Assyrian text, ישמע for ישמעאל. Groff, *Revue égypt.*, vol. v., p. 87, note v.

|| See Gesenius, *Thes.*, p. 1283.

¶ Compare with Genesis, ch. xvii., v. 17, 19; ch. xviii., v. 12; ch. xxi., v. 6; ch. xxvi., v. 8.

It may be that the holy tribe was so designated at a certain epoch; or the Isaakel may perhaps have been a Puritan group, anterior to that of the Jakobel. What is certain is that these pious people would only call the Supreme Being, summed up in *Elohim*, El or El*elion* (the most High God),† or *Saddaï* (the Almighty God).‡ At the epoch of the internal religious struggles they had their encampments in Palestine; Bethel was their favourite sanctuary. The altars, or rather the pillars § which they left behind them were called *El Elohé Israel*, "El is the God of Israel."

We can see at once the analogy between a moral and religious condition of this kind and that of the Mussulman. It was a kind of prehistoric *Islam*. The Jakobelite patriarch was a true *Moslem*, one who gave himself up to God, who made of God the centre of his life, a devout man we might say, were it not that in its modern meaning this term implies practices which the ancient Semitic *Moslem* repudiated with horror. The Israelite tribe seems, then, to have been formed by a religious motive, and to have had a religious standard. The type of Abraham, "the friend of God," as the Mussulmans call him, stands out at the dawn of Judaism and Islamism as the ideal of grandiose piety

* *El* has not the same root as *Elohim*.
† Genesis, ch. xiv., v. 18 and following.
‡ Genesis, ch. xxv., v. 11; ch. xlviii., v. 3 and following; Exodus, ch. vi., v. 2, 3.
§ Genesis, ch. xxxiii., v. 20. The Jehovist compiler always makes the mistake of substituting altars for pillars in the old patriarchal legends. But the verb *wayyasseb*, which he uses, applies rather to a pillar than an altar.

and perfect faith. Abraham is a *Moslem*, but he is above all else a *Moumin*, a believer, a pious hero, a kind of Ali, brave, generous, polygamous, a man of honour. He is an Arab saint, who will have great difficulty in securing his place among the monks, the virgins, and the ascetics, more Buddhist than Semitic, who people the Christian heaven.

The Beni-Israel, in conception differing but little from the Jakobelites and the Isaakites, were thus a phenomenon, not unique, but remarkable and transcendent in the midst of the Hebraic family; just as Rome stands out among all the Latin and Italiot populations, as an almost miraculous case. Rome was in Latium a sort of asylum of selection. The tribe of the Beni-Israel appears to have been something of the same kind among the Hebraic tribes. We may fancy Israel as being a sort of Geneva in the midst of the varied populations, a rendezvous of the pure, a sect— or an order if that expression be preferred—analogous to the *Khouan* Mussulmans, much more than as a distinct *ethnos*. The Edomites and Moabites, in fact, were already permanently settled in the east and west of the Dead Sea, when the Beni-Israel found their way as vagrant pastors to the same region. It is possible that these latter may have remained systematically and from religious motives attached to the nomad life, which tended more than any other to preserve the antique habits. The Beni-Rékab were still more tenacious, inasmuch as they continued up to at least the sixth century B.C. to live under the tent, and to lead their ancient mode of life. We shall find, moreover, this lofty ideal of the nomad life remaining a sort of magnetic pole, towards which Israel will constantly gravitate.* In a very real sense the fixed settlement in the land of Canaan was a degradation and a religious decadence for Israel, and subsequently progress was embodied in a return by reflection to the ideas and sentiments of the antique genius of the Hebrews, so true is it that the first glimmering perceptions of races are those which control their whole history and contain the secret of their destinies!

This difference between the nomad and fixed populations, which is so capital a one nowaday, had not, however, in those distant ages, the importance which we attribute to it. Edom, Moab, Israel, and Amalek were brothers. Edom and Moab do not reveal themselves to us in the nomad state at any stage of their existence. Israel led in succession both modes of life. Amalek, a member of the Edomite family,† and Midian, connected with Abraham through Cethura, never settled down in one place. The Amalekites continued to roam over all the peninsula of Sinaï and to the east of Palestine when the rest of Edom had for centuries settled down in one place. They then lived mingled with the other populations of Palestine until they were absorbed by the Israelites. It may be said that these peoples went through three successive stages of existence: first the pure nomad

* See above, pp. 51—53.
† Genesis, ch. xxxvi., v. 12, 16.

stage, like that of the Hebrew patriarchs; then the stage of mixture with sedentary populations, analogous to the life now led by the metualis of Syria — this being the condition of Israel from its entry into Canaan up to the time of David, and of Amalek among the Israelites until its absorption; and lastly, the stage of small nationalities more or less compact, with a national god, this being the state in which we always find Edom and Moab, and in which Israel is found from the date of its being formed into a nation about the time of David.

The Hebraic tribe soon came to be broken up into sub-tribes, under the influence of polygamy, which created great rivalry between the half-brothers. The Jakobelites became divided from a very early period into ten families: Reuben, Judah, Simeon, Dan, Issachar, Naphtali, Asher, Zebulun, and Gad. It is impossible to say in what chronological order these various families appeared in Israel. Reuben is always represented as the oldest and Benjamin as the youngest of the house.

Side by side with Jacob, and upon the closest intimacy with him, we find mentioned at a very early epoch, the clan of Joseph or Josefel,* which seems to designate an addition or adjunction of congeners,†

* Grof, *Revue égypt.*, iv., pp. 95 and following; Stade, *Zeitschrift*, 1886, pp. 1 and following, 16.

† Comp. יוספיה. Esdras, ch. viii., v. 10. As an individual name *Joseph* means the child which is born some time after the others, when no more are expected. Genesis, ch. xxx., v. 24, and ch. xlviii., v. 1 and following.

who became afterwards annexed to Israel. These late comers, these grandsons of Father Jacob, became divided into two families, Ephraim and Manasseh. We shall see later that a very reasonable hypothesis suggests itself with regard to this annexation. After the settlement of Israel in Canaan, we shall be struck by the superiority of the Josephites over the rest of Beni-Israel, and we shall even see that Joseph will often be spoken of to designate the whole of the family, and will become synonymous with Jacob.* If, as I believe, the Israelites really came from Padan-Aram, it must be confessed that nothing is known of their long journey from Harran to Shechem. Shechem appears to have been one of the points to which they returned the oftenest, and up to the period within the limits of history a number of holy places were pointed out as being connected with their sojourn there. The Canaanite Hivvites, who inhabited Samaria, appear to have lived on good terms with them, though the memory of a bloody episode which occurred between a fraction of the Beni-Jacob and the people of Shechem had not died out.†

* Jacob and Joseph are constantly spoken of in parallel terms in the Psalms. See Psalms lxxx., v. 2, and lxxxi., v. 6; Amos, ch. v., v. 15; ch. vi., v. 6. These instances of polynomia are of frequent occurrence among ancient peoples. Thus the Greeks are named Πελασγοί, *Graii*, Ἀχαιοί, Μυρμιδόνες, &c., the Trojans, Τρῶες, Δάρδανοι; their town called Ἴλιον, Πέργαμον, &c.

† Genesis, ch. xxxiv.; Genesis, ch. xlix., v. 5—7, a poetical fragment, which may be regarded as the origin of the prose narrative. In this narrative we may detect the desire to extenuate the misconduct of the Beni-Jacob. The passage in verse, upon the con

Hebron was a not less important centre of initiation for the wandering Israelites.* They lived with the Hittites or Khetas upon the most friendly footing.† The important well of Beer-Sheba, where they halted like so many generations of pastors, left profound recollections upon them,‡ Gerar§ and Kadès-Barné were their last halting-places before entering Egypt. A terrible desert lay before them, and beyond this desert of fifty miles they sniffed the land of the Nile, with its abundance, its wealth, and its delights. A sort of powerful attraction thereupon took possession of these poverty-stricken beings, who were reduced to struggling with the other Bedouins for a few drops of water, and whom anything like famine brought to a terrible plight.

The numerous episodes of the charming pastoral epopœa which was afterwards built upon this golden age had little that was historical about it; and the artificial method attending the composition of each episode is easy to gather, but the colour of the narratives is truth itself. It is analogous with the Kitâb-el-Aghâni of the Arabs, which is an incomparable picture of ancient life, though a picture containing

trary, suggests the commission of a frightful crime, which for a long time rendered Israel odious to its neighbours.

* Genesis, ch. xiii., v. 18.

† Note particularly Genesis, ch. xiv., v. 13 (an almost pre-historic passage), and ch. xxiii.

‡ Genesis, ch. xxi., v. 28 and following.

§ Genesis, ch. xx., v. 2; ch. xxvi. v. 1, taking into account the anachronism. The Philistines were not yet established in Palestine at the patriarchal epoch.

THE BENI-JACOB, OR BENI-ISRAEL. 97

few elements worthy of credit. There is only one fragment in these legends which has the appearance of being taken from authentic ancient books, and this is the passage relating to the war of the four Chaldæan kings, which one of the narrators has adapted more or less skilfully into his story.* According to this fragment, "Abraham the Hebrew, who dwelt in the plain of Mamré the Amorite," took part in the invasion of the countries of the Dead Sea, of Kudur-Lagamar, King of Elami, and his allies. In order to deliver Lot, his nephew, whom the invaders had carried off, Abraham the Hebrew is said to have formed a small army consisting of 318 of his servants, and had rescued his nephew from the hands of the four kings. This is not to be taken literally; Lot and Abraham doubtless had an ethnographical meaning, and were intended to designate, upon one hand, the general body of the Hebrew tribes, and, upon the other hand, the populations in the neighbourhood of the Dead Sea, whom the Egyptians called Rotenu,† and who, according to the Israelite ethnographers, were the near relatives of Abraham.

The Beni-Israel thought too that they could remember a time when the southern part of the Dead Sea was a valley, in which were situated towns the history of which was connected with the campaign of the Chaldæan kings, and which were destroyed by a conflagration of bitumen.‡ The geographical theory upon

---

* Genesis, ch. xiv.   † See above, p. 10.
‡ Genesis, ch. xiv.

which these stories are based is one that cannot be admitted, inasmuch as it is proved that the waters of the Lake Asphaltites have been constantly falling, and that the lake has, in consequence, been gradually getting smaller.* The strange aspect of the valley, with its pillars of salt, resembling veiled statues,† the peculiar properties of the waters of the Dead Sea, suffice to explain the birth of these legends.‡ It is dangerous to look too closely after history in ancient dreams, where spectres are indistinguishable from men. But the Israelitish imagination retained a strong impression of these narratives, and they believed that the *Refaïm*,§ phantoms of vanished races, and the *Enakim* giants peopled this "valley of the dead," where they still thought they could discern the living traces of the terrible vengeance of the just *elohim*.

* Lartet's *Expl. géol. de la mer Morte*, pp. 174 and following, 266 and following,

† Robinson, *Pal.*, ii., 435 ; iii., 22 and following; Seetzen, i., 428 ; ii., 227, 240 ; Lynch, *Narrative*, ch. xiv.

‡ Genesis, ch. xiv., xviii., xix.

§ Job, ch. xxvi., v. 5. The name *Siddim*, said to have been given to the ancient valley, is perhaps a mispronunciation for *Sedim*, "the Valley of Demons."

CHAPTER IX.

RELIGION OF THE BENI-ISRAEL.

A RELIGION without a dogma, without a book, and without a priest is of necessity very open to external influences. Thus the ancient Hebrews were inclined to accept, with a facility which the graver among them severely blamed, the rites of neighbouring peoples. The habit of throwing kisses of adoration to the sun and moon struck them with astonishment, and they were inclined to imitate it.* The holy places of the Canaanites more especially inspired them with a mingled feeling of respect and dread. The Canaanite town of Luz contained a spot which popular belief associated with terrors and visions. It was regarded as the gate of heaven, as the foot of a vast staircase or pyramid, with steps (*sullam*) which ascended from earth to heaven.† The elohim occupied the summit, and their messengers were continually descending and ascending it, bringing the earth into communication with the world above. The ancient Hebrew patriarchs held this place in great veneration; they called it, as everyone else did, *Bethel;* that is to say, the house or

* Job, ch. xxxi., v. 26 and following.

† Genesis, ch. xxviii., v. 12, 13. For the meaning of סלם compare the Palmyra Inscription, No. 11. (Vogüé).

temple of God.* Luz, in addition to its *sullam*, possessed one of the pillars, or *ansab*, anointed with oil, erected by unknown adorers, but which the newcomers regarded as being quite as sacred as if they had raised them themselves. The Israelites adopted the pillar of Bethel, as Mahomet was in after days obliged to adopt the Caaba. It was asserted that the stela in question had been raised by the patriarch Jacob,† the consequence being that this spot became the chief sanctuary in Palestine. The God of Bethel, in particular, was looked upon as the supreme master of the country, with power to dispose of it as his own property. Subsequently he was identified with Iahveh, and it was supposed that the Israelites had received from this powerful local god a formal donation, which constituted their title to the possession of Palestine.‡ It was admitted that each people held the land of which it was owner from its own god, though it should be added that this same god often took the land from others to give it to his chosen people.§

The masses are always idolatrous, and the puritans

* Genesis, ch. xii., v. 8; ch. xiii., v. 3, 4; ch. xxviii., v. 10—22; ch. xxxi., v. 9—15; ch. xxxv., v. 1 and following. All these passages in the history of Jacob are strongly polytheistic.

† Genesis, ch. xxviii., v. 19. It is not the stone but the place which Jacob calls Bethel. The connection with *betyle* (Sanchoniathon) remains doubtful.

‡ Genesis, ch. xiii., v. 3—4; ch. xxviii., v. 13—16; 20—21. See above, p. 80.

§ Judges, ch. xi., v. 24, and the whole of the supposed message of Jephthah.

of the Israelitish clan had great difficulty in preventing the unenlightened, women more especially, from practising the Aramaic and Canaanite superstitions. The chief abuse was with the *teraphim*, a kind of idol, probably made of carved wood, which were carried on the person, and were regarded as a sort of household gods and domestic oracles.* The wise men protested against these follies. The name of *Iahou*, or Iahveh, the equivalent of El, was no doubt much respected, but the sages of these very ancient times seemed to descry a danger in this proper name, and preferred the names of *El, Elion, Saddaï,* and *Elohim*. The name of *Abir Iakob*, "the Fort of Iakob,"† was for a long time preferred, and was in common use some time before that of Iahveh. The offering of the first-fruits, and therefore of the first-born, to the Divinity was one of the oldest ideas of the so-called Semitic peoples. Moloch and Iahveh, more especially, were conceived as being the fire which devours that which is offered to it, so that to give to God was to give food to the fire. What was consumed by the fire was consumed by God. In this way the most revolting misapprehensions took root. Moloch was a terrible bull of fire,‡ and to offer the first-born to Moloch was to offer them to the fire,

* Genesis, ch. xxxi., v. 19, 30, 34 (compare Genesis, ch. xxxv., v. 2, 4); Judges, ch. xviii., v. 14 and following (compare ch. xvii., v. 5); First Book of Samuel, ch. xix., v. 13, 16.

† The Blessing of Jacob, a very ancient fragment, Genesis, ch. xlix., v. 24.

‡ Diodorus Siculus, XX., xiv., 6.

either by allowing them to be burnt outright or to be passed through the flames.

The consequence of these hideous chimeras was human sacrifice upon so appalling a scale that the idea of looking for some substitute soon suggested itself. The first-born was replaced by an animal or a sum of money.* This was called "the money of the lives." † The wise King of Ur-Casdim seems to have owed some of the respect with which he was treated to the fact of his having immolated a ram in the stead of his son, when circumstances called for the sacrifice of the latter.‡ Real immolations were not rare with the Phœnicians, § especially among the Carthaginians.‖ The Hebrews or Terachites also sullied themselves sometimes with these abominations.¶ In the event of pressing danger in Phœnicia, Carthage, and the land of Moab, the sovereigns and the great made, in compliance with the cruel popular prejudice, the sacrifice of some one dear to them or of their eldest son. We have a striking example of this among the Moabites at the time of Elijah and Elisha. The example of Jephthah and the legend of Abraham's sacrifice show that the Beni-Israel were no more exempt than their congeners from this odious rite.

* Numbers, ch. xviii., v. 15 and following.
† כסף נפשות. Second Book of Kings, ch. xii., v. 4.
‡ See above, pp. 63, 64.
§ Sanchoniathon, p. 36 (Orelli).
‖ *Corpus inscr. semit.*, Nos. 171, 194.
¶ Mesa, Second Book of Kings, ch. iii., v. 27; Comp. Diodorus Siculus, XX., xiv.

I believe that the perilous idea of the offering of the first-born did not bear fruit previous to the national epoch, when the people were established in Canaan, and when Iahveh had become their local god, as Camos was the local god of Moab. The national religion is always the bloodiest one. In the primitive elohism, monstrosities of this kind were condemned, and they must have been extremely rare among the nomads. Among the pagan practices reproved by Job, human sacrifices are not mentioned, doubtless because that horror hardly ever occurred. In any event, the civilising attempt of the Israelite prophets succeeded, at a very early period, in substituting for this blood-stained rite the inoffensive offering up of the first-born of the flock. A ransom, not clearly explained, represented the primitive immolation of "that which opens the womb."* The God of Abraham was always credited with having a strong aversion from human sacrifices. The horrible sacrifices of children, which were the disgrace of the seventh century B.C., remained unknown, it would appear, to the patriarchal tent.

The agents of civilisation were, even thus early, endeavouring by well-considered practices to extend culture and restrain barbarism. Their purpose was

* Book of the alliance, Exodus, ch. xxii., v. 28. Compare the Elohist passage, Exodus, ch. xiii., v. 1—2, 10 and following. The expression העברת (v. 12) is the expression employed everywhere else to express the act of passing children through the fire in honour of Moloch. See Second Book of Kings, ch. xii., v. 3; Gesenius, *Thes.*, p. 985.

to effect the education of the body as well as that of the mind. One of the causes of physical and moral filth was the habit of eating carrion and diseased animals. The distinction between clean and unclean animals is a very old one, although the list of those which were prohibited was only drawn up later and has varied considerably.* Swine, which in the East are very subject to trichinosis, were among the very earliest meats to be avoided. A direction followed by all those who were afraid of doing wrong was not to drink blood, and to avoid eating animals which had not been bled.† The blood was regarded as the constitutive element of the person. It was a maxim that "the soul is in the blood;" so that to assimilate a man's blood was to absorb him and to devour his very self.

Among the observances which, under the cover of the Semitic religions, have made the round of the world, and which seem to go back to the Terachite period, must be included, as it would seem, that of circumcision. The unvarying custom of the Elohist narrator is to ascribe the origin of circumcision to ante-Mosaic times;‡ and his reason for doing so was probably based upon the observation that most of the Terachite peoples practised circumcision, though not

---

* See lists in Leviticus and Deuteronomy.

† First Book of Samuel, ch. xiv., v. 31 and following, ancient text, forming part of a whole in which the instructions of the Thora properly so called are ignored.

‡ Genesis, ch. xvii.; xxi., v. 4; xxxiv., v. 15 and following.

nearly so regularly as the Beni-Israel.* The populations of Syria and Arabia, in particular, practised the operation long before Islam. The ancient Greeks remarked this; only they were wrong in believing that Egypt was the sole origin of this custom.† As to the Israelites, they never classed the Moabites and Edomites as *garelim*, or uncircumcised.‡ This qualification was originally applied by them only to the Philistines,§ who were undoubtedly Cretans or Carians.

At first this custom was not so general and had not the religious signification which was given to it afterwards. It was an operation resorted to by many tribes, and it was one which had its physiological reasons.‖

* Circumcision of Ishmael, Genesis, ch. xvii., v. 23, 25 and following. Jos., *Ant.*, I., xii., 2.

† Herodotus, ii., 30, 36, 37, 104; Diodorus Siculus, I., xxviii., 3; III., xxxii., 5; Agatharchidas, *De mari Erythr.*, 61; Strabo, XVI., iv., 17; XVII., iii., 5. Comp. Jos., *Ant.*, VIII., x., 3; *Contre Apion*, I., 22; Epiph., Hær. i., 33; ix., 30; Origen, *Comment. in Gen.*, 10; Eusebius, *Præp. evang.*, vi., 11; Philostratus, *H. E.*, iii., 4; Schahristani, trans. Haarbrücker, ii., 354.—Upon the other hand, see Jos., *Ant.*, XIII., ix., 1; xi., 3; *Vita*, 23. "Circumcision was practised, but was not compulsory, in Egypt. The royal mummies whose generative parts have not been removed are many of them uncircumcised. A statue at Boulaq, appertaining to the first dynasty, is circumcised." (Remark of M. Maspero.)

‡ Jeremiah, ix. 26 does not prove anything on this head.

§ Iashar, in 2nd Book of Samuel, ch. i., v. 20; Judges, ch. xiv., v. 3, and in general throughout the Books of Judges and of Samuel. The Canaanites were for the most part uncircumcised. Genesis, xxxiv. Sanchoniathon (Orelli), p. 36, is scarcely worth attention. The idea of a connection between the sacrifice of the first-born and circumcision is quite superficial.

‖ Philo, *De circumcisione*, Opp., ii., 210 and following.

Without it, certain races of the East would have been to a certain extent impotent, and would have been doomed to acts of lamentable impurity.* The operation was often performed just before marriage.† The young man was then called *hatan damim*, "the bleeding betrothed."‡ The same custom still exists among some Arab tribes.§ With other tribes the circumcision was an annual festival, and all the adults born in the same year were circumcised upon the same day. This was their introduction to sexual connection, which had hitherto been debarred them, and from this date they were at liberty to marry.∥ But this mode of proceeding had great drawbacks. As the operation is a much more serious one for adults than for children¶ the circumcision of children became the rule. The reasoning which led to this was analogous to that which has in our day led to compulsory education. It was not unreasonably regarded as a fault for parents to omit doing what would prevent their

---

* Quia pueris præputium apud eos multo longius est quam apud nos, quod in re venerea multum nocet. J. de Thevenot, *Voyages* I., ch. xxxii.; Niebuhr, *Descr. de l'Arabie*, p. 69; Winer, *Bibl. Realw.*, i., p. 159. The root غـرل signifies "to be too long," and has no meaning, either religious or irreligious.

† Genesis, ch. xxxiv., Elohist part.

‡ Exodus, ch. iv., v. 25 and following. With regard to the varied meaning of ختن, signifying at once "to circumcise, son-in-law, father-in-law," see Stade and Wellhausen quoted below; Gesenius, *Thes.*, p. 539.

§ Wellhausen, *Prol.*, p. 360.

∥ Stade, *Zeitschrift für die alttest. Wiss.*, 1885, p. 135 and following (after Ploss).

¶ Genesis, ch. xxxiv., v. 24 and following.

RELIGION OF THE BENI-ISRAEL.

children from suffering from a far more painful operation in after life.

The word *garel*, indicating the natural state of the organs,* in time became synonymous with sullied; and this was a gross insult, especially when addressed to the Philistines.† The operation of removing the *gorla* assumed a ritual meaning, and, as generally happens in a case of this kind, the distinction between the sacramental accessory and the principal was lost sight of. In very ancient times the operation was performed with flint knives, because there was no such a thing as a metal blade.‡ It was for a long time believed that the use of the flint knife was essential, and it was still employed even after the free use of metals. Moreover, the original reason for the operation was lost sight of, and races which from a physiological point of view had no need of it adopted it, regarding it as a religious initiation and a purification. Circumcision, in a word, after being a useful precaution in certain cases, became a practice deemed good for all men, and eventually compulsory upon all. This is what one so often finds in the history of religions. A precept

---

* It is curious that the uncircumcised should never be designated in Hebrew by the negation of circumcision, לֹא־נִמּוֹל, for instance.

† עֲרֵלִים is already found in use as a word of insult to the Philistines, in an authentic chant of the time of David (Second Book of Samuel, ch. i., v. 20.)

‡ Exodus, ch. iv., v. 25; Joshua, ch. v., v. 2 and following; Herodotus, ii., 86. This usage is still prevalent in Abyssinia. Ludolf, *Hist. æth.*, i., 21.

which has its local and individual use becomes, once that it has been treated as sacred, a universal precept, which is adhered to in climates and by peoples which have no need for it.

Islamism intensified the error of Judaism. A custom which had its use for certain Eastern races made differently from what we are, spread among races to whom it brought more drawbacks than advantages. The idea that the peoples who had not undergone this operation were in some measure impure, and that all contact with them should be avoided, was a particularly unfortunate one, for it led the Israelites to commit the most revolting acts of intolerance,* for which those whom they maltreated avenged themselves by jests, and for their taunt of *longus*† was thrown back the epithet *curtus*.

The adoption of this usage by the Israelites may be regarded, then, as a great historical blunder. Circumcision was in the religious life of Israel an act in contradiction with its true vocation, and was very nearly causing it to miss its providential function. The rigorists took advantage of this practice to preach total sequestration. When the genius of propaganda and the dream of a universal religion for the human race became the dominant idea of Israel, circumcision stood in the way as the great obstacle. It was very nearly causing the whole scheme to fail. If St. Paul

---

* The compulsory circumcisions in the time of the Asmoneans; idea that the allies of Israel ought to be circumcised. Sanchoniathon (Orelli), p. 86.

† This is the meaning of the words ערל = غـل.

had not got the better in his struggle with James, Christianity (that is to say, universal Judaism) would have had no future before it.

Like nearly all the primitive peoples,* the Hebrews believed in a sort of doubling of the person, — a shadow, a pale and vacuous figure, which, after death, went beneath the earth, and there led a sad and gloomy existence in dark and sombre chambers.† These were the *Manes* of the Latins, the νέκυες of the Greeks. The Hebrews called them *Refaïm*, a word which seems to have meant phantoms, and to have been employed much in the same way as *heroes*.‡ signifying at once heroes and the dead. The abode of these poor exhausted beings was called *scheol*. It was conceived upon the analogy of the family tombs, where the dead rested side by side, so much so that to descend into *scheol* was synonymous with being gathered to one's fathers.§ The dead existed there unconscious, without knowledge, without memory, in a world without light, abandoned of God.‖ There was no recompense, no punishment. "God doth not heed them." Those

---

* See above, pp. 24, 84 and following; Reville, *Relig. des peuples non-civilisés*, vol. i., pp. 67 and following; vol. ii., pp. 89 and following, 203 and following.

† Inscription of Esmunazar, *Corpus insc. semit.*, part i., No. 3; inscr. of Tabnith, *Acad. des Inscr. et Belles-Lettres*, June 24, 1887.

‡ Heroopolis = בעל-צפון, Typhonian fables; Valley of the *Refaïm* or Heroes = Fables of the Dead Sea.

§ Genesis, ch. xv., v. 15; ch. xxxv., v. 29.

‖ Psalm vi., v. 6; lxxxviii., v. 6 and following; cxv., v. 17 and 18; Isaiah, ch. xxxviii., v. 18 and following; Job, ch. xiv., v. 21, 22.

persons who had any sort of enlightenment saw very clearly that an existence of this kind was very much like annihilation; but most people, nevertheless, bethought themselves of securing a good place, a comfortable bed, against the day that they should join the Refaïm. What gave the greatest comfort was to think that one would be among one's ancestors and resting with them.* Ideas of this kind seem to have had a stronger hold upon the imagination of the Canaanites than of the Hebrews.† It would appear as if the wiser of the Hebrews took precautions to prevent the masses from being engrossed by these ideas, which as a rule have such a fascination for the people. The descent into hell and the peregrinations athwart the circles of the other world, such as absorbed the thoughts of the Assyrians and Egyptians, savoured to them of impiety.‡

All this was due to the profound separation which the Hebraic conscience from the first laid down between man and God. With the Aryan the *Pitris*, or

* Genesis, ch. xxv., v. 8; xxxv., v. 29; ch. xlix., v. 29; Numbers, ch. xx., v. 26; Judges, ch. ii., v. 10; First Book of Kings, ch. xiii., v. 23; Second Book of Kings, ch. xxii., v. 20; Ezekiel, ch. xxxii., v. 18 and following.

† Esmunazar and Tabnith inscriptions, texts of priceless value, because they give us a fair idea of what a *rafa's* reasoning was like.

‡ It may be added that the Egyptians and Assyrians appear to have formed, successively or simultaneously, the two conceptions, of a sad and gloomy *scheol*, and that of an after life full of rewards and expiations. Maspero, in the *Revue de l'histoire des religions*, 1885, vol. xiii., pp. 125 and following; *Etudes égyptiennes*, vol. i., pp. 185—190.

RELIGION OF THE BENI-ISRAEL.

ancestors, were gods, and consequently immortal. In Egypt the dead man becomes an Osiris, a divine and eternal spirit. The Hebrew patriarch regarded such ideas as highly indecorous. God alone is eternal; an eternal being would be God. Man is essentially fleeting. He lives a few brief days and then disappears for ever. There are, no doubt, some very virtuous men, friends of God, whom God carries up that they may be with him.* But, apart from these elect, it is the fate of man to disappear in oblivion. He has no reason to complain if he has been accorded a fair length of years, if he leaves children to perpetuate his family; if, after his death, his name is pronounced with respect at the gate of his place.† In default of all that, an *iad*, a pillar bearing his name, is some consolation;‡ not much, it is true, but better than none at all. What else is there for you?

The latent consequences of such a conception of life were that the justice of God did not extend beyond this lower world, a fact which must have perplexed the simple patriarch with much astonishment. The Book of Job was not written for another thousand years, but even at the early age of which I am speaking it must have been thought. The sage was perplexed to know what to say when he saw a wicked man prosperous, a just man rebuked. But the world was still very

---

* Enoch: Genesis, ch. v., v. 22. But this legend appears to be of Babylonian origin.
† Ruth, ch. iv., v. 10, 14.
‡ Isaiah, ch. lvi., v. 5.

simple-minded, and the solutions, which were at a later date regarded as insufficient, were accepted as giving a more or less reasonable explanation of the providential government of the universe.

The belief was that evil produced evil of itself, and perforce entailed punishment, even when the law was transgressed unwillingly.* There was no distinction between sin and error.† The family was regarded as a thing so sacred that a breach of the conjugal tie, even in ignorance, entailed death and the most terrible chastisements.‡ Good, upon the contrary, was recompensed by long life and a numerous posterity.§ This took place almost automatically, so to speak. God slew the man who did any peculiarly evil deed.‖ Life was a good gift, a favour of God. Long life was the reward of the just. The man without reproach might be severely tried, but God would avenge him; he saw his children and his children's children, even to the fourth generation, and he died at the age of six score years, full of days.¶

---

* Double meaning of words עמל, שוא, &c., signifying at the same time the evil and the punishment. Genesis, ch. xlii., v. 21, 22, 28; Second Book of Samuel, ch. xiv., v. 9 and following; Isaiah, ch. v., v. 18.

† Note carefully the shades of meaning of the verb חמא.

‡ Genesis, ch. xii., v. 17 and following; ch. xviii., xix.; ch. xx., v. 6; ch. xxvi., v. 10.

§ Exodus, ch. i., v. 21.

‖ Genesis, ch. xxxviii., v. 7, 10.

¶ Job, last verse. It was the same with Tobias and Judith.

CHAPTER X.

THE BENI-ISRAEL IN EGYPT.

THE counter-influence of the arrival of the Semites in the regions of the Mediterranean promptly made itself felt in Egypt. Egyptian civilisation was from two to three thousand years old when this great event in the world's history took place. Up to that time Egypt had been familiar, in the Sinaitic peninsula and in the regions bordering upon the isthmus, with bands of plunderers (*sati* or *shasus*), differing very little in their habits from the low-class Bedouin,* but of doubtful race. But there can be no doubt, upon the contrary, as to the Semitic character of these *Hyksos*, or Shepherds,† who, more than two thousand years B.C., interrupted in a measure the current of Egyptian civilisation, and

* Maspero, *Hist. anc. des peuples de l'Orient*, pp. 101 and following. (About 2,400 or 2,500 B.C. at latest.)

† The learned Jews of Alexandria, having heard of Manethon's *History of Egypt*, sought in it a connecting link of the relations of Israel with Egypt. The comparison with the Hyksos struck them, and this was the starting point of interpolations in Manethon's text, some intended to favour the Jewish system, the others, upon the contrary, conceived in a spirit of depreciation towards Israel. See Josephus, *Contre Apion*, i., 14, 26; Müller, *Fragm. hist. gr.*, ii., pp. 514, 566, 578, 579.

founded at Zoan (Tanis),* near the Isthmus, the centre of a powerful Semitic state. These Hyksos were to all appearances Canaanites, near relations of the Hittites of Hebron. Hebron was in close community with Zoan, and there is a tradition, probably based upon historical data, that the two cities were built nearly at the same time.† As invariably happens when barbarians enter into an ancient and powerful civilisation the Hyksos soon became Egyptianised. They raised Egyptian temples to the Semitic god Sutekh (Sydyk), and adapted Egyptian hieroglyphics to their requirements.

It seems indeed that it was in this mixed country of Zoan that the so-called Phœnician or Semitic writing was invented.‡ The necessity of transcribing Semitic names into Egyptian led to phonetism, that is to say to a choice of hieroglyphic characters which were stripped of their meaning, and retained only their sounding signs.§ This was exactly what the Chinese Buddhists did to render the Sanskrit words,|| and especially

* The great retrenched camp of the Hyksos Hâouârou (Avaris), is probably Baal-Saphon or Heroopolis.

† Numbers, ch. xiii., v. 22.

‡ Memoir of M. de Rougé upon the *Origine égyptienne de l'alphabet phénicien*, read before the Académie des Inscriptions, published in 1874, after the author's death.

§ Phonetics had long been in existence among the Egyptians. What the Semites did was, first, to suppress the ideographical part and the consonantical syllabic part of words; second, to select a single sign for each sound, in place of the Egyptian homophones. This is rather a systematisation of the principle of phonetism than a discovery of the principle itself. (Note of M. Maspero.)

|| Stanislas Julien, *Noms sanscrits dans les livres chinois.* (Paris, 1861).

what was done by the Japanese, the Coreans, and the Annamites, when they extracted very reduced alphabets from the infinite variety of Chinese characters. The Hyksos thus laid down the principles of alphabetic writing, and their selection of twenty-two characters, made with a very accurate appreciation of Semitic phonetics, has remained an established fact. Governed by the habits of Egyptian hieroglyphics, which takes account of the articulation alone, they wrote the consonant only, which is a quite insignificant omission from the Semitic point of view, but which became of capital importance when the alphabet of twenty-two letters was adopted by other races. The Greeks, a thousand years later, made good this deficiency by forming vowels from the Semitic aspirates, and thus was constituted the writing which all peoples have adopted. Hebron no doubt was acquainted with the invention of the Hittites of Zoan, adopted it, and possessed writings from a very remote date.* This was probably the source whence the Moabites† and the Israelites‡ derived it, unless we prefer to suppose that they copied it direct from Zoan, which is assuredly not an inadmissible hypothesis.

The Hyksos of Zoan could not fail to exercise a great

---

* Hence perhaps the narrative of the fourteenth chapter of Genesis. The Khetas were familiar with handwriting about 1800 B.C. Maspero's *Histoire*, pp. 224, 225.

† The oldest Moabite inscription is that of Mesa, about 875 B.C.

‡ The oldest known Israelite inscription is that of the tunnel of Siloh, at Jerusalem, about 700 B.C.

influence upon the Hebrews who were encamped around Hebron, the Dead Sea, and in the southern districts of Palestine. The antipathy which afterwards existed between the Hebrews and the Canaanites was not as yet very perceptible. The harvests in Egypt being much more regular than in southern Syria, the Khetas sometimes received from the Egyptian kings gifts of corn.* From Kadès-Barné or Gerar to the cantons fertilised by the Pelusiac branches of the Nile it was not much more than a hundred and fifty miles. The Bedouin, as I have already said,† had a double feeling towards organised civilisation: upon the one hand aversion, due to the keenest of all jealous motives, that of impotence; upon the other hand an almost excessive admiration. The products of civilisation were quite beyond him; he regarded them as being really miraculous. The resultant of these contradictory sentiments was upon the whole an attracting influence; for the greatest delight of the semi-barbarian is to gather where he has not planted. The comfort enjoyed and the profit made in this to him unknown world fascinated him like a mirage. He admired everything, down to the bread which he ate and the onions on which he fed; but he soon grew dissatisfied with the small value attached to his services and the amount of work expected from him in return. A kind of nostalgia gained hold upon him; and finding himself treated as a labourer, his one thought was how he

* Maspero, p. 255.
† See above, p. 54 and following.

should effect his exodus at any sacrifice, only to regret as soon as he had succeeded the wages which he received and the onions which he ate in what he calls his "house of bondage."[*]

Things are still much the same in the present day. The infiltration of Arabs into Lower Egypt is going on upon a large scale. The Arab remains for a while distinct, and is exempted from forced labour, but in time he becomes assimilated with the fellah, and is not in any way to be distinguished from the rest of the population.

There are the best of reasons for believing that the immigration of the Beni-Israel took place at two separate times.[†] A first batch of Israelites seems to have been attracted by the Hittites of Egypt, while the bulk of the tribe was living upon the best of terms with the Hittites of Hebron. These first immigrants found favour with the Egyptianised Hittites of Memphis and Zoan; they secured very good positions, had children, and constituted a distinct family in Israel. This was what was afterwards called the *clan of the Josephel*, or the *Beni-Joseph*. Finding themselves well off in Lower Egypt, they sent for their brethren, who, impelled perhaps by famine, joined them there, and were received also favourably by the Hittite dynasties. These new-comers never went to Memphis. They remained in the vicinity of Zoan, where there is a land

---

[*] Exodus, ch. xiii., v. 8, 14; ch. xx., v. 2.
[†] Read carefully Genesis, ch. xlviii., v. 1 and following.

of Goshen,* which was allotted to them, and in which they could continue their pastoral life. The land of Goshen, in fact, was as it were a transition between Egypt and the desert. The Egyptians, very hostile to herdsmen,† as sedentary agriculturists always are, abandoned it to the populations who earned their livelihood by the rearing of flocks.

The whole of these ancient days, concerning which Israel possesses only legends and contradictory traditions, is enveloped in doubt; one thing, however, is certain, viz., that Israel entered Egypt under a dynasty favourable to the Semites, and left it under one which was hostile.‡ The presence of a nomad tribe upon the extreme confines of Egypt must have been a matter of very small importance for this latter country.§ There is no certain trace of it in the Egyptian texts.‖ The kingdom of Zoan, upon the contrary, left a deep impression upon the Israelites. Zoan became nearly synonymous with Egypt.¶ The relations between

* What is now the Wadi, near Ismaïlia.

† Genesis, ch. xliii., v. 32; ch. xlvi., v. 34; ch. xlvii., v. 6.

‡ The incoherent narrative which Josephus (*Contre Apion*, i., 26, 27) attributes to Manethon implies at all events the connexity of the Hebrews and the Hyksos.

§ The views which have been often put forward as to the Semitic origin of the religious reformation of Amenhotep IV. (worship of Khunaten, at Tell el-Amarna), must be abandoned. *Aten*, which has been compared to *Adon*, is one of the oldest words in the Egyptian language. It is found in the texts of the Pyramids, the wording of which is possibly anterior to Ménès. (Note of M. Maspero.)

‖ Errors of Messrs. Lauth and Chabas.

¶ Isaiah, ch. xix., v. 11, 13; ch. xxx., v. 4; Psalm lxxviii.,

Zoan and Hebron were kept up, and although it is very doubtful whether the chiefs of the Beni-Israel at this remote epoch had their burial-places at Hebron,* it may easily be believed that the two capitals of the Hittites retained the consciousness of their common origin. Hebron was proud of the synchronism, which made it out seven years older than Zoan.†

The first-comers, the Josephites, always assumed an air of superiority over their brethren, whose position they had been instrumental in establishing.‡ These Josephites were, it would appear, men of higher cultivation than their fellows. Their children, born in Egypt, possibly of Egyptian mothers, were scarcely Israelites. An agreement was come to, however; it was agreed that the Josephites should rank as Israelites with the rest. They formed two distinct tribes, those of Ephraim and Manasseh. Outside these two families there were also the sporadic Josephites, who several times set up their claims. But it was decided that they should attach themselves as best they could to the two families of Ephraim and Manasseh.§ It is not impossible that the origin of the name of *Joseph* (addi-

---

v. 11, 43. It should be added that this is mainly owing to the important part which the Tanite dynasty (the 21st) played in the time of Solomon, and to the power of the feudal princes of Zoan under the 22nd, 24th, and 25th dynasties. (Note of M. Maspero.)

* Genesis, ch. xxiii.
† Numbers, ch. xiii., v. 22.
‡ Genesis, ch. xxxvii., v. 8, &c.
§ Genesis, ch. xlviii.

tion, adjunction, annexation) may have arisen from the circumstance that the first emigrants and their families, having become strangers to their brethren, needed some sort of adjunction to become again part and parcel of the family of Israel.

CHAPTER XI.

INFLUENCE OF EGYPT UPON ISRAEL.

This peaceful sojourn of Israel in the land of Goshen may have been a somewhat lengthy one, but infinitely less so than is generally supposed.* I will put it at a century. The position of Israel during this sojourn was a stable and organised one, but not sufficiently so to exercise upon the spirit of the people an action deep enough to modify their patriarchal ideas, or to substitute for the old stock of Babylonian traditions which they carried with them the fables of Egypt. Just as the Hyksos had given to their worship of Sydyk the forms of the Egyptian religion, so, in a certain measure, the Beni-Israel must have brought their ancient worship into keeping with the taste of their new country; or rather they must have added to this worship of Bedouin simplicity observances which they saw practised around them, with a complete belief in their efficacy. Some parts, afterwards regarded as essential, of the religion of Israel, date from this period, and so it was that Egypt, although profoundly

* There is no reliable chronology in regard to this. The texts are uncertain, contradictory, and, in addition, devoid of historical value.

pagan, came to introduce several important elements into the religious tradition of humanity.

Egypt had possessed, from the earliest times, sacred texts and a somewhat extensive religious literature. There is no ground for believing that these texts had the slightest influence upon the Israelites. The latter did not understand Egyptian, and even if the alphabet of twenty-two letters existed they did not make use of it. The probability is that not one of the Hebrew emigrants had anything to do with the priests who taught the more or less elevated mysteries of Egyptian theology. They would doubtless not have come across a single one of these hierophants in the district, itself scarcely Egyptian, in which they dwelt. Moreover, speculative doctrines such as these, even supposing them to be serious, were not at all in keeping with the bent of their intellect. Nothing of what was rare or learned came to their ears. The Israelite saw Egypt as the Mussulman Arab sees pagan countries, entirely from the outside, perceiving only the surface and external things. Everything underwent a singular transformation as seen through their narrow range of vision.

The comparisons between the Bible and Egyptian learning which would imply a thorough knowledge of the secrets of Egypt must then be rejected. What is called the Decalogue is very analogous to the negative confession of the dead man before Osiris at the hour of judgment.[*] But there is no date for these little codes

---

[*] Book of the Dead, ch. 125.

INFLUENCE OF EGYPT UPON ISRAEL. 123

of eternal moral philosophy; as a rule they exist long before they are committed to writing. Egypt, far from having perfected the Israelitish religion, in my opinion altered it in many respects for the worse.

The Egyptian worship was a very idolatrous one; the god dwelt in a fixed place, a temple, an ark, or statues, and the rites celebrated in his honour were very complicated. There can be no doubt that Israel, like the Hyksos, were affected by the contagion of these ideas. It is not likely that the desire to return to the nomad life had so far abandoned them that they built temples in the land of Goshen; but one usage which they adopted was that of arks or tabernacles, shielding behind the hawks which faced each other, and under another large oblique wing, forming a kind of veil, the image of the god, invisible to the profane. In the Egyptian rite this small closed chapel was always placed upon a bark which the priests carried upon their shoulders in procession or during the peregrinations of the god. It was a portable *naos*, by means of which the god could at times undertake long journeys without being deprived on the way of any of his honours.* From the time of their sojourn in the land of Goshen the Israelites no doubt made for themselves an ark of this kind to serve as a centre for the somewhat eclectic worship which they performed.

---

* De Rougé, *Etude sur une stèle égyptienne de la Bibl. Imp.* Paris, 1858; de Vogüé, *le Temple de Jérusalem*, p. 33. Lepsius, *Denkm.* Abth. iii., Bl. 189 *b*; Wilkinson, *A Popular Account of the Ancient Egyptians*, vol. i., pp. 267, 270.

They probably carried it with them when they left the country. This ark was the most appropriate thing possible for nomad life. It followed them in all their wanderings through the peninsula of Sinai, and we shall find it assuming extraordinary importance and becoming the cradle of all the religious institutions of Israel. The bark, which was an essential part of the Egyptian ark, disappeared, and its place was taken by a species of large chest, fitted with staves for the bearers and covered by the sphinxes or hawks facing one another and folding back their wings on both sides, so as to constitute in the space between a sort of divine throne.* As, in the popular language of the Israelites, a sphinx was called a *cherub*, the privilege of being seated between the cherubim became as a matter of course the essential privilege of the national god.†

The consecrated loaves, placed upon a table before the god, were one of the bases of Egyptian worship.‡ The Israelites adopted this rite and put it in practice as soon as it was applicable, that is to say as soon as their worship had some sort of stability about it. These loaves were without leaven, this being regarded as a special condition of purity.§ To put them to a secular use was regarded as a sacrilege which the only extremest necessity could justify.

---

* Exodus, ch. xxv., xxxvii.
† First Book of Samuel, ch. iv., v. 4 ; Second Book of Samuel ch. vi., v. 2 ; Psalm lxxx., v. 2 ; xcix., v. i., &c.
‡ Vogüé, see above.
§ First Book of Samuel, ch. xxi. ; Hosea, ch. ix., v. 4.

INFLUENCE OF EGYPT UPON ISRAEL.

Thus the Israelites became acquainted with the externals only of the Egyptian religion, its mummeries and its fetiches. The serpent god haunted them for centuries, both as a nightmare and a talisman.* The sacred bulls, the Apis of Memphis, the Mnevis of Heliopolis,† and the Hathor calves seemed to strike them more even than anything else. ‡ The unenlightened part of the Beni-Israel adopted these gilded images almost as gods of the tribe, and we shall find the people, whenever they could elude the pressure of the puritans, reverting to these visible protectors, to whom a pompous worship was paid. The usage of cries (*teroua*), § of loud music, of dancing around the god—customs which seem in nowise patriarchal—probably date from these times. Circumcision among the Beni-Israel was anterior to their coming into the land of Goshen, but it is not impossible that their sojourn in this country, where the practice was almost endemic,‖ contributed to make it a more regular custom.

* Numbers, ch. xxi., v. 8 and following; Second Book of Kings, ch. xviii., v. 4.

† Herodotus, iii., 28; Diodorus Siculus, I., xxi., 10; Strabo, xvii., 22.

‡ Although the fact has been denied, "there are Apis and Mnevis bulls in stone and metal, some of the stone ones being of very large size, like the Apis of the Louvre, which belongs to the Saïte epoch, or the Mnevis of Boulacq, which dates from the 20th dynasty." (Maspero.) The reproductions of Hathor are still more numerous.

§ תרועה, perhaps θρίαμβος, *triumphus*, which do not appear to be Aryan words.

‖ See above, pp. 105, 106.

The winged disk, flanked by the *uræus*, which made so great an impression upon the Phœnicians and became the essential feature of their art,* was doubtless also adopted by the Israelites. The oldest Jewish seals bear this symbol.† The sphinxes certainly remained impressed upon the imagination of the Israelites. The *cherubim* are in part derived from them, though these chimerical beings have several times changed in shape, in accordance with the caprices of Oriental fashion, and although the very name of *cherub* seems to come rather from the direction of Assyria. What relates to the *ephod*, the *urim*, and the *thummim* in the Hebrew writings is so obscure that no accurate idea of them can be formed. Here, however, the influence of the winged globe, flanked by the uræus, seems to show itself again.‡ The replies of Iahveh, when he was consulted by the *urim-thummim* of the ancient shape, resembled very much those of the Egyptian gods.§ Upon the other hand, the *urim-thummim* of the breast-plate of the Jewish priests was quite analogous with the costume of the Egyptian judges. ‖ The sacerdotal vestments of Jerusalem were,

---

* *Mission de Phénicie*, index, p. 883.

† Levy, *Siegel und Gemmen* (Breslau, 1869), pp. 83 and following, pl. iii.; de Vogüé, *Mél. d'arch. orient.*, pp. 131 and following; Clermont-Ganneau, in the *Journal asiatique*, Feb.-March, 1883, pp. 128 and following.

‡ See below, p. 228.

§ See below, p. 229.

‖ Diodorus Siculus, I., xlviii., 6; lxxv., 5; Elien, *Var. hist.*, xiv., 34.

like all articles of luxury, borrowed from Egypt.*
At the remote epoch of which I am speaking there is
nothing to show that any such vestments existed,
though the use of linen for the sacerdotal surplices
seems to have been an imitation from Egypt, and a
very ancient one too.†

What also appears to be distinctly Egyptian is the
idea of persons being called by a sort of divine hereditary vocation to have charge of religious things, and
of their alone knowing how to offer worship and do
honour to the gods. The clergy is of unquestionable
Egyptian origin. Nothing could be more opposed to
the spirit of the patriarchal society in which the
family itself kept its own *sacra*. From the time of
their sojourn in Goshen the Israelites probably had
ministers of this kind, of Egyptian origin, whom each
family kept in return for their religious services. This
was what was called a *levi*, a word which appears to
signify *inquilinus*, an adherent, an adjunct to the tribe,
an alien. ‡

It may be that this word was only produced later,
when the *levis* formed a sort of tribe apart, without
any land of their own, and when it was agreed
that Levi had been a son of Jacob to whom God
assigned no lot because his descendants were scattered

---

* See Ancessi's *Vêtements du grand prêtre et des lévites*, &c.
Paris, 1875.

† Herodotus, ii., 87; First Book of Samuel, ch. ii., v. 18; Second
Book of Samuel, ch. vi., v. 14, &c.

‡ יָלְוּ *qui adhæserunt* or *adjuncti sunt.* Isaiah, xiv., v. 1; ch.
lvi., v. 3.

among the other tribes and sustained by them. The name of Gershom, borne by more or less fabulous founders of the Levitical order, apparently alludes to the state of things which made members of that order strangers wherever they went.* It is well, in any event, to observe that the *levi* is not in any way the patriarchal *cohen*. Every head of a family was *cohen*. In many pious tribes the chief of it was called *cohen*,† while the notables were called *cohanim*.‡ These names were regarded with the utmost respect. The *Levite*, on the contrary, was little more than a sexton, having to do with the material side of the worship only. Thus the tribe of Levi (to employ the expression generally used) contributed very little, at all events up to the captivity, towards religious progress,§ and none of the great prophets were Levites. Inferior divination, on the contrary, had much in common with Egypt. The habit of consulting the gods, who replied by signs, was one of the traits of the Egyptian religion.‖ The ephods and the diviners who drew lots, after the manner of the Levite Micah,¶ are probably derived thence.

In fine, Egypt, far from contributing to the reli-

---

* Note the singular points of resemblance between Exodus, ch. ii., v. 22; Judges, ch. xvii., v. 7; ch. xviii., v. 30.

† Exodus, ch. iii., v. 1.

‡ Job, xii., v. 19.

§ The Levitical origin of Moses is an *à priori* supposition of comparatively modern date.

‖ See p. 229.

¶ Judges, ch. xvii., xviii.

INFLUENCE OF EGYPT UPON ISRAEL.

gious progress of Israel, put obstacles and dangers in the path that the people of God was to tread. It was in Egypt that originated the "golden calf," that perpetual stumbling-block of the masses, the brazen serpent which the puritans abhorred,* the lying oracles, the Levite, who was the leper of Israel, and perhaps circumcision, which was its greatest error, and was at one time very nearly upsetting its destinies. With the exception of the ark, Egypt introduced nothing but disturbing elements, which had afterwards to be eliminated, in some cases by violent means. It was not the same with the data borrowed from the Chaldæans. All of these were fruitful, and, with the exception perhaps of the unpronounceable name, remained pillars of the religion. The believing part of humanity finds its life in them still, and owes to these ancient fables a whole prehistoric epoch in which it finds much delight, and a cosmogony of which it is very proud. The genius of Israel does not come from Chaldæa, but Chaldæa supplied it with the ten first pages of the book which has enabled it to gain so unrivalled a success.

Egypt, upon the contrary, furnished it with few fruitful germs. And how many exquisite creations it nipped in the bud! In Egypt we see the last of the stately Jakobelite life, and of those grand types of aristocrats, proud, honourable, and serious in religion. Authority passed out of the hands of the chief of the

* Second Book of Kings, ch. xviii., v. 4 ; and Ezekiel believed that Israel was idolatrous in Egypt, ch. xx., v. 7 and following.

tribe, and became in a measure democratised. Henceforward the masses were to have a voice in affairs, and this voice would not always be raised in favour of religious puritanism. The worship of the Elohim came to be regarded as insipid, and with the people ever looking back regretfully to the vulgarities of Egypt, it was found necessary to appease them by raising statues of Apis with golden horns.

In the social and political order, the change which took place in Israel from its sojourn in the land of Goshen was a very considerable one. During the century which it passed in Egypt Israel had multiplied exceedingly. The spirit of the nomad tribe had gradually been fading away. At the patriarchal epoch we do not find a single instance of a revolt against the patriarch, for his authority was a purely moral one. But now absolute government had begotten its counterpart: the revolutionary spirit. The masses, soured by the functionaries of Pharaoh, frequently revolted against their chiefs. These mild pastoral families, whose passage the sedentary populations used to welcome with delight, had become a hard, obstinate, and "stiff-necked" people. Their approach excited universal apprehension; they were an enemy. Fierce towards all whom they found in their path, the transformation had taken place: Israel was no longer a tribe, but a nation. Alas! we have never, since the world began, seen or read of a merciful nation!

CHAPTER XII.

EXODUS OF ISRAEL.

EGYPTIAN civilisation, the history of which has so many analogies with that of China, has this peculiarity, that, often as it has been invaded by the stranger, it has invariably absorbed the invader, and has always, after a given time, gone back to the original level which the invasion had displaced. While the Hyksos were reigning in Lower Egypt, ancient Egypt, sometimes tributary but in reality autonomous, continued to lead an unaltered life at Thebes. A long series of wars resulted in a victory for the native party. The 18th and 19th dynasty founded a new empire, more powerful than all those which had succeeded one another in the Nile Valley. From being conquered, Egypt in her turn became conqueror, and the armies of Thotmes and Rameses marched in triumph over Syria.

The distinguishing features of these civilisations, the origin of which is lost in the night of time, are an immense pride and an utter contempt for the barbarian, who is often their superior in energy and morality, and who has an abhorrence of mandarin-like habits and of the mania for administrative routine. Victorious by her perseverance, Egypt treated the Semites of Egypt and Syria as a Chinese governor would treat barbarian rebels. The finest Arab tribes seemed to them only fit to throw up trenches and make bricks. The true Egyptians had the deepest antipathy for these herders. There is ground for believing that some of the Beni-Israel, at all events the Josephites, had participated in the acts and favours of the Hyksos. But all this was changed when there arose, in the words of the ancient narrator, "a king who knew not Joseph." The Israelites lost all the privileges which they had obtained from the fallen dynasty. They fell into deep distress, and in order to gain their living they were obliged to become labourers and do the hardest of all drudgery.

Public works were at this time assuming an extraordinary development in Egypt.* In the region of the Isthmus, more particularly, Rameses II. built two large towns, Pa-toum, a vast assemblage of warehouses and the ordinary fortified buildings,† and *Pa-Rameses-Aanakhtu* (the city of the very brave Rameses), which was in a way his northern capital.‡ He also went on with the execution of the canal which connected

---

* Maspero, *Hist. anc. des peuples d'Orient*, pp. 227 and following.

† Πάτουμος of Herodotus, ii., 158. It is Tell-el-Mashkutah. See E. Naville, *The Store-city of Pithom* (London, 1885). A great number of towns in this region were named *Pa-toum*. Tell-el-Mashkutah was undoubtedly the Pa-toum which at the epoch of the Alexandrian translators was identified with the Pithom of the Bible.

‡ Maspero, *op. cit.*, pp. 221, 224, 228, 229.

Lake Ballah and the Nile.* In order to execute these works, in which it is said that the native Egyptians took no part,† it was necessary to call in the help of the Bedouins of the Sinaitic peninsula and of southern Canaan. The store-houses of Pithom (or Pa-toum) were built of bricks made out of clay and chopped straw, dried in the sun. The Beni-Israel were employed in making these bricks, which would not have been a very difficult task if they had not at times been obliged to go and find straw. For noble tribes, which regarded all labour as degrading, this was the height of shame and misery. Perpetual quarrels went on between the poor wretches who declared that they were overdone with work, and the rigid taskmasters who met each complaint with the unvarying reply ever addressed to servile labour, "Be off with you; you are idle fellows."

During the long reign of Rameses II., all idea of a revolt was out of the question, but the military achievements of this reign, and the extraordinary amount of building that marked its progress, produced their ordinary effect. The last years of the Egyptian Louis XIV. were marked by a very decided decadence. The reign of Menephtah, his successor, witnessed the commencement of the reverses which were to follow. Barbarians of every kind, Carians, Lycians, Pelasgi, Mæonians, Tyrrhenians, Lydians, and Libyans, swooped down upon the west of the Delta, desirous not only of

---

* Maspero, p. 228.
† Diodorus Siculus, I., lvi., 2.

plundering but of establishing themselves there.*
Menephtah defeated them at first, but eventually the
barbarians gained their ends. It is from this invasion
that I date the establishment of the Philistines† upon
the coast adjoining Egypt, a country in which the Canaanite race was very scanty. Under Seti II. the Pharaohs' power had become very weakened, and Egypt
was practically powerless beyond her frontiers, while
at home she was a prey to social decomposition. The
slaves rose in revolt, and in many places the Asiatics
who had been taken prisoners and condemned to very
severe labour, declared themselves masters of the
country.‡ Large bands of them reached the Sinaitic
peninsula, a poverty-stricken country no doubt, but
one in which they at all events escaped the taskmaster's whip.

Among the fugitives were the Beni-Israel, who,
while domiciled in Goshen, had never quite lost their

* De Rougé, *Revue archéol.*, July and August, 1867.

† Maspero, *Hist. anc.*, pp. 267, 270. The relationship between this name and the Pelasgi is very doubtful; the Cretan origin of the Philistines is, upon the contrary, almost certain. The language of the Philistines appears to have been a Greco-Latin dialect. The comparisons Akis = *Anchises*, Goliath = *Galeatus*, and some others are also very conjectural. But in the second volume of this work I shall endeavour to show that certain Greek and Latin words which have existed in Hebrew from a very remote date, such as parbar = *peribolos*, mekéra = μάχαιρα, mekoné = *machina*, pilegs = *pellex*, liska = λέσχη, were introduced in David's time by the influence of the Philistines. See the typical portrait of the Philistines in Lepsius, *Denkm.*, iii., 211.

‡ Diodorus Siculus, I., lvi., 3 and following; Maspero, pp. 261, 262.

nomad habits. The Bedouins, like the Amalekites, whom they constantly saw encamped in the neighbourhood of the Bitter Lakes, excited their envy and brought with them, so to speak, the wind of the desert. It would seem that it was at Pa-Rameses, where they were assembled for brickmaking, that the Israelites formed their plan for escaping. The Levis and other low-class Egyptians who had got mixed up with them, and had become more or less incorporated with them, entered into the plot. A few of the free Egyptians who had reason to be discontented with the dynasty may also have joined in it.* The singular thing is that the Beni-Israel should afterwards have prided themselves on having spoiled the Egyptians of Pa-Rameses by carrying off with them valuable objects which they had borrowed of them.†

What are we to think of the man who has come to stand out as a colossus among the great mythical figures of humanity, and to whom the ancient narratives attribute the principal part in this exodus of Israel.‡ It is very difficult to give an answer. Moses is completely buried by the legends which have grown up over him, and though he very probably existed, it is impossible to speak of him as we

* Exodus, ch. xii., v. 38; Numbers, ch. xi., v. 4.

† A detail which now seems incomprehensible. It formed part, however, of the oldest narrative. See Dillmann upon Exodus, ch. iii., v. 21, 22. Exodus, ch. xi., v. 1 and following; Exodus, ch. xii., v. 36.

‡ The alleged Egyptian texts relating to Moses have none of them stood the test of careful criticism.

do of other deified or transformed men.* His name appears to be Egyptian.† *Mosé* is probably the name of Ahmos, Amosis, shortened at the beginning.‡ According to the prevalent tradition, Moses was a *Levi*,§ and we have seen that this name probably was used to designate the Egyptians whose services were required for the worship and who followed Israel into the desert. The name of Aharon, perhaps, is derived in a similar way. Moses appears to us at first as having been brought up by, and being a functionary of, the Egyptians. The fact of his killing an Egyptian in a moment of instinctive indignation has

---

* Moses, from the historic point of view, cannot be at all compared with Jesus. St. Paul admits Jesus to have been a person who in reality existed. Now St. Paul was a contemporary of Jesus; he was converted to the sect four or five years after the death of Jesus (see Epistles to the Galatians). The oldest documents relating to Moses are four or five centuries posterior to the epoch in which he must have lived.

† The Alexandrian Jews had some suspicion of this. Gesenius, *Thes.*, p. 824.

‡ It is difficult, at all events, to overlook the element *mos*, "son," which is found in Thotmos, Amenmos, &c. The shortened form *Mosu* is sometimes met with in the Egyptian onomasticon. It is true that one would expect to find in the Hebraic transcription the simple sibilant, and not the *chuintante*. See de Rougé, *Revue archéol.*, November, 1861, p. 354; August, 1867, pp. 87—89. But where are we to learn how the Hebrews, who first wrote the name of משה about 1000 or 1100 B.C., pronounced the *schin* ? It was just the time when one-half of Israel used the word *sibboleth*. The שׁ and the שׂ also are used indifferently in the old way of writing the name of Israel (*Iesurun*, &c.). See above, p. 90, Note *. As a rule, in ante-scriptural Semitic etymology, the *hé* and the *heth*, the *schin* and the *sin* may be regarded as one single letter.

§ Exodus, ch. ii., v. 1.

nothing improbable about it. His relations with the Arab Midianites, a species of Hebrews not reduced to servitude by Egypt, and with the Idumean Kenites, especially with a certain Ieter or Jethro,* whose daughter he is said to have married, also seem to have a semi-historical character. With regard to whether he was really the leader of the revolt and the guide of fugitive Israel, it is unquestionably quite possible that an Egyptian functionary of mixed race, told off to keep watch over his brethren, may have played a part similar to that of the mulattos of St. Domingo and been the author of the deliverance. But it is also possible that all these narratives of the Exodus, into which fable has penetrated so deeply, may be even more mythical than is generally supposed, and that the only fact which can be depended upon out of them all is the departure from Egypt of Israel and its entry into the peninsula of Sinai.

It does not seem as if the Israelites and their companions had any other object in view, before they left Pa-Rameses, except to escape the tyranny of Pharaoh. If they had then the idea of conquering that land of Canaan in which their ancestors had wandered as nomads, it must have been in a very crude form. The first thing was to get out of Egypt, and two routes lay before them, one being in a north-

* Exodus, ch. iv., xviii. The termination *o* is a peculiarity of the Arameo-Arabic dialects of the Midianite region (Sinaitic and Nabathean inscriptions). Upon the other hand the forms יתר, יתרו, יתרי, יתרא lead one to take יתראל as the name of a tribe. See above, pp. 80, 81, 89.

easterly direction to the Mediterranean coast, and then along the one high road which had from the earliest times connected Syria and Egypt along the sea-shore. But the nomads did not like following a highway, while the capital reason which prevented them from taking this direction was that they would after a few days' march have encountered the Philistines, then in the full flush of their military organisation.* The Israelites and the emigrants who accompanied them were scarcely armed at all, and a struggle with these rude warriors would, therefore, have been a hopeless one.† So it was resolved to go in a south-easterly direction, and reach the peninsula of Sinai as quickly as possible. In three days' march they reached what the Semites called Pi-hahirot (to-day Kalaat-Agrud), opposite the entrenched camp of the Hyksos, abandoned or destroyed since the time of Ahmos I.

That branch of the Red Sea which in our days terminates at Suez on a very shallow shore, then reached, in the form of lagoons, much farther inland,‡ and extended by a chain of lakes or underground infiltrations to the basin of the Bitter Lakes. In reality the waters of the Red Sea reached to what is now known as the ridge of Serapeum. To pass from Egypt into Asia leaving this to the north, it was necessary to cross pools of water belonging to the Red Sea, though at

* See above, pp. 134, 135.
† Exodus, ch. xiii., v. 17, 18.
‡ The ruins of Colzoum (Clysma), where people embarked for India up to the Middle Ages, are now two leagues inland. Suez has only been in existence since the Arab conquest.

certain points, owing to the accumulation of sand, the water was not ankle-deep. The passage, however, was not without its danger, for the tide in these narrow channels would, when the wind was in a certain direction, and at certain seasons of the year, be very capricious, and those who were not careful in the selection of their time might well be surrounded by the waters and exposed to sink in the quicksands. No doubt the popular fancy exaggerated the list of accidents which really happened, and found pleasure in relating fictitious episodes of caravans and armies being submerged.* It may reasonably be imagined, too, that at this critical moment of the journey the mass of fugitives was seized with a panic which left a deep impression behind it. But the popular tales alone about the dangers of the passage would have furnished a sufficient basis for the sacred legend, marked with the most exuberant spirit of the marvellous which afterwards came out in it.

Among the fables with which this legend teems, none is more improbable than that of a pursuit of the fugitives by the Egyptians, ending in a hopeless disaster to Pharaoh's army. Owing to the dynastic weakness of Egypt, the rule of the sovereigns was little more than nominal in the Isthmus, and a fugitive who had got beyond the Bitter Lakes was certain of his freedom. Moreover, there is nothing to indicate that the Egyptian Government had any desire to keep

* Compare with the legends of the "Lieue de grève," in Brittany.

by force within its borders a band of foreigners whose presence had become, to say the least of it, useless. All that was afterwards related about the exodus of Israel proves that there was no direct record of it, and that in the age and place where the legend was built up no one had any precise idea of the time and circumstances amid which the event occurred.*

* The song of Moses in Exodus xv. is a literary and artificial composition of much later date.

CHAPTER XIII.

ISRAEL IN THE DESERT OF PHARAN.

HAVING escaped from what they always called "the house of bondage," the people of Israel found themselves face to face with what is perhaps the most inhospitable desert under heaven.* In its western part it is known as the Desert of Sur,† while farther east it was called Pharan. Had they continued their route due east they would have found nothing but vacuity‡ and death. They turned towards the south-east, following very closely the sea, or rather the ancient route which the Egyptians had traced more than a thousand years before for working the Sinai copper mines.§ The want of water was the most cruel deprivation. At the end of three days the fugitives reached a place called Mara, on account of its brackish

---

* Notwithstanding the entirely legendary character of the narratives about the Sinaitic period, the diary of the desert contains many serious elements which cannot be altogether disregarded. See Robinson, Dillmann, and the Ordnance Survey of the Peninsula of Sinai, by Wilson, Palmer, &c. (1869.)

† Pococke (*Descr.*, vol. i., p. 139) has heard it called Shedur. Perhaps this may be right; שור might be a mistake for שדר.

‡ תחו, still in the present day تِيه, *Tih*.

§ Serbout el-Qadim, Wadi-Maghara.

waters.* They endeavoured, by the infusion of certain boughs,† to render it potable, but only with indifferent success. The encampment at Elim ‡ was a less trying one, for they found there twelve springs, seventy palm-trees and tamarisk-trees, which afforded them a welcome shade. The tribe then approached nearer to the sea, as far as the first spurs of the vast mountain chain of Sinai. The desert of Sin again subjected them to severe hardships, for it is a terrible country, bare and waterless, where even in winter the flocks of sheep can scarcely find sufficient food.

The narratives of the incidents which occurred during this march, which afterwards became the basis of a religion, or, to speak more correctly, of universal religion, all of them attribute the principal part to Mosé. I have already pointed out that this theory can only be accepted with considerable reserve, but it is probable, nevertheless, that the activity of the semi-Egyptian Hebrew, who seems to have had much to do with the preparations for the exodus, was again manifested during the marches through the desert. Another *Levite*, named Ahron, or Aharon (an Egyptian name, perhaps), stands out side by side with him, as well as a woman named Miriam, who, according to the legend, were his brother and sister. Some narratives§ attached more importance to these persons than do the versions which have come down to us.

* Now called Aïn-Howara.
† Compare with Lesseps's *l'Isthme de Suez* (Paris, 1864), p. 10.
‡ Wadi Gharondel.
§ Micah, ch. vi., v. 4.

There is perhaps some foundation for what we are told as to the relations which Moses established with the tribes to the east of Egypt,* and these relations would have been useful to him in the difficult task which he had assumed. But one hesitates about speaking of the shadows dimly outlined in the darkness of profound night as real personages. We shall see later on that the name of Aharon, in particular, is open to quite a different explanation. The only historical lines which we possess with regard to these times—the Song of Beër,† in which we can trace a clear allusion to what was afterwards cited as a miracle of Moses—show us the *sarim* (princes) and the *nedibé ha-am* (nobles of the people), carrying staves of command, and effecting with these staves, without any supernatural intervention, the act which more modern legends attributed to Moses. Nothing can be further removed than this short song from the idea of a single leader inspired of God.

Even if the legendary narratives did not relate to us the murmurings and daily revolts of the people against the leaders who had brought them out of Egypt, such scenes might be inferred *à priori*. Man is sensitive to his present misfortunes only. What he *has* suffered always appears to him of small account by comparison with what he *is* suffering. Hunger and thirst caused the slaves of yesterday to regret the onions of Egypt and the life of relative abundance which they had

* See above, pp. 136, 137.
† Numbers, ch. xxi., v. 17, 18 (taken from the Jasher).

enjoyed there. The leaders did not, in these circumstances, hesitate to resort to any of the impostures which the ancients regarded as perfectly legitimate. It was necessary to persuade these poor waifs that the god of their tribe was watching over them. All the incidents of the route were made to serve this end. Whenever a spring of water was discovered, the discovery was attributed to a miracle. Now and again the wind would bring upon their track a flock of quails, and this, they were told, was due to the god who watched over them and wished to relieve their distress.

A trifling source of relief which these solitudes offer the traveller was afterwards exaggerated, to a remarkable degree, by the legend. It often happens that, at certain seasons, the shrubs in the desert are covered with a sort of gummy exudation, by means of which the wanderers succeed in slightly appeasing their hunger. This is what the Arabs call *mann es-semà*, "the gift of heaven," or simply *mann*, "the gift," believing that this excrescence falls from heaven like a kind of white frost. The Israelites had their share of this trifling succour, and in after days, in lands where it was not known what *mann* was, the most fantastic narratives were spun upon this subject. Manna was described as the bread which the sons of God eat in heaven, and it was generally accepted that God, as an act of special favour, had for some time fed his chosen people with angels' food.*

* Psalm lxxviii., v. 25.

The real miracle would have been that the Israelites were able to live in the desert of Sinai if they had been as numerous and their sojourn had been as long as the legend asserts. But the traditional story on this point is certainly full of exaggerations. The band of fugitives was infinitely smaller than the hyperbolical figures of the existing text would lead us to believe; in the second place, the duration of their wanderings was not nearly so long as is supposed.* The fugitives may have brought away with them some corn and provisions from Egypt. With the valuable objects which they laid hands upon, if the narratives are to be believed,† they may have procured something in exchange from the Ishmaelite or Midianite traders, and so have formed a flock. Perhaps, too, the peninsula was not so denuded three thousand years ago as it is now. ‡ The vegetable mould appears to have spread from wadis to the neighbouring plains.§ Certain valleys were formerly dammed so as to serve as a reservoir for the winter rains.‖

---

* The forty years (Amos, ch. ii., v. 10) recall the forty days' journey of Elijah to Horeb (First Book of Kings, ch. xix., v. 8). The oldest texts did not make any calculation of the length of sojourn in the desert.

† Numbers, ch. xx., v. 19 (taken, it would seem, from the book of the *Wars of Iahveh*), would lead one to infer that they had articles of value with them.

‡ *Ordnance Survey*, part i., pp. 28, 194, and following.

§ I owe this information to the Suez Canal Company.

‖ Dykes have been found which, at the time of the 5th, 6th and 12th dynasties, formed lakes, around which were clustered the villages of the Egyptian miners. (Note of M. Maspero.)

At the present day the peninsula, if we except the convent of St. Catherine, is peopled by a few hundred Bedouins, who are plunged in the deepest poverty. Formerly the population was beyond doubt larger. The Amalekites and the Midianites, who appear to have been very numerous tribes, lived there for centuries.* Pharan, which is identical with Raphidim, afterwards gave its name to the Pharanites,† who, in their time, were of almost as much importance as the Saracens.

The route of Israel through the desert was a passage, not a sojourn; but the impression which this short period of miserable existence left upon the minds of the people was very deep. All the circumstances, of which a more or less distorted recollection was preserved, were regarded as sacramental, and the theocratic caste afterwards moulded them to the purposes of its religious policy. The slightest incidents were magnified, and the manna and the quails were adduced as proofs that the people had been miraculously fed, and that God himself had been their guide, and had marched before them in the way. Upon these vast solitary plains, where the atmosphere is so luminous, the presence of a tribe can be detected from afar by the smoke which ascends straight up towards the sky. Night time is often chosen for a march, and in that case a lighted beacon, fastened on to the end

* Genesis, ch. xxv., v. 18; First Book of Samuel, ch. xv., v. 7; ch. xxvii., v. 8.

† Ptolemæus, V., xvii. 8.

of a long pole, is often used as a rallying sign.* This column, invisible by day, luminous by night, was the very God of Israel, guiding His people through these solitudes.† This good genius of the desert had shown such a special affection for Israel that the people came to invoke him in a quite personal way. The God who had brought Israel out of Egypt and enabled them to live in "the land of thirst" was not the absolute Elohim, the great God, King, and Providence of the whole universe. He was a god who had a special affection for Israel, who had bought them as merchandise. How far we are here from the ancient patriarchal God, just and universal! The new god of whom I am speaking is in the highest degree partial. His providence has only one aim, and that is to watch over Israel. He is not as yet the god of a nation, for a nation is the produce of the marriage of a group of men with some land, and Israel has no land; but he is the god of a tribe in every sense of the word. Great is the decadence from the ancient Jakobelite, whose genius finds fresh expression in the Book of Job and who had a far higher idea of God and of the universe.

A protecting god needs a proper name, for the protecting god is a person; he becomes identified with those whom he protects. Israel had in their religious vocabulary but one proper name for God. The name of Iahveh which the ancient nomads had brought back

* Quintus-Curtius, V., ii., 7; numerous modern testimonies, particularly the French expedition to Egypt.
† Exodus, ch. xxxiii., v. 9.

from Padan-Aram, or Ur-Casdim, was not, like El or Elohim, a generic name; it was an undeclinable, inflexible name, analogous to the *Camos* of the Moabites. By a process of ideas which it is impossible now to follow out, the protecting god of Israel was called Iahveh.* Each step towards the formation of the national idea was, it will be seen, accompanied by a degradation in the theology of Israel. The national idea was in favour of a god who would think only of the nation, who in the interests of the nation would be cruel, unjust, and hostile to the whole human race. Iahvéism commenced, to all intents and purposes, when Israel adopted self-interest as a national principle; and it grew with the nation, causing the obliteration of the sublime and true idea of the primitive Elohism. Fortunately there was in the genius of Israel something superior to national prejudices. The old Elohism was never to die; it was to survive Iahvéism, or rather to assimilate it. The wart was to be extirpated. The prophets, and especially Jesus, the last of them, will expel Iahveh,† the exclusive god of Israel,

---

* Iahveh appears as the military protector of Israel immediately after their coming out of Egypt. It is true that such a conception may have been retrospective. In the fragment which has been preserved of the song to celebrate the capture of Heshbon, the victory of Israel is not attributed to Iahveh. It no doubt was in the complete song, inasmuch as Moab is called in it "the people of Chemosh." (Numbers, xxi., v. 29.)

† This is the deep-rooted idea of the Gnostics; but they falsified it by shutting their eyes to the fact that all this occurred within the limits of Judaism. The German anti-Semites of our day are guilty of the same historical injustice.

and revert to the noble patriarchal formula of one good and just father for the universe and the human race.

The transition from idealism to nationalism is never effected with impunity. Israel was not the only people to whom the adoption of a protecting god brought decadency; and Israel, at all events, had the courage to try and counteract the effects of their error. By a series of efforts long sustained, Israel at length returned to the truth, and established, in place of the idea of the national god, the universal idea of the Elion, or El-Shaddai, of the patriarchs. El was just towards men, though his justice was enveloped in mystery. Iahveh is not just, being monstrously partial towards Israel and cruelly severe upon other peoples. He loved Israel and hated the rest of the world. He slew, lied, deceived, and robbed, all for the benefit of Israel. And what good reasons were there for believing that it was this particular god who had made heaven and earth? All this constituted a tissue of contradictions which the genius of the prophets gradually overcame. The work of the prophets consisted in re-creating, by reflection, the ancient Elohism, in forcibly identifying Iahveh with El-Elion, and in rectifying the twist which the adoption of a particular god had given to the religious direction of Israel.

A special god, being, in fact, the gravest of all philosophical errors, becomes a source of constant deviations for the people who give themselves over to one. Just in proportion as El had given good advice to the ancient patriarchs and had inspired them with an elevated notion of life, so did Iahveh pervert Israel, rendering them cruel, iniquitous, bloodthirsty, and treacherous where their own interests were concerned. Ezekiel [*] asserts that Iahveh, wishing to chastise his people, commanded them at one time to sacrifice their children, so that they might be punished with their own hands. Assuredly Iahveh, at this remote age, did not differ very much from Moloch. The good of the nation whom he protected was the supreme good; all the rest being as nothing in comparison. The world existed for Israel's sake. Iahveh was a national, that is to say a very malign god.

If the religion of Israel had not gone beyond this phase, it is assuredly the last religion to which the world would have rallied. It might as well have adopted that of Camos. But, in spite of appearances, elohism retained its inward vitality, and was to prevail again, until Iahveh had lost all special characteristics and his very name had been succeeded by an equivalent of Elohim, the harmless Adonaï, "the Lord." To declare that a name is unpronounceable is very much the same as to eliminate this name altogether. As a matter of fact, the usage which became prevalent in the centuries immediately preceding the Christian era marked the close of the struggle between Iahveh and Elohim, or rather was tantamount to an admission that Iahveh no longer existed. The

[*] Ezekiel, ch. xx., v. 25 and following.

Greek and Christian translators almost ignore the word *Iahveh*. Κύριος, the equivalent of Adonaï, has more or less supplanted the old divine proper name. If the Alexandrian translators had adopted the transcription Ιευάς, that would have been a tremendous obstacle to the monotheistic propaganda; people would have said that this was another Jupiter, and that it was not worth while to make any change.

What the worship of a national god may lead to is not monotheism, but what we in our day call *henotheism*. The national god is a jealous god, and will not hear of any rivalry, so that it becomes necessary to abandon all the other gods for him. It is probable that in Daibon or Ar-Moab Camos was as exclusive as Iahveh became in Jerusalem, and that a pious Moabite supposed him to be as susceptible as Iahveh was. It was the same with Melqarth at Tyr, because the name of the "King of the town" was an adaptation of the supreme God to a national past.* The habit of repeating upon every occasion, "Our God is so great that all the other gods are nothing by comparison with Him," of necessity provoked the retort, "Our God is the only god in the world." But the intellect of peoples is so sluggish that it took them centuries to draw this conclusion.

The man who is in distress or trouble takes a false view in religion; for he must needs believe that a

* For the analogies between the worship of the Tyrian Melqarth and that of the Israelite Jahveh, see *Miss. de Phén*, pp. 574, 575.

God cares for him and will be his avenger. He readily becomes superstitious. Idolatry, reduced during the ancient patriarchal period to the minimum compatible with the intellect of unlettered people, had acquired a great hold upon them while in Egypt. The people clamoured for Mnévis and Hathor.* It is doubtful whether Mosé was so much opposed to this idolatrous worship as was afterwards asserted, for we find that a brazen serpent said to have been set up by him was in existence until the reign of Hezekiah, who broke it in pieces. This serpent, which the people called *Nehustan*, and to which they offered sacrifices,† was probably an ancient idol of Iahveh. The serpent was, in Egypt, not so much a god of itself, as a manner of representing the gods and goddesses. One of the points which constituted the great inferiority of Iahveh was this degrading promiscuity with the gods of low degree. There was never any image of Saddaï, Elion, or Elohim. There were images of Iahveh.

At a later date it was asserted that Moses had lifted up and placed upon a pole, as a talisman against the bite of the serpents, this mysterious *Nehustan*.‡ Both versions may be true, for it is not at all impossible that Moses may have been, in some ways, one of those sorcerers whom Egypt possessed, or who came from the

* It is remarkable that Hathor holds a very important place in the Egyptian inscriptions of the peninsula of Sinai. (*Ordnance Survey*, part i., pp. 168 and following.)

† Second Book of Kings, ch. xviii., v. 4.

‡ Numbers, ch. xxi., v 4—9.

ISRAEL IN THE DESERT OF PHARAN.

banks of the Euphrates.* No alterations are too great to have taken place after the lapse of five or six centuries, when a religious genius as powerful as that of the Hebrews is working upon an oral tradition which is above all things non-resistent and susceptible of any degree of transformation.

The *aron*, or ark, in the course of these peregrinations, became more and more the central piece of the tribes. The bearers of the wooden staves which acted as handles were probably *Levites*. They were highly esteemed, and were in a measure the guides and the leaders of the nation. They were called Beni-Aron or Ahron,† so, in accordance with the custom of genealogies, Aron, or Ahron, became a personage, a guide of the people like Moses, and in time the latter's brother. This is how many savants explain Aaron's being made the head of the priesthood and the supposed leader of the so-called tribe of Levi. I give their opinion just to show how, in difficult matters of this kind, views may differ, without on that account exceeding the bounds of possibility.

Upon reaching the first slopes of Sinai, the Israelites ceased to follow the sea. Veering to the east, they marched round the base of the mountain and struck inland as far as the place called Rephidim.‡ It is almost the only spot in the peninsula where nature

* Balaam.

† אהרן for ארן would be an ancient way of spelling, יהוסף, יהושע, יהוח.

‡ Now called Feirân. It is the Φαράν of the ancients.

deigns to smile.* There are a few palm-trees and a little water, but the name of these pools is characteristic, for they were called the waters of *Meriba*, that is "of strife," on account of the incessant fights which took place there between the Bedouins when they came to let their flocks drink of them.

It was, too, at this spot that the Israelites appear to have had to fight their first battle with the hordes who were seeking, like them, to eke out a bare existence in these regions. The Amalekites, closely related to the Edomites, and consequently very nearly connected with the Jacobite group, fell upon them while they were at rest under the palm-trees of the oasis. The Israelites got the upper hand, and this fact, followed no doubt by many others of a like kind,† was the origin of a terrible feud between Israel and Amalek. Israel swore that they would not cease their warfare against the Amalekites until they had exterminated them,‡ and they kept their word.

With the battle of Rephidim commence, in all probability, the borrowings of the compilers of Sacred History from the ancient book of the *Wars of Iahveh*.§

---

* *Rephidim* means the "place of repose." The site of the convent of St. Catherine is much better, but the Israelites do not appear to have gone in this direction.

† The Jehovist narrator seems to have magnified into a miraculous victory several stories of skirmishes and captures of fugitives. (Deuteronomy, ch. xxv., v. 17 and following; First Book of Samuel, ch. xv., v. 2.)

‡ Exodus, ch. xvii., v. 8—16.

§ I shall endeavour to show, in vol. ii., that the first compilation of a Sacred History, constituting the framework of the

At this battle there appears for the first time a companion of Mosé, upon whom devolved more especially the military part. This was Hosea or Iosua (the conqueror), known under the name of Joshua. The bias of the pious compilers is so visible in all these narratives that the name of Joshua, like that of Moses, can only be used in a historical narrative with the utmost precaution.* Caleb,† one of the most highly extolled heroes of the book of the *Wars of Iahveh*, may have only existed in the imagination of the collectors of popular songs who were responsible for the epic souvenirs of the nation. It was the same with Hur, whose name appears originally to have designated a sub-tribe in the south of Judah, in relation with the Calebites.‡

The sojourn at Rephidim may have lasted some time. Three months had elapsed since the coming

present Hexateuch, took place about 800 B.C., but that this compilation was made from still earlier books, the *Iasar*, the book of the *Wars of Iahveh*, the book of the patriarchal legends, which may be assigned the approximate date of 900 B.C.

* By reasoning of this kind, it is urged, it would be possible to prove that Napoleon never existed. The two things do not run on parallel lines. The first sources of the history of Moses and Joshua are nearly 500 years posterior to Moses and Joshua. Handwriting was not known in Israel until three or four hundred years after the time of Moses and Joshua. The ages which do not possess handwriting transmit only fables.

† This name is more Canaanite than Hebrew. *Corpus inscr. semit.*, part i., Nos. 29, 52. See above, pp. 89, 90, and below, pp. 205, 206.

‡ Exodus, ch. xvii., v. 10 ; ch. xxiv., v. 14 ; First Book of Chronicles, ch. ii., v. 19 and following, 50 and following ; ch. iv., v. 1, 4.

out of Egypt,* when the Beni-Israel raised their camp and penetrated into the rocky gorges which lead to the Wadi, and which were designated by the generic name of Horeb.† This was what was called "the desert of Sinai," an austere and imposing region, for which the genius of Israel was to secure the first rank among the holy places of humanity.

* Exodus, ch. xix., v. 1.
† Exodus, ch. iii., v. 1.; ch. xvii., v. 6; ch. xxxiii., v. 6.

CHAPTER XIV.

SINAI.

The mountain of Sinai, formed of dark granite, which the sun, gilding every object upon which it shines, has bathed for centuries without penetrating, is one of the most singular phenomena on the surface of the globe.* It is the exact likeness of those landscapes of a world without water, such as one imagines the moon, or any other celestial body devoid of atmosphere, to be. It is not that frequent and terrible storms do not gather round its summit. But the storm, in other places beneficent, is here merely terrible, a kind of inorganic phenomenon, in a manner metallic, a concert entirely composed of the sound of the cannon, the drum, the trumpet, and the bell. Its summits must be inhabited by severe gods; it is Olympus without its waters and forests, Iceland or Jan Mayen without snow. Of all that constitutes nature—sun, clouds, water, trees, verdure, man, beast—there is nothing here but stone, seamed by lodes of metal, sometimes condensed into sparkling gems, always resisting life and stifling it all around. Copper, turquoises, all the residues of a kind of natural vitrifaction, these are the products of Sinai.

* *Ordnance Survey*, part i., p. 28.

The Thora, also, is said to have come from there, but never life. If one excepts the little oasis of the convent of St. Catherine, placed beyond the parts seen by the Hebrews, the barrenness is absolute; this unnatural country yields neither fruit, nor corn, nor a drop of water. On the other hand, nowhere is the light so intense, the air so transparent, the snow so dazzling. The silence of these solitudes is appalling; a whisper awakens curious echoes, the traveller is alarmed by the sound of his own footsteps.* It is indeed the mountain of the Elohim,† with their indistinct outlines, their deceptive transparencies, their strange reflections.

Sinai is, in a way, the mountain of Egypt. Egypt properly speaking has no mountains.‡ What are called the Arabian or Libyan chains are merely mountains in appearance; their uniform heights have no reverse; they are banks formed by the hollow of an enormous valley. The shores of the Red Sea, which runs like a canal through the desert, resemble each other. Sinai is therefore throughout the region of Sahara an *unique* object, an isolated accident, a throne, a pedestal for something divine. Egypt, shut up in its valley and caring nothing for the aspect of the country, paid little attention to it; but it was otherwise with the nomad tribes in the neighbourhood. Horeb, or Sinai, from the most remote antiquity, was the object of religious worship on the part

* *Ordnance Survey*, part i., p. 80.

† הר האלהים. Exodus, ch. iii., v. 1.

‡ One must except the Djebel-Ataka and its chain, running to the monastery of St. Paul, forming, as it were, small Sinais.

of the people of Hebrew or of Arab origin who roamed about those parts.* They made pilgrimages there.† The Semites of Egypt went there frequently to offer up sacrifices.‡ They believed that their god resided there. The holy mountain spread terror a long way around it. It was called *par excellence* "the mountain of Elohim," or "the mountain of God."§ It was admitted that the Elohim resided on its summits,‖ snowy or shining, limpid as crystal or gloomy and enveloped with a terrible covering of mist. Up to the first centuries of our era the tribes from the north of Arabia made pilgrimages to Feiran and Serbal. The names of the pilgrims written in hundreds on the rocks of the valley leading there, bear witness to the persistency with which the worship attached to these rocks was carried on for centuries.¶ The worship of mountains is one of the most ancient among the Semitic races.** Tabor, Casius, Horan, Hermon, and Lebanon had their worship and their

* Exodus, ch. iii., v. 1 and following.

† Exodus, ch. iii., v. 18.

‡ Exodus, ch. iii., v. 18.

§ Exodus, ch. iii., v. 1; ch. iv., v. 27; ch. xviii., v. 5; ch. xxiv., v. 13; First Book of Kings, ch. xix., v. 8; Numbers, ch. x., v. 33; Psalm xxxvi., v. 7; lviii., v. 16 and following.

‖ Note expression משׁה עלה אל האלהים. Exodus, ch. xix., v. 3, "Moses went up into the *Elohim*."

¶ Inscriptions called Sinaitic. See the dissertation of Tuch, in the *Zeitschrift der d. m. G.*, 1849, pp. 129 and following; that of Levy of Breslau, same collection, 1860, pp. 363 and following, 594 and following There are among the pilgrims Christians, Jews, and pagans. *Journal asiat.*, January, February, and March, 1859.

** Baudissin, *Studien zum semit. Rel.*, ii., pp. 232 and following.

god.* Sinai had its god, who had the greatest possible affinity with lightning. The summits where such terrible storms were brewed appeared to be the dwelling-place of a fiery deity with the pinions of an eagle or a hawk,† riding on the wings of the wind, with angels for messengers and his ministers a flaming fire.‡ The *Arafel*, the dark cloud, was his veil. He rent it to show himself in lightning. A god of flame resided there. What is very striking is that in the five or six really ancient paragraphs which we have concerning the life of Moses, the future chief of Israel, exiled among the Midianites and keeping the sheep of his father-in-law Jethro, he visits "Horeb, the mountain of God," and sees there the vision of a bush which burns without being consumed.§

The god of Sinai was, at all events, redoubtable, and was not to be disturbed with impunity in his retreat. When you met him in the gorges of his mountain he endeavoured to kill you. Such appears at least to be the explanation of the following curious episode. We must be satisfied with translating it, for we cannot fathom its real meaning. "And it

* Baal-Hermon, Baal Lebanon, Baal-Horan, Deus Carmelus, the name of *Cassiodore*. See *Corpus inscr. semit.*, part i., p. 26.

† Exodus, ch. xix., v. 14. See the curious coin in the British Museum, a little anterior to Alexander, representing a god of lightning on a kind of winged velocipede, with the legend יהו; De Luynes, *Numism. des satrapies*, pl. iv., No. 4; Combe, *Vet. Numi*, in British Museum, pl. xiii., No. 12; Six, in *Numism. Chronicle*, 1877, p. 229. It is not impossible that a satrap of the Jewish or Samaritan countries put the god of the country on these coins.

‡ Psalm civ., v. 4.

§ Exodus, ch. iii., v. 1 and following.

SINAI.

came to pass by the way in the inn, that Iahveh met him and sought to kill him. Then Zippora* took a sharp stone and cut off the foreskin of her son, and cast it at his feet, and said, Surely a bloody husband art thou to me. Then Iahveh let Moses go."† This appears to me the counterpart of the struggle between Jacob and an angel. When a person passed through the territory of a god it was not rare for the god to attack him in the dark, and he did not escape without being emasculated, unnerved, or undergoing some sanguinary expiation.

Sinai was therefore above all a mountain of terror. Certain spots were considered holy, and one could not walk on them without taking off one's shoes. ‡ The general belief was that one could not see the god and live. § Even his presence killed. || The common people could not approach him. ¶ His face, a kind of distinct hypostasis of himself,** was the head of Medusa which no living person could see.†† Even those

* The wife of Moses.
† Exodus, ch. iv., v. 24—26.
‡ Exodus, ch. iii., v. 5.
§ Exodus, ch. iii., v. 6.
|| Exodus, ch. xix., v. 12 and following, 21; ch. xx., v. 18 and following; ch. xxviii., v. 35; ch. xxx., v. 21; ch. xxxiii., v. 20; Leviticus, ch. xvi., v. 13. Exception: Exodus, ch. xxiv., v. 9—11, which confirms rule. Note Genesis, ch. xvi., v. 13.

¶ Exodus, ch. xxiv., v. 2
** Exodus, ch. xxxiii., v. 14. Compare the Θεοῦ πρόσωπον with the פן־בעל of the Phœnicians. Concerning Maleak Iahveh see further on, p. 234.

†† Legend of Elijah, First Book of Kings, ch. xix., v. 13; Isaiah, ch. vi., v. 2.

who enjoyed the honour of conversing with him face to face expiated that honour by death. It was related that one day, in Horeb, Moses wished to see the glory of this terrible god. The god took him, placed him in the cleft of a rock, made him stand up, covered him with his large open hand, and passed by. Then he withdrew his hand so that Moses saw him from behind. If Moses had seen his face he would have died.* Elijah afterwards saw the god of Horeb under similar circumstances.† To catch a stealthy glimpse of this hidden god, was the supreme privilege of the elect. Other visions, such as the dazzling nature of the sky,‡ confirmed the impressions held with regard to the top of the mountain. It was related that one day the elders of Israel ascended the mountain and saw the divinity of the place, "and there was under his feet as it were a paved work of sapphire stone, and as it were the splendour of heaven itself."

The god of Sinai, it will be seen, was a god of lightning. His *theophanies* took place in the storm, in the midst of the flashing of lightning.§ The ancient Iahveh had already perhaps possessed some of these characteristics. Iahveh besides was decidedly beginning to play the part of the tutelary god of Israel, and was replacing the old *elohim* in the imagination of the people. ‖ It was therefore only natural that they

* Exodus, ch. xxxiii., v. 17—23 (very old).
† First Book of Kings, ch. xix.
‡ Exodus, ch. xxiv., v. 1, 2, 9—11.
§ Exodus, ch. xix.; Job, ch. xxxviii., v. 1.
‖ The fact of Sinai being called the "Mountain of Iahveh"

should identify Iahveh with the God through whose lands they were passing and whose terrible influence they thought that they felt.* Egypt carried the belief in local divinities to the uttermost limit; each district had its special god. Sinai was henceforward the basis of all the theology of the Israelites, and it was obstinately declared that Iahveh appeared there for the first time under the form of fire.†

What really happened when, from the camp of Rephidim, the tribe entered the rocky defiles of the Horeb? ‡ Impossible to say. Did there take place, in fact, opposite to Serbal, a religious act, a sort of consecration of the people to the god of the mountain,

does not authorise the conclusion that Iahveh was primitively the name of the god of the mountain.

* Exodus, ch. iii., v. 14; ch. vi., v. 3.

† Exodus, ch. iii., v. 1 and following.

‡ The critic who holds that all the stories relative to Horeb and Sinai are legends, can hardly attach any value to the topographical researches which have been made in order to localise the Biblical *mise en scène*. The author, writing in Palestine, did not have in view this or that site in preference to another. It is, however, far more natural to connect the Biblical traditions with Serbal, beyond Feiran, than with Djebel Mousa or Djebel Katherin. This latter region is in fact fertile, well watered, and in no way deserves the name of the "desert of Sinai," by which the place of the *theophanie* is designated. Let me add that *Horeb* and *Sinai* were considered synonymous; now *Horeb* certainly meant the mountainous region which overlooked Rephidim. Exodus, ch. iii., v. 1; ch. xvii., v. 6.

The inscriptions of Wadi Mokatteb are also a serious indication. They show that the immemorial pilgrimage was made to Feiran and to the heights which overlook it. Feiran (Rephidim) is, if one can so express oneself, the religious and historical centre of Sinai.

so that from that day forward the god of Sinai was the special god of Israel? Did Moses, the chief of the people, take advantage of one of those fearful storms so frequent in the country to make the people believe in a revelation of the "god-lightning" who resided on the heights? The manner in which the Law was connected with Sinai, towards the nineteenth century B.C., had it any foundation in fact? Or, in the four or five hundred years which followed this grandiose legend, did it swell like a soap bubble, all the more brilliant and coloured because it was empty?

Two things only can be perceived. The first is that from the commencement of the Sinaitic epoch it became the custom to regard Iahveh as appearing in the form of a vision of flame.* For clothing he had a thick cloud, for voice the thunder. In the storm he rode upon the wind and made the clouds his chariot.† Sometimes he is represented in an automatic car furnished with wings.‡ A second well-ascertained fact, not less remarkable, is that the Iahveh of the Hebrews, when definitely constituted, lived in Sinai,§ as Jupiter and the Grecian gods lived in Olympus. His dwelling was on the mountain top, especially when the summit was hidden from sight by heavy

* Genesis, ch. xv., v. 17; Exodus, ch. iii., v. 2; ch. xix., v. 18; ch. xxiv., v. 17; First Book of Kings, ch. xix., v. 12; Ezekiel, ch. i., v. 27; ch. viii., v. 2. I am led to believe that in Deuteronomy, ch. xxxiii., v. 16 (Blessing of Moses), one must read שכני סיני.

† Psalm xviii., v. 11; civ., v. 8, 4.

‡ Coin in British Museum (see p. 160).

§ Exodus, ch. xix., 3, 4; ch. xxxiii., v. 21.

clouds. From thence he burst forth with horrible sounds, lightning, flames of fire, and thunder. The fundamental image of the Hebrew religion and poetry is the *theophany* of Iahveh appearing like an aurora borealis to judge the world.* This apparition always came from the south, higher up than Paran and Seir, starting from Sinai. Thus in the most ancient piece of Hebrew poetry which we possess in a complete form—†

> O Iahveh, when thou wentest out of Seir,
> When thou marchest out of the field of Edom,
> The earth trembled, and the heavens dropped,
> The clouds also dropped water;
> That Sinai! . . . . at the sight of Iahveh;
> At the sight of Iahveh, the God of Israel.

And in another very old piece artificially inserted to form the "Blessing of Moses"—‡

> Iahveh came from Sinai,
> And rose up from Seir against them;
> He shined forth from Mount Paran;
> He comes from Meriboth-Kadesh,§
> From the south side, the fire shines.‖

---

* See descriptions of *day of Iahveh* in all the prophets, beginning with Amos, and those of the apparition of the Messiah (the *parousie*) in the synoptic Gospels.

† The Song of Deborah, Judges, ch. v. Remark that these verses, like those which follow, are anterior to the accounts contained in Exodus.

‡ Deuteronomy, ch. xxxiii., v. 2.

§ Deuteronomy, ch. xxxiii., v. 2; one must surely read קָדֵשׁ ממדבר קָדֵשׁ or ממריבות. Compare Ezekiel, ch. xlvii., v. 19. See Gesen., *Thes.*, at words מריבה and קדש. The Greek translator has read, like us, Καδής. Compare Psalm xxix., v. 8. The *meriba* or *meriboth* of Kadesh was a well-known spring.

‖ Passage altered by copyist. I suppose one should read מִיָּמִין,

And in the original portions of the Psalm "Let God arise"—*

> O God, when thou wentest forth before thy people,
> When thou didst march through the wilderness,
> The earth shook, the heavens also dropped,
> At the presence of God. . . . .
> Even Sinai! . . . .
> At the presence of God, the God of Israel;

and in the Psalm of Habakkuk—

> God came from Teman,
> The Holy One came from Mount Paran.†

Sinai became therefore the Olympus of Israel, the place from whence all the luminous apparitions of Iahveh issued. It was only natural that when they desired a Thora from Iahveh that they made him reveal it on Mount Sinai or Mount Horeb. At this remote epoch, that is to say when Israel went up to the mountain of God, did the people think that they heard some lesson? Did Moses take advantage of the circumstance to inculcate certain precepts? The little influence exercised by those precepts in the daily life of Israel, during the six or seven hundred years which followed, favours the belief that they never existed. It appears probable at least that the people left the holy mountain filled with terror and persuaded that a powerful god inhabited its peaks. There were no

---

"On the south side." Compare First Book of Samuel, ch. xxiii., v. 19. Perhaps the real text of our passage is מימין הישימון.

* Psalm lxviii., v. 8, 9. At verse 18 read אדני בא מסיני.

† Habakkuk, ch. iii., v. 3; Psalm lxxvii., v. 17, &c., passage which appears imitated from Habakkuk.

SINAI.

doubt sacrifices offered and altars erected.* There was, above all, a startling recollection. The people had really seen the god of the holy mountain. This vision, like a flash of lightning, had blinded them. Deep in their inflamed retinas there remained a kind of aurora borealis whose vision they could not shake off. Not one of the old Hebrew poems but commenced with this persistent impression. The chief image which dominated the religious feeling of Israel was the apparition of Sinai.

Primitive man has always lodged his gods in the mountains of eternal snow. Those untrodden heights left a great latitude for mystery. People could well imagine that the muses (kind of fairies) inhabited Parnassus, that Jupiter held his court upon Olympus, before the summits of those mountains had been explored.† But directly the ascent was made it was clearly seen that the immortals were not there.

Iahveh, like the other gods, lived in the highest mountain of the region consecrated to his worship. Sinai was marvellously adapted to play the part of a divine mountain for the tribes roaming to the east of Egypt, in the north of Arabia, and in the south of Palestine. In middle Palestine the volcanic mountains of Horan, whose appearance is so striking, might have been selected. In fact the poet supposes the

* Exodus, ch. xvii., v. 15, 16.
† The people of antiquity and of the Middle Ages had not the same taste for ascending mountains as people of modern times. The first ascent of Mont Blanc took place in 1788.

mountains of Horan to have been jealous of the preference shown by Iahveh for the little hill of Sion.* In the north part of Palestine it was certainly Hermon which would have been chosen. That superb isolated cone, always streaked with snow, the highest in Syria, seemed expressly made for the residence of the god of the region. The fact that the god of Israel had his dwelling in Sinai, a mountain so far from the ken of Palestine, is the best proof of the religious importance which the children of Israel attached to that mountain. For the seers and the poets the aurora of the divine apparition came always from "the south." If Iahveh was not, as may be supposed, the special god of Sinai, it is at all events at Sinai that must be placed the intermediary station where he became the special god of Israel. This was a terrible fall; the old æon of the Chaldeans, the master of life, descended to the inferior part of protector of a little nation. But this nation was Israel, and what Israel adopted had the good fortune of being adopted by humanity. In this sense Iahveh really appeared in Sinai, and the ancient Hebrew poet was right in saying—

> Iahveh came from Sinai,
> He rose up from Seir,
> He shined forth from Mount Paran.†

The adoption of Iahveh which appears to have been consummated at the Sinaitic epoch,‡ was it regarded

---

* Psalm lxviii., v. 16.
† Deuteronomy, ch. xxxiii., v. 2.
‡ The Jehovist account of the battle of Rephidim (Exodus,

SINAI.

as a conversion, as something as marked as were afterwards the construction of the temple, the reform of Hezekiah, and especially the fanatical organisation of Josiah? This must be accepted with great caution. One of the signs of the complete nationalisation of a god is the introduction of his name into the proper names of men. Now the name of Iahveh, either as initial component (*Ieho* or *Io*) or as final component (*Iah*), seldom appears in proper names before the day of Samuel and of Saul.* More than that: a great number of Israelites at the time of the Judges and of David bore names into which entered the component Baal,† such as Jarebaal, Meribaal, Ishbaal, Baaliada. ‡ This name of Baal, the equivalent of Adonai, but in great favour among the Phœnicians, was not considered improper or idolatrous until the days of the prophets of the school of Elijah. Up to that time a broad

---

ch. xvii., v. 15, 16), seems to have been borrowed from the *Wars of Iahveh*, which, written in the ninth or tenth century, may have exaggerated the Jehovist character of those accounts.

* Apparent exception: Jokebed, mother of Moses (name no doubt fabricated afterwards; the name of Iahveh is not found in the name of any woman of really ancient times; *Athalia* is a feminine adjective). It is not at all sure that the name of *Joshua* includes the name of Iahveh, and then the personage is quite legendary. Joel and Abiah, names of the sons of Samuel, are doubtful. As regards Joas and Jotham, father and son of Gideon, see below (p. 260). With regard to Micah or Michaihon, see below (p. 285).

† Afterwards *boset* (shame) was substituted for *baal*, or else *El* was put in the place of *Baal*. A great number of pagan names have been thus obliterated.

‡ Other examples: Gesenius, *Thes.*, pp., 229, 230.

eclecticism had been the religious rule of Israel. It is remarkable that the names formed of the components *Milik* or *Baal* are to be found particularly in the families of Gideon, of Saul, and of David,* or among their followers.

* Gesenius, already quoted.

CHAPTER XV.

JOURNEYING TOWARDS CANAAN.

It is strange that once among the mountains of Sinai, in the direction of the Serbal of to-day, the children of Israel did not push on a little to the south-west. There they would have found higher peaks than those of Serbal, and, in the valley between those lofty summits, an oasis which would certainly have appeared to them like the Paradise of God; we mean the upper valley in which is now situated the convent of St. Catherine. It is probable that this lovely spot was occupied by a stronger tribe; for, after a visit to the "desert of Sinai," the people of Israel returned to the "desert of Paran," [*] and, after twenty days' journey, arrived at the extremity of the Elanitic gulf, at Asion-Gaber. This was a Midianite emporium.[†] Fearing to sojourn in towns, like all nomad tribes, the Beni-Israel avoided entering that place.

The route of Israel appears to have been up to that time very uncertain. It is probable that if the fugitives had encountered some fruitful land on their way they would have halted. On arriving at Asion-

---

[*] Numbers, ch. xii., v. 16.
[†] Deuteronomy, ch. ii., v. 8.

Gaber they had Arabia before them, a not very enviable land, peopled besides, as far as it could be, by Ishmaelites and Ketureans. It is probable that the idea occurred to them at this moment of returning to Canaan, the dwelling place of their ancestors, no longer as foreigners who were tolerated, but as lawful owners. Gratitude is not a national virtue. The kindness of the Hivites and the Hittites towards their fathers was forgotten. It was perhaps at this time that they circulated the pretended oracles of the God of Bethel, local divinity of Palestine, or of Iahveh, who had promised the ancestors of the nation to give them this land. Each country belonged to a god who bestowed it on whom he wished. If the god of Bethel had really promised the land of Canaan to Beni-Israel, that was decisive. The people must have had preconceived ideas on this subject; for, between the desert where they wandered and the land of Canaan, there were populations established, Edom and Moab, over whose territory they would be obliged to pass in order to reach Canaan, and who, according to all appearances, would be little friendly towards brothers from whom they were separated by centuries and different adventures.

What leads one to believe that this idea occurred to the Israelites when they had arrived near Asion-Gaber is that their route was no longer capricious. Canaan was clearly their objective. The shortest road was to reach Canaan by Negeb, that is to say by the south. In fact, from Asion-Gaber the Israelites went

JOURNEYING TOWARDS CANAAN.

to Kades-Barnea, the last place where their ancestors had halted before entering Egypt. This must have been the most trying part of their journey. They retained no recollection of any intermediary halting-place between Asion-Gaber and Kades-Barnea, because in fact along this terrible road, devoid of all the necessaries of life, there was no resting-place.

Kades-Barnea had a fine spring called "the Spring of Judgment," perhaps because people consulted it for the purpose of obtaining certain oracles or judgments of God.* Kades was on the border of Edom, but it was a sort of common halting-place, and not an Edomite town. It was there, it appears, that the elders formed precise plans for the conquest of Canaan.† It was there above all that they opened negotiations with Edom. The Edomites had already organised a kingdom. The Israelites wished to pass through their territory on the footing of perfect neutrality. The Edomites refused.‡ The situation became critical. The Amalekites threatened their rear.§ The Canaanites, finding their position menaced, prepared to defend themselves. Arad,‖ the King of Canaan, who appears to have been at that

---

* Gesenius, at words, קדש and מריבה.

† The details which follow appear historical, and were probably borrowed from the book of *Wars of Iahveh*. Judges, ch. ix.

‡ Numbers, ch. xx., v. 14 and following.

§ Numbers, ch. xiv., v. 39 and following.

‖ Numbers, ch. xxi., v. 1 and following; ch. xxiii., v. 40 (characteristic omission).

time the most powerful monarch in those countries, attacked the Israelites and made some of them prisoners. The King of Sefat inflicted a terrible reverse upon them, in consequence of which they made a vow to Iahveh to exterminate that city and all the surrounding villages of the Canaanites.*

Finding it impossible to pass from the south to the north of Edom, the Israelites determined to turn the country, and, passing to the south of the Dead Sea, to reach the country of Moab. The route which they pursued from Kades to the frontier of Moab is very uncertain. It appears that the Israelites turned off sharp to the east, crossed the Wadi Arabah, wandered to the east of the Arabah, in countries but little known, and approached the country of Moab by its eastern frontier, at a place named *Iyyé ha-Abarim*, "the ruins of Abarim." Abarim was the name of the mountains or rather the lofty tableland which forms the eastern bank of the Dead Sea. The *Iyyim* of the Abarim were perhaps the lesser chains of the Abarim on the desert side.†

What, under these circumstances, were the relations between Israel and their Moabite brethren? Probably similar to the relations which had existed between Israel and their Edomite brethren.‡ Distrust was the ruling passion of this people, full of hatred and

* Numbers, ch. xiv., v. 45; ch. xxi., v. 1—8; Deuteronomy, ch. i., v. 44; Judges, ch. i., v. 17.

† Numbers, ch. xxi., v. 10. There was a place called *Iyyim* in Judah.

‡ Numbers, ch. xx., v. 14. Compare Judges, ch. ix.

JOURNEYING TOWARDS CANAAN. 175

coveteousness. It seems, in fact, that the Israelites avoided passing through the land of Moab.* From Iyyé ha-Abarim they went and pitched their camps in the ravine of Zared. Thence, instead of entering into Moab, they went by way of the desert. At Béer, the discovery of a spring, by means of a divining rod, gave rise to the following song, which one must suppose to have been sung in chorus.†

Spring up, O well; sing ye unto it. The princes digged the well, the nobles of the people digged it. . . . .

This song afterwards became the origin of miraculous stories. It was pretended that Moses caused the water to flow by striking the rock with his wand.

The people afterwards encamped in the ravine of the upper bed of the Aron, which they called Nahaliel, "the ravine of God." Here the situation became more serious. They were on the frontier of Moab, of Ammon, and of the country occupied by the Canaanites. Ammon was too strong for them to dream of attacking it.‡ Israel professed friendly feelings towards Moab at that moment. It was therefore decided to attack the Canaanites, and an armed body rushed boldly on Bamoth and on Daibon, which seem to have been carried without resistance.

On debouching from Nahaliel the Israelites left the desert, the land of nomads, for countries more regularly

---

* The list of halting-places in Numbers, ch. xxxiii., is in contradiction with that of Numbers, ch. xxi.

† Numbers, ch. xxi., v. 15. Borrowed from *Wars of Iahveh*.

‡ Numbers, ch. xxi., v. 24.

inhabited. Here we see them entered into that land, the object of their aspirations, which they were going to appropriate by violence, but whose conquest they legitimised, because they were about to make of a moderately favoured district perhaps the most celebrated spot on the surface of our planet, the holy land *par excellence*, the land the most loved, the most regretted, that ever existed.

How long was it since they had left Egypt? Perhaps only a very short time. We may willingly suppose a year or eighteen months. It was a passage, not a sojourn. But never was a journey more fruitful. Each impression of those months of crisis was rich in consequences for the future. Judaism was destined entirely, some centuries later, to found itself on the legends relating to the flight from Egypt to the desert and to Sinai.

Worship during this period must have returned to patriarchal simplicity. In remarkable places altars or pillars were raised, which were called *iad* (finger post), or *nès* (rallying post).* The ark, a sacred piece of furniture of Egyptian origin, assumed importance. They shut up in it everything of general interest; it formed, so to speak, the portable archives of the nation. According to conceptions which obtained at least to the ninth century, the ark at some distance went before the people while they were going from one camp to another. According to the same traditions, when the ark set forward they cried, "Rise up, Lord, and let

* Exodus, ch. xvii., v. 15, 16.

JOURNEYING TOWARDS CANAAN. 177

thine enemies be scattered." And, on the contrary, when it rested, "Return, O Lord, unto the many thousands of Israel."

We possess, in fact, a religious song of which this cry forms as it were the principal note.* It is the most singular composition in Hebrew literature. We seem to hear the distant echo of the triumphal peregrinations of the travelling deity across the desert.† In it Sinai figures as the place of the highest theophany, not as the place where the Thora was given. The extreme obscurity of the style of this dithyrambic is a sign of its antiquity, although certainly more modern sentiments penetrate here and there. It would not be surprising if we had here a specimen altered, or rather adapted to the liturgic forms‡ of some of the canticles of the *Wars of Iahveh*, or of *Jasar*.§ The old collection opened, in fact, with canticles descriptive of the approach to the land of Canaan and of the last marches in the desert.

The probability is that where a halt was made the Ark was placed outside the camp under a tent. This was what they called *ohel moëd*, the tent of meeting, or *ohel edouth*, the tent of the covenant. Perhaps they

---

* Psalm lxviii.

† Especially v. 1—25.

‡ This song may have served for the inauguration of the temple (v. 16, 25—28). The passage v. 18 ought surely to be corrected רבתים אלפי ישראל, according to Numbers, ch. x., v. 36.

§ Especially the passage v. 12—15 is full of the epic spirit of the ancient *sirim*.

already went there for judgments, divine oracles, and to take oaths. God was supposed to be there in person. They believed that a cloud descended, remained at the entrance, and conversed with the leaders.*
More communicative than that of Sinai this God allowed them to approach him; they spoke with him. The God of Israel became human; he made himself the companion of men, more especially the companion of the poor and needy.† The *tabernaculum Dei cum hominibus* existed from that moment.

But this was only a germ. The institutions had still something undefined about them. The barbarism was extreme; there was nothing civilising nor moralising in the teaching of the Levites. The Israelites did not employ writing. What took place among them, although already exceedingly remarkable, did not differ much from the domestic life, so original, of the other Terachite, Ishmaelite, and Keturean tribes, which spread over the southern confines of Syria. Their philosophy wavered between two contradictory assertions, " God is eternal; man lives four days; God governs the world with justice and omnipotence; and yet there is injustice everywhere. Man is audacious to complain; and yet he has a right to complain." The patriarchal era was drawing to a close; nations were beginning; human society was losing its nobility and its goodness; it demanded a wider and more vigorous range.

* Exodus, ch. xxxiii., v. 7-11.
† Psalm lxviii., v. 6, 7.

BOOK II.

THE BENI-ISRAEL AS FIXED TRIBES FROM THE OCCUPATION OF THE COUNTRY OF CANAAN TO THE DEFINITIVE ESTABLISHMENT OF THE KINGDOM OF DAVID.

CHAPTER I.

THE BENI-ISRAEL BEYOND THE DEAD SEA AND THE JORDAN.

WHEN the tribes of Israel appeared on the heights above the wells of Nahaliel (towards 1350 B.C.) the country beyond the Dead Sea had just been the theatre of memorable events.* The Canaanite section of the Amorites, who appear to have come from Hebron and Hasason-Tamar (afterwards called Engaddi), had assumed, in becoming the centre of a confederation of tribes previously known under other names, a very considerable position. Enclosed up to that time, on the east, by the Jordan and the Dead Sea, the Amorites had overflowed eastward, and had formed two trans-Jordan kingdoms: the kingdom of Basan (Batanée), whose capital was Astaroth-Carnaïm, and a kingdom further south, bounded on the north by the Iabbok, on the south by the Arnon, and whose capital was Heshbon.

* Numbers, ch. xxi.; Judges, ch. xi., v. 18 and following.

Heshbon and all the country to the north of the Arnon had up to that time belonged to the kingdom of Moab, which thus lost, by the Amorite invasion, all the southern portion of its territory. This was probably the cause of the favour with which the Moabites received Israel when it made its appearance in the regions of Abarim.

Sihon, the founder of the Amorite kingdom of Heshbon, assembled his army to meet the new invaders. The battle took place at Iahas. The defeat of Sihon was complete. The Israelites seized on all the country from Arnon to Iabok.

Heshbon fell into their hands. This was the first great victory won in the name of Iahveh. Heshbon was a beautiful *acropolis* in the middle of a fertile and well-watered country. The conquest of this important place gave rise to a song of which some *strophes* have been preserved.* The poet first of all shows the power of Sihon, and relates the defeat of Moab. He supposes an appeal made by the conqueror to the neighbouring populations to come and rebuild Heshbon.

Come unto Heshbon; let the city of Sihon be built and prepared.

* * * * *

Woe to thee, Moab! Thou art undone, O people of Chermosh; he hath given his sons that escaped, and his daughters, into captivity unto Sihon, king of the Amorites.

* * * * *

But Israel was stronger than the conquerors of Moab.

* Numbers, ch. xxi., v. 27—30. Taken from the *Wars of Iahveh.*

"We have shot at them; Heshbon is perished even unto Dibon, and we laid them waste even unto Nophah, which reacheth unto Medebah."

The town of Jaazer, which formed part of the city of Sihon, fell after Heshbon, and from that time Israel was master of the country from Jabbok to the Arnon. This was what was called by the generic name of the country of Gilead. This conquest, rapidly executed, leads one to suppose that the chiefs who planned it were endowed with real military talent. According to the authors of the Thora, Moses was still alive at this epoch, having at his side his lieutenant Joshua. In the book of the *Wars of Iahveh*, Moses had disappeared before the country of Moab was approached. The Song of Beer, the whole episode of Baalam supposes his absence; and certainly, if the old text had admitted that Moses still existed during the wars between Sihon and Og, some miraculous intervention would have been attributed to him in the battles, as at Rephidim.

The destruction of the Amorite kingdom of Bashan closely followed the destruction of the Amorite kingdom of Heshbon and of Jaazer. Og,[*] King of Bashan, was defeated at Edrei. The rich country which stretches from the mountains of Hor to the Lake of Tiberias and to the Jordan became the possession of the children of Israel. A powerful family animated with military instincts, that of the Makarites, contributed in a great degree to this conquest, and thenceforth settled

[*] Og was enveloped in legends (Deuteronomy, ch. iii., v. 2). It is possible that when the *Wars of Iahveh* was written the name of the last king of Bashan was not known.

in the plains of Hor. The Makarites formed part of the Manasseh branch of the family of Joseph, which preserved more than ever its ascendency over the rest of Israel.

These two great wars had given a very advantageous position to Beni-Israel. The two kingdoms of Sihon and of Og, become their domain, brought them an extent of territory over thirty-five leagues in length, which amply sufficed for their numbers. It is probable, in fact, that after the conquest of the kingdom of Bashan there was a breathing time. The tribes no doubt waited, before passing the Jordan, until the fertile country they occupied had come to be too small for them. These were years of youth and vigour. The centre of Israel at this epoch was what was called *Arboth-Moab*, "the plains of Moab." This was a plain situated on the banks of the Jordan, opposite Jericho, at the foot of Mount Nebo, and, more strictly speaking, the place called Shittim, "the acacias." The ark remained at this place under a tent, and constituted as it were the vital knot of the nation.

This apparition of a new force in the little world of Palestine, already overcrowded, naturally excited the most lively apprehensions on the part of the primitive settlers. Ammon does not appear to have been very much alarmed; Moab, already so weakened by the Amorites, was obliged to confine itself to intrigues. In the oldest historical books is to be found a curious tale on this subject, attributed to Balak, the son of Zippor, an assumed King of Moab. The *nabi* existed at this epoch among the Semitic races, but of a very different character to that which he afterwards assumed. He was still the sorcerer, the man possessing mysterious secrets, who was in daily communication with the *elohim*. These *nabis* constituted a redoubtable power. Supernatural gifts were attributed to them, as also a profound knowledge in the art of divination. Their curse was supposed to operate infallibly and without any aid. Sometimes they were called upon to curse certain days which were regarded as unlucky.* On other occasions they were highly paid to curse those whose perdition was desired.† It was believed that their curses struck home, and these howlers were engaged to pour out against the enemy torrents of abuse, supposed to be efficacious.‡ It was almost always by powerful parallelisms, by *carmina* in parabolic style, that these magic spells, considered infallible in their effects, were expressed.§

The most celebrated of these sorcerers at that time was, according to the legend, a certain Baalam, the son of Beor, who came from a town called Pethor. Balak sent for him, gave him large sums of money, and made him the most superb promises. He was taken to a high place called Bamoth-Baal, near Ataroth, in that part of ancient Moab which Israel has just conquered. From thence could be seen the

* Job, ch. iii.
† Numbers, ch. xxii., v. 7—17.
‡ See Isaiah, ch. xv. and xvi., the lamentation of Moab.
§ Numbers, ch. xxii., v. 6.

first encampments of Israel. Now it is related that in spite of all the efforts which Baalam made to curse Israel, the words were in his mouth converted into blessings. Later on, this episode became the foundation for some curious tales. About the time of David, the oracles which Balaam was supposed to have pronounced were written in the finest rhythm of ancient poetry, and with these compositions a sibylline framework was constructed for the predictions relative to the future of Israel and of other nations.*

The intimate relationship between Moab and Israel prevented any sanguinary war between them. It was not the same with Midian.† The Midianites had not managed to make any fixed conquest. Like the Amalekites they were everywhere to be found in the deserts to the east of the Dead Sea. We have seen them, during the flight from Egypt, entering into relations with Moses, through their *cohen* Jethro. Then we saw them struggling with the Edomites in the land of Moab.‡ It was this northern branch of the Midianites which got into a serious conflict with

---

* The episode of Balaam, in its present form (Numbers, ch. xxii., xxiii., xxiv.), is a Jehovist and Elohist combination, after the manner of ancient records, that of the deluge for example. The foundation is borrowed from the *Wars of Iahveh* like what precedes it in Numbers, ch. xxi. It will be remarked that Moses is not mentioned there, when it was only natural that he should have performed his part. There is nothing authentic in the *masal* but the form. From ch. xxiv., v. 20, the interpolations are clear.

† Midian was only connected to Abraham by the slave Cethura, like Ishmael by the slave Hagar.

‡ Genesis, ch. xxxvi., v. 35.

Israel. The war was a terrible one. The branch of Midian engaged in the battle was exterminated with its five kings. All the males were put to death; the women and the flocks were carried away captive.*

These military successes on the part of Israel surprise one at first sight. Israel had no warlike proclivities during its patriarchal period, nor during its sojourn in Egypt. At the epoch of the Judges it often exhibited weakness towards its neighbours. Later on, if one excepts the time of Saul and of David, the qualities displayed by Israel were not of a military order. One is tempted to believe that the military superiority shown by this band of fugitives in regard to the tribes in the region of Jordan was derived from the Egyptians which it counted in its ranks, and particularly to Moses, who must be considered as almost an Egyptian, whose real part was much more, it would appear, that of a chief after the fashion of Abd-el-Kader than that of a prophet like Mahomet. Their arms may have been better than those of the tribes they fought with. Between barbarians, the smallest element of civilisation gives to the tribe which possesses it immense advantages over the tribes who have nothing but the primitive weapons handed down from the past.

During that long sojourn, intermixed with campaigns always successful, in a country then rich, there was no doubt in the bosom of Israel a powerful work of internal organisation going on. A number of

* Numbers, ch. xxxi.; Joshua, ch. xiii., v. 21.

families established themselves in a permanent manner.* We have seen how the Manassite family of Makir took the principal part in the conquest of Hor. A great portion of it remained in the land it had conquered. The lands of Jaazer and Gilead were exceedingly good for the rearing of cattle. The Reubenites and the Gadites, who had large flocks, appropriated them. The first established themselves in the ancient country of Moab situated to the north of the Arnon, which the Amorites had taken from Moab, and which the Israelites had recaptured from the Amorites. The cities of Ataroth, Daibon, Heshbon, Eleale, Baal-Meon fell to Reuben. The cities of Jaazer, Nimra, and the intersected tableland to the east of Jordan fell to Gad. On its left bank the valley of the Jordan is narrow. Agriculture could not flourish in such a country; it remained always essentially pastoral.

Besides, the ancient race was far from having disappeared. The population of Israel was very inconsiderable. Shut up in strong cities, it saw itself surrounded by hostile tribes† who wanted only a patriotic rallying point. The names of a certain number of places were changed and called after their new proprietors.‡ But they did not long endure. The old names were restored. Thus Kenath, at the foot of the mountain of Hor, which

---

* Numbers, ch. xxxii., v. 16 and following.
† Numbers, ch. xxxii., v. 17.
‡ Numbers, ch. xxxii., v. 38, 41, 42.

was captured by the Manassite Nobah, was for some time called *Nobah*,* then it resumed its ancient name Canatha or Canotha, which still exists as Kenawat.

* Judges, ch. viii., v. 11.

CHAPTER II.

THE CONQUEST OF THE REGION BEYOND JORDAN.

In the plain of Shittim the people had under their eyes a spectacle which perpetually excited their greed. The Jordan alone separated them from a land which was even superior to that which they occupied; more and more they imagined that this land had been promised to them by the God of their fathers. Opposite to them the important city of Jericho stood out like a challenge. These old excitable races drew no line between their desire and their duty. The Moabite king Mesa made no conquest unless it were ordered by his god Camos.* It is probable that upon divers occasions the national God, Iahveh, commanded the Israelites to cross the Jordan by signs which were considered as compulsory.

The land which Israel had in view was a ridge, sixty miles broad at its base, separating the Mediterranean from the deep bed in which the Jordan flows, and of which the Dead Sea is as it were the central basin. The height above the Mediterranean is nearly 3,300 feet; the height above the Dead Sea and the lower Jordan is 4,600 feet; for there is

* Inscription, lines 9, 12, 13, 14, 18, 32.

CONQUEST OF REGION BEYOND JORDAN.

a deep depression at this spot. The foot of the slopes reaches neither to the Mediterranean nor to the Jordan. Like a continuation of the sands of the Mediterranean, these plains stretch to the west, and are susceptible of being richly cultivated (the Saron). On the side of Jordan the lesser mountain chains fall away in an abrupt manner to within ten or twelve miles from the river, and at their foot is formed an alluvial plain, which would, one might suppose, be a source of wealth to the country. It is not so. This plain (Ghôr) is unhealthy, and has never played a considerable part in the history of the country. Israel, on the other hand, showed no tendency to approach the bank. The Saron remained always in the hands of the Canaanites. It is the hog's back stretching between Saron and Ghôr, which was the theatre of the astonishing history I am now writing.

As the country of Gilead, beyond Jordan, is designed by nature for a pastoral life, so is Palestine on this side of Jordan designed for agriculture and living in cities.* One must not look at these matters after our European ideas of a deep, black soil, unceasingly watered and covered with rich verdue. These ridges, in appearance arid, are rich after their fashion. To half-starved people coming from Africa they must appear sparkling with wealth. The vine, the olive, and the fig-tree prosper there. Corn grows in sufficient quantities. There is no want of water. The

* Josephus, *B. J.*, III., x. 7.

cold is never excessive, and it rains a great deal in the winter; all through the year the altitude at which one lives renders the heat very supportable. No great city could have developed itself on these heights, deprived of large waterways; but an agricultural population, grouped in small towns lying close to each other, could find there the essential conditions of material welfare without which no human society can accomplish an original evolution.

The Canaanite populations which, as it appears, already occupied the country when the Hebrews passed there the first time had lost a great deal of their ancient vigour. The Amorites had exhausted themselves in concentrating all their forces to the east of Jordan; the Hittites of Debir, of Kiriat-Arba, or Hebron, had also lost much of their importance since the time when their name erroneously represented for the Egyptians the whole of Syria. The victories of Ramses had greatly diminished them. The Hivites lived peacefully at Gabaon and in the neighbourhood of Sichem. Little is known of the Perizzites; it is even a question whether they had any fixed territory. The *Girgishites* resided obscurely in their city of *Gergesa*, on the eastern shore of the Lake of Genesareth.* The Jebusites were much more powerful. Their territory was not large, but their city of Jebus, or Jerusalem,† was

* See *Vie de Jesus*, p. 151, note 1.
† It may with equal force be urged that this name was given by David or by the Canaanites. The root *slm* appears to mean "place of safety."

considered in those days as an exceedingly strong place.

In the midst of these Canaanites regularly established in the towns, there roamed, as in the times of the patriarchs, nomads without any fixed dwelling, such as the Amalekites, and other tribes leading a miserable existence, like gipsies without hearth or home.* People saw survivors of the ancient indigenous populations, anterior to the Canaanites (*Emim, Zomzommim, Anakim*), in individuals of lofty stature whom they believed to be dwellers in certain particular places.† But popular imagination revels in giants; it willingly creates them. These Anakim were surrounded by legends; ‡ they sometimes called them *refaïm* (the dead, the giants, the phantoms, the heroes); a plain to the south-west of Jerusalem bore their name, and they were confounded with the Titanic races buried beneath the sea.

The language of the Canaanites, as we have already observed, was the same as that of the Sidonians or the Phœnicians, and consequently very little different from that of the Hebrew people. Writing was not employed among them. We have, however, an authentic and considerable specimen of their language; it is the *onomasticon* of the geography of Palestine, especially the names of the towns. The

* Job, ch. xxx.
† Numbers, ch. xiii., v. 28, 32 and following.
‡ The Book of Joshua, ch. xii., xiii., xiv., xv., greatly exaggerates the importance of the Anakims.

Israelites changed hardly any names of villages or towns, as is proved by the localities pointed out in the Book of Joshua itself as having remained Canaanite. In the countries where the Israelites became masters, the names were seldom modified; even the words *Jerusalem* and *Sion* appear to belong to a previous period. This holds even truer of the names of rivers and mountains and words employed to denote things characteristic of the country. Now these old Canaanite names, often obscure, which is only natural, when we bear in mind their great antiquity, do not materially differ from the language of the Israelite invaders, not more indeed than from the more ancient invaders, Moabites, Edomites, Ammonites, &c. The Philistines alone, in this linguistic region, present an exception. A mixed marriage between Israelite and Philistine is never spoken of.*

Although identical, as far as race goes, with the populations of the coast, who became so celebrated under the name of Phœnicians, and with the Canaanites of Africa, or Carthaginians, † the Canaanites of the interior appear to have remained far below the Phœnicians and the Carthaginians in the matter of civilisation. Their ornaments of dress and of worship must have come from the Phœnician cities of the coast. The inhabitants of Laish, at the foot of

---

* Remark the omission of Philistine women, First Book of Kings, ch. xi., v. 1. It was not considered necessary to prohibit such marriages. The two races were too different.

† Passages of St. Augustine often quoted.

Hermon, are pointed out as an exception, because they lived in the interior "after the manner of the Sidonians," that is to say in the midst of ease and luxury, the fruit of industry. All the archeological vestiges of the Canaanites to be found in the Palestine of to-day are rude without art. The aspect of a Canaanite city could not have differed much from the poorest locality of Syria of the present time. Sumptuous buildings were rare, or were apparently entirely wanting.

The worship of the Canaanites was also very little different from that of the Phœnicians, especially from that of the Carthaginians. According to the Egyptians,* Baal and Sydyk were the supreme gods of the Khetas. Sydyk, in fact, seems to reappear in the names of the Jebusite kings, *Malkisedeq*, *Adonisedeq*. Baal assumed a double form, and took the shape of a woman, of Astoreth or Astarte, goddess of love and of voluptuousness, origin of the Aphrodite of the Greeks. They called her *Asera*, that is to say the Happy Woman. Her images or symbols† were spread through the country.‡ The worship of Baal and of Astoreth or Asera was performed chiefly on

---

* Maspero, *Hist. anc. de l'Orient*, p. 232.

† Probably the sign ⛩ so frequently seen on Phœnician and Carthaginian monuments. See *Corpus inscr. semit.*, part i., t. 1, pp. 281 and following, 428 and following.

‡ *Mission de Phénicie*, pp. 508, 509, 640, 653, 662, 663, 666, 691. These images were called *aserim* or *azeroth*, as the images of Baal were called *baalim*. In the same way we speak of *des christs*, *des bons-dieux*, *des saintes-vierges*.

the tops of hills, in the midst of sacred bowers and of green trees. This was what was called *bamoth*, or high places. They are still to be found at every step in Phœnicia, especially in the country of Tyre, in the ancient territory of the tribe of Asher.* Sacred prostitution† and the practice of making their first-born pass through the fire‡ were among the bases of these religions, which the nomad Hebrews viewed with horror, but which they imitated directly they were settled. So true is it that living in tents alone had preserved them from those rites.

In addition to the high places of the Canaanites there were places of worship of unknown origin, such as Bethel, Sichem, Garizim, some localities in Gilead, certain places called Galgal, which the Hebrews adopted much more willingly, for they were held to be very ancient, and it was related that the fathers had sacrificed there. The title upon which Israel laid the most stress in order to establish its right over Palestine was a sort of charter of Iahveh, regarded as god of Bethel.§ It was quite in the spirit of antiquity, on entering a country, to adopt the local god, and to endeavour to serve him according to his tastes.‖

* *Mission de Phénicie*, Book IV., ch. iv.

† Ibid., pp. 518, 585, 647—653, 662, 663.

‡ Second Book of Kings, ch. xvi., v. 3 and following.

§ Genesis, ch. xxviii., v. 13 and following; ch. xxxi., v. 13 and following.

‖ First Book of Samuel, ch. xxvi., v. 19; Second Book of Kings, ch. xvii., v. 27; Ruth, ch. i., v. 16.

CONQUEST OF REGION BEYOND JORDAN. 195

What grieved David, when he foresaw his exile, was that he would be forced to sacrifice to other gods than Iahveh.* Later on Naaman the Syrian, wishing to offer up sacrifices to Iahveh, at Damascus, asked leave to carry with him two mule loads of Canaanite earth, for no real sacrifice could be made to Iahveh except upon that earth.†

In reality these Canaanites represented but an indifferent form of human society. There was no central organisation. Every fortified hamlet had a *melek*, or king, a little military chief whose authority extended two or three leagues round.‡ Certain tribes, like the Gibeonites, formed confederations several leagues in extent. Each city trusted in its fortifications. Although we have no authentic specimen of these military works, one can form an idea of them from the innumerable *tells* of Palestine, their summits covered with ruins and their flanks carved out of the rock.

The resistance offered by the Canaanite tribes was very different, according as they lived in mountain or plain. In the mountains the Canaanites everywhere fell before the Israelites; in the plains, on the contrary, at Saron, at Naphoth Dor, in the plain of Jezrael, at Beth-Sean, in Ghor, the Canaanites defended themselves victoriously. The cause of this difference lay in the chariots of war, protected with iron, which

---

* First Book of Samuel, ch. xxvi., v. 19.
† Second Book of Kings, ch. v., v. 17.
‡ Joshua, ch. xii., v. 7.

the natives possessed, but not the invaders. These chariots, terrible in the plains, were useless in the mountains. There the Canaanites had nothing to defend them but the walls of their towns. The Israelites had no knowledge of the art of military engineering. They waited and finally entered the place by surprise or treason.*

The Canaanites do not appear to have had any cavalry, in the sense in which we understand the word, nor had the assailants any. Personal courage consisted, on both sides, of that furious dash, sometimes artificially excited, in which still lies the force of the Arab. It seems to have been greater and more obstinate on the part of the Israelites.

Both sides were alike cruel. All antiquity was cruel. Cruelty was an advantage not to be dispensed with. Ferocity is one of the forces of barbarians. The fear inspired by their atrocities makes people submit to them. One of the essential points of Carthaginian strategy was to frighten the enemy by their tortures.† The custom of cutting off the thumbs, the hands, and the feet of the conquered was usual among the Canaanites. One of their little tyrants boasted that he had seen seventy kings, mutilated in this manner, pick up what fell from his table.‡

As for the Israelites, their cruelty, if one is to believe

---

* Thus fell Ai and Bethel.
† Example of Agathocles.
‡ Judges, ch. i., v. 7.

the ancient records, was systematically dictated by religious motives, by a kind of moral puritanism produced by the crimes committed by the natives. This is doubtless an exaggeration on the part of later historians. The invaders do not appear to have drawn up any plan for the extermination of the Canaanite race. Later, this extermination became an act of piety, commanded by Iahveh. In a number of instances there was an understanding arrived at between the two races. The Canaanites accepted a situation analogous to that of the rajahs under the Mussulmans. We do not see that they ever revolted. Under the Judges we read of wars against the Philistines, against the Ammonites, &c. We do not read of any against the Jebusites, the Hivites, &c. The first wars, those of Joshua, were terrible. After the victory all the male inhabitants of the Canaanites were slain; the kings were massacred, then the dead bodies were crucified. Human ferocity assumed the form of a compact with, of a vow to, the Divinity: oaths of extermination were taken; reason and pity were prohibited. A city or a country was condemned to destruction, and it would have been considered an insult to their god not to have kept this hideous oath.* Fearful examples were related of the vengeance wreaked by the god on those who wavered in the execution of these fearful engagements.

* This is the meaning of the word *herem*, so deplorably repeated in these books. See Joshua, ch. vi., vii.; First Book of Samuel, ch. xv.

The contrast is strange between these Red Indian customs, reproduced with fearful sincerity in ancient Israelite history, and the picture of patriarchal life, so noble, so humane, so pure, traced in Genesis. Of a truth this picture is too ideal for us not to suspect that it has been embellished. In fact, however, seeing the low scale of Eastern morality, tent life, in the Semitique or Semitised countries, has always been preferable to that in the towns. A nation which has a territory to conquer or to defend is always more cruel than the tribe which is not yet attached to the soil, and it is thus that people at times, merciful while living together in families, become cruel when they form a nation. Then, it appears that people in ancient times on losing their simplicity became harsh and vindictive. Nations at their birth are ferocious. Now, about this date, 1,200 or 1,300 years before Jesus Christ, nations began to be born in the East. Principles, true under the patriarchal epoch, could no longer be applied.* The bases of justice were changed. What was true in the days of pastoral life was no longer so in an age of iron, in which a man, honest according to the ancient acceptation of the term, was at every instant misunderstood and a victim.

I do not know if Joshua had a greater historical reality than Jacob. But of a truth the tender-hearted Jacob would have been disgusted had he been able to witness many of the acts of Joshua,

* Five hundred years later this was the cause of Job's deep despair.

afterwards reputed to be glorious. Jacob on his death-bed is supposed to have cursed Simeon and Levi for their misdeeds, which, as compared with those of the conquest, might well have passed for moderate reprisals.*

* Genesis, ch. xlix., v. 5, 7 ; ch. xxxiv.

CHAPTER III.

JUDAH AND BENJAMIN.

The passage of the Jordan certainly took place opposite to Jericho.* The Jordan at this place is about as wide as the Thames at Windsor. In spring it cannot be forded; towards the end of summer and in autumn it is little more than two feet deep. It was easy to effect a passage, though only a few would cross over at the same time. Since the establishment of their principal camp at Arboth Moab, detachments more or less considerable of Beni-Israel incessantly passed the fords. These raids merely excited the cupidity of their brethren. The rich oasis of Jericho, with its palm-trees and its perfumes, tempted the tribes. The city was taken, probably by treason, and destroyed. It was afterwards rebuilt; but no doubt at some distance from where the Canaanite city stood.

After the capture of Jericho, the central camp of Israel was removed to a place called Gilgal, in that well-watered plain which stretches from the foot of the mountain to the mouth of the Jordan. Gilgal or Galgal† means a heap of stones dedicated to a religious

---

* Second Book of Samuel, ch. xvii., v. 22, 24; ch. xix., v. 16, 17, 89. In order to bring in his miracle, the narrator of *Joshua* is obliged to suppose circumstances derived from the season.

† Equivalent of *gal*.

JUDAH AND BENJAMIN.

purpose. The Gilgal in question was probably a sacred mound of the Canaanites; but perhaps it owed its origin to an Israelitish encampment, or it may have been a mound raised for sacrifices. Afterwards it was supposed that in these megalithic monuments had been found a souvenir of the miraculous passage of the Jordan.* The puritans saw in them the remains of pagan worship, and in this way the Galgal of Jericho became a religious centre greatly revered by some, very obnoxious to others,† so much so that this name has often been given to various localities. However that may be, the Gilgal of Jordan became the starting point for a series of expeditions into the mountains. It is a very false idea‡ to look upon Israel at this moment as an organised army, having only a single aim. Nearly all the expeditions were undertaken by bands of adventurers, acting on their own account.§ Sometimes a band was composed of men belonging to various tribes; the expedition then assumed a kind of federal character; but these operations must have been rare, and they produced no serious consequences in the ulterior institutions of the nation.

An expedition which appears to have been made

* Joshua, ch. iv.

† Judges, ch. iii., v. 19, 26; Hosea, ch. iv., v. 15; ch. ix; v. 15; ch. xii., v. 12; Amos, ch. iv., v. 4.

‡ This is owing to the fictitious form of the story in the Book of Joshua.

§ Numbers, ch. xxxii., v. 33—42.

by an army composed of the men of all the tribes was that which ended in the destruction of the Canaanite city which was afterwards called *ha-Aï*, "the heap of ruins," near Bethel. The real name of the city was forgotten; but the recollection of the skilful stratagems attributed to Joshua, the chief who personified all this period of military raids, was preserved. The city, like Jericho, was laid under a *herem* or anathema. Every one was killed, and the king was nailed to a tree until the evening. The execution was still more atrocious than that of Jericho, since the town was never rebuilt, and even its name was obliterated.

Terror spread through the country. Many tribes submitted and accepted the yoke in order to escape death. The division of the Canaanite tribes aided the invaders. Every town followed its own policy without troubling itself about others. This was particularly the case in the confederation of the Gibeonites. This little tribe, of Hivite origin,* possessed four or five towns, Gibeon,† Kefira, Beeroth,‡ Kiriath-Iearim.§ These towns had no kings, and consequently no military force; they accepted the new-comers and concluded a treaty with them, which reserved all their rights, but which little by little was for-

* Joshua, ch. xi., v. 19
† To-day *El-Djib*.
‡ To-day *Bireh*.
§ To-day *Abu-Gosch*.

JUDAH AND BENJAMIN.

gotten, or rather transformed into a tolerably hard bondage.*

The town which became the centre of this history, and which perhaps from that time was called *Ierousalaim*, "place of safety," and *Sion* (fortress),† served as fortress to a small tribe named *Iebousim*. It was a fortified summit on the brink of a ravine, much deeper then than now.‡ The Jebusites' city was built on the spot now occupied by the *haram*, stretching along the crest of the mountains to the south. A little spring, called Gihon, § was no doubt the cause of the selection of this locality, which afterwards held an exceptional position among the sacred pilgrimages. The Jebusites considered themselves menaced by the arrival of the Israelites.|| Their king, Adonisedek,¶ especially, was alarmed at the alliance which the Gibeonites had formed with these dangerous strangers. He opened negotiations with four neighbouring Amorite kings, to wit, the King of Hebron, the King of Jarmut, the King of Lakish, the King of Eglon, and the five kings laid siege to Gibeon. Joshua, or whoever was the

* Joshua, ch. ix. The bondage was not complete until under Solomon.

† See Gesenius, *Thes.*, p. 1154. The meaning of Sion is doubtful.

‡ Josephus, *Ant.*, XX., ix., p. 7. English excavations have shown the description given by Josephus to have been true.

§ Called Fountain of the Virgin.

|| Joshua, ch. x.

¶ Adoni, in these old names, is always followed by the name of a god, as Adoni-Iah, Adoni-Ram, Adonibezek, who seems to be the same person as Adonisedek.

chief of Israel, had still his camp at Gilgal, near the place where the passage of the Jordan had been effected. The Israelite army marched in a body to force the five kings to raise the siege of Gibeon. A panic seized on the Canaanite army; it fled towards Bethoran as far as Maqqeda. Joshua pursued it, cut it in pieces, killed, it is said, the five kings and crucified them. A popular song[*] celebrated this victory; in it were found these two lines:—

> Sun, stand thou still upon Gibeon,
> And thou, moon, in the valley of Ajalon.

The poet wished to express the astonishment of nature at the prodigious effort of the Israelites. This rhetorical figure[†] afterwards gave rise to some curious mistakes. The two lines were placed in the mouth of Joshua, and in changing the meaning of the word, which signifies "stood still with astonishment,"[‡] it was supposed that the sun really stood still at the order of Joshua.

The capture of Maqqeda, of Libna, of Lakish, of Gezer, of Eglon, took place rapidly one after the other. More important still was the capture of Hebron[§] and of Debir, which were the capitals of the southern

---

[*] Preserved in the *Iasher*.

[†] In the Song of Deborah the stars fought against Sisera.

[‡] The verb *damam* means "to be silent, struck with terror." The mistake is created by the substitution of *amad*, which means, materially speaking, "to stop."

[§] Judges, ch. i., v. 9—15; Joshua, ch. x., v. 36 and following; ch. xii., v. 10; ch. xv., v. 13; ch. xx., v. 7.

Canaanites, who seemed to have possessed a culture superior to that of the rest of the country. It was asserted that Hebron was given as a fief to a legendary hero of Judah, to a certain Caleb,* concerning whom many wonderful tales were told. In reality Caleb appears, like Judah, to have signified a tribe, that of Calbiel (dogs of God),† specially devoted to war, and almost synonymous to Judah.

Thus in a series of successful raids, which probably followed each other rapidly, the whole country which afterwards formed that of Benjamin and Judah was conquered. As these two tribes always acted together, and as the first conquest just corresponds to their frontiers, we are led to believe that the conquest itself was their work. Judah was one of the principal divisions of Beni-Israel. The Benjamites appear to us to have been a smaller division of youthful warriors, bearing a bad reputation for morality,‡ forming a sort of body of light infantry, from among whom were chosen the archers and slingers. The name, which signifies "left-handed," was derived from the habit they had contracted of making use of the left instead of the right hand, which was advantageous in handling the sling.§ The two divisions,

* Judges, ch. i., v. 20.

† *Corpus inscr. semit.*, part i., Nos. 49, 52, 86. Caleb is surely the short for כלבאל. Othoniel is nephew of Caleb; now Othoniel means Lion of God, equivalent to *Ariel*.

‡ Horrible stories, Judges, ch. xx., xxi.

§ Judges, ch. iii., v. 15; ch. xx., v. 16; First Book of Chronicles, ch. viii., v. 39; ch. xii., v. 2; Second Book of Chronicles, ch. xiv., v. 7.

at any rate, acted together and shared the fruit of the campaign.

The Benjamites, far less numerous, had their capital at Gibeah,* a league north of Jerusalem. They were very important as fighting men; but they had hardly any territory. They failed in several attempts to take the city of the Jebusites.† On the other hand the Gibeonites lived independent beside them, and Gezer was never taken.‡ The other tribes were obliged once or twice to punish them terribly, which almost led to their destruction.§

The Judahites occupied in a much more effective manner the territory which henceforth bore their name. The whole of Palestine sloping to the south of Jerusalem belonged to them, but they were powerless against the men of the plain along the sea coast, who possessed iron war-chariots.‖ The Philistines also formed a barrier to the west which they did not attempt to attack.¶

* To-day *Toleil-el-foul*. Robinson, i., pp. 577 and following.
† Judges, ch. i., v. 21.
‡ Judges, ch. i., v. 29.
§ Judges, ch. xx., xxi.
‖ Judges, ch. i., v. 19.
¶ Judges, ch. i., v. 18, is surely a mistake or an interpolation.

CHAPTER IV.

THE CONQUEST OF MOUNT EPHRAIM AND THE NORTH.

THE triumph of Benjamin and Judah over a great number of the Canaanite tribes of the south had the most important consequences. Under the protection of the Judahites, and always aided by them,* the Simeonites took possession of the cities to the extreme south, Arad, Beershebah, all the celebrated places of the last patriarchal days. The hostility shown by the King of Sefat to the Israelites will be remembered. The city condemned to *herem* was annihilated; it was called *Horma*.† Simeon never separated itself from Judah;‡ a number of towns are represented at the same time as Judahite and Simeonite; the limits on the south between Simeon and Edom remained undefined. These regions were the pastures of the nomads; the ownership of the soil hardly existed. The Amalekites and the Shemites § continued to live both as shepherds and brigands. Simeon conquered them; he reappears in the time of Hezekiah, then

---

* Joshua, ch. xix., v. 9.
† Judges, ch. i., v. 17.
‡ Judges, ch. i., v. 2 and following, **17**.
§ First Book of Chronicles, ch. iv., v. 40 and following.

his trace vanishes, absorbed as the tribe was on one side by Judah, on the other by Edom.

Dan, also, under the protection of Benjamin and Judah, found a fixed dwelling place, at least for a time. This was the weakest of the tribes of Israel. The Danites encamped between Jerusalem and the Mediterranean, to the north of the Philistines and the west of the Gibeonites.* They never succeeded in subduing the Canaanites, or even in establishing themselves, and they almost all migrated to the north.† Aijalon, Bethsemes, Saalbim remained Canaanite, and the Ephraimites were afterwards obliged to conquer them.‡ Jaffa always remained a purely Phœnician city, without any continuous connection with the Israelites.

The Josephites continued to hold the first rank in the family of Israel. We have seen a fraction of Manasseh, the Makirites, conquer Hor and Bataneh and colonise them. The other Manassehites, among whom were also found many Makirites and Ephraimites, the second branch of Joseph, established themselves in the country which was afterwards called Samaria.§ The war was fierce and cruel: the Canaanites of the plain, especially those on the side of Beth-Sean and Jezrael, had war chariots plated with iron, which filled with fear the Bedouins accus-

* Song of Deborah, v. 17.
† Joshua, ch. xix., v. 47, 48.
‡ Judges, ch., v. 34, 35.
§ It is curious that the Book of Joshua, which relates the conquests of Joshua, does not mention that of Samaria.

tomed to fight in mountain and ravine. The clearing of the forests occupied by the Perizzites and the remainder of the Anakim was also a matter of difficulty and danger.*

The valley of Sichem, with its abundant streams, seemed marked as the site of the capital of this splendid country. The Ephraimites built a very strong position there, perhaps after coming to terms with the Hivites of the district. A great many legends were circulated to show that Jacob, wandering in this region, had acquired a regular claim to it,† that Joseph was buried there,‡ that the patriarchs had made of this place the centre of the worship of Iahveh.§ Sichem, in fact, was always the religious centre of the Josephites, and often the rallying point for all Israel, before the genius of this singular people had been centred solely on Jerusalem.

It was in some respects the same as regards Shiloh. Shiloh may be regarded as having been the first central point of the whole family of Israel.‖ As soon as the great temporary camp of Gilgal was raised the ark was established there, and it remained there for centuries.¶ Shiloh was, in this way, a common city.

* Joshua, ch. xvii., v. 14—18.

† Genesis, ch. xxxiii., v. 18; ch. xxxiv., v. 2; ch. xxxvii., v. 12 and following.

‡ Joshua, ch. xxiv., v. 32; Genesis, ch. l., v. 25.

§ Genesis, ch. xii., v. 7; ch. xxxiii., v. 20; Joshua, ch. xxiv., v. 26.

‖ Joshua, ch. xix., v. 9 and following; ch. xxi., v. 22; ch. xxii., v. 9, 12.

¶ Up to Eli and Samuel.

The fine stretch of plain was a favourable place of meeting of all Israel.

Bethel was also a federal point, half-way between the Benjamites and the Josephites.* Its conquest seems to have been accomplished by the Josephites by surprise.† As we have said, it was a place of great religious importance. The God of Bethel was the God of the whole land of Palestine. He was in this way one of the elements which entered into the composition of Iahveh. The old Canaanite sanctuary of Bethel (perhaps a graduated pyramid like the substructure of the Assyrian temples) was not destroyed until a rather recent period, and for a long time proved a formidable rival to Jerusalem.

Issachar had the ill-defined territory between the house of Joseph and the tribes of the north. The large number of properties running the one into the other to be found in this country shows that the division of land was due to the chances of conquest, and not to a topographical operation executed deliberately, as the Book of Joshua, always so artificial, would have us believe.

The Israelitish occupation in these regions was still more incomplete than in the south. Ghor and the plain of Jezrael defended themselves with their iron chariots. The Phœnician town of Dor was the metropolis of the whole shore from Carmel to Jaffa. The coast known under the name of Naphoth-Dor, and

---

* Judges, ch. xvii., v. 81.
† Judges, ch. i., v. 22 and following.

the southern slope of Carmel,* remained Phœnician. The native populations of Taanach, Megiddo, Endor, Jibleam, Beth-Sean, and all the right bank of Jordan as far as the point at which it leaves the Lake of Genesareth, resisted Manasseh and Issachar† victoriously. The whole plain of Jezrael also escaped them.

Zabulon and Naphtali took what was afterwards called the "circle of the Gentiles," Galilee.‡ But their occupation was in reality merely a cohabitation with the previously established races. The towns of Kitron and Nahalol remained Canaanite.§ Laish or Lesem, until the posterior invasion of the Danites, was an industrial and trading town, living after the manner of Sidon.‖ The Canaanite King of Hazor continued to reign to the west of Lake Houlé and along the upper banks of the Jordan.¶

Asher possessed still less effectively the country where it established itself. The Phœnicians always remained masters of the coast, and the children of Asher were never more than tolerated by them.**

The establishment of Israel in the countries north of Palestine was slow.†† A long time passed between the passage of the Jordan and the day when Asher, as a

* A piece of a Phœnician inscription was found there.
† Joshua, ch. xvii., v. 11 and following; Judges, ch. i., v. 27.
‡ Isaiah, ch. xviii., v. 23.
§ Judges, ch. i., v. 30—32.
‖ Judges, ch. xviii., v. 7.
¶ Joshua, ch. xi., v. 10.
** Judges, ch. i., v. 31; ch. v., v. 17.
†† The campaign of Joshua against Jabin is a repetition of what is related in the Book of Judges, ch. iv.

tribe, really came into existence. It required, in fact, two or three centuries to complete this conquest; it was a daily struggle, the battle of the iron and the earthen pot. The element the least capable of resistance was broken. The Book of Joshua, which attributes the conquest of the whole of Palestine to one great captain, is the least historical of the books of the Bible. If one excepts the taking of Jericho, the establishment of the Benjamites at Gibeah, and the occupation in force of several towns by the tribe of Judah, the conquests set down to the account of Joshua (an alleged series of overwhelming victories and monstrous exterminations), never took place. By some successful raids Israel established its ascendency over the little Canaanite kings of the south. Some towns were effectually occupied together with their territories, and some sections of tribes, like the Gibeonites, treated with the new-comers. Lastly, a great number of towns, like the *Ierousalaïm* of the Jebusites,* like Gezar,† like Beth-Sean,‡ resisted successfully. The two populations combined with each other like a sponge and water. Their language was the same, and they could have had little difficulty in coming to an understanding.§ The religious fanaticism which was destined afterwards to render the Israelites such bad neighbours as yet existed only in a latent condition.

---

* Joshua, ch. xv., v. 63.
† Joshua, ch. xvi., v. 10.
‡ Joshua, ch. xvii., v. 12, 13.
§ Isaiah, ch. xix., v. 18.

CONQUEST OF MOUNT EPHRAIM.   213

In order to understand this one must have seen how the *métualis* of Syria, who are the new-comers, inasmuch as their arrival in the region of Lebanon dates only from the time of the Crusades, have mixed with the other races of the country. One must have seen the mixed or rather double villages, where two populations live together hating and yet tolerating one another. Nearly the whole of Turkey presents a similar spectacle. It is impossible to draw the map of such countries. A map gives one only the well-defined divisions of states and provinces. Now, in the time of the human societies to which I refer, there was no such a thing as a state. There was the tribe and the town. The tribe and the town represent only an enlarged family. None of those powerful influences which trace such deep lines of demarcation in humanity had as yet made themselves felt.

Among excitable and capricious peoples, enmity is not often very durable, and the foe of one day often became the ally of the next. In the districts where the Canaanites and the Israelites were mixed, marriages between the two races were not rare.[*] Such and such a person was called "the son of the Canaanite woman."[†] The mixture of religions was still more common. There was no religious hatred between the populations. The Israelites, especially those in the mixed country, did not scruple to worship the Baalims and the Astartés of

[*] Judges, ch. iii., v. 6.
[†] Exodus, ch. vi., v. 15.

the place.* Iahveh appeared only during federal manifestations, and these were not frequent.

Israel was not yet a nation; it was an agglomeration of tribes which never lost sight of their common origin. And, among their relations, these tribes often included sections still nomad, with whom their ancestors had been on terms of friendship or had indulged in neighbourly intercourse. This especially applies to the Edomite tribes and the Arabs of the south and the east. The Kenites, who during the journey through the desert had rendered service to the fugitives, came and settled near Arad, among the children of Judah and of Simeon.† It is supposed to have been the same with the Edomite tribe of Quenizzis.‡ The Jerahmelites and other remnants of patriarchal tribes, who continued to wander through the deserts of the south, affiliated themselves with the already strongly coagulated mass of Judah.§

The position of the Israelitish conquerors was very similar to that of the Franks in the north of France in the sixth century. Here and there were to be found small but compact bodies of new race, but more frequently simple military fiefs, not to speak of places of refuge, where the old race continued to live as of yore. In addition to all this there existed a sort of Dooms-

* Judges, ch. iii., v. 6, 7.

† Judges, ch. i., v. 16, and the large Hebrew lexicons at word קני.

‡ Judges, ch. i., v. 12, and the large Hebrew lexicons at words קנזי and קנז.

§ Lexicons at words ירחם and ירחמאל.

CONQUEST OF MOUNT EPHRAIM.

day Book of the epoch, a primitive partition among the families of the conquerors, founded upon genealogies which were recorded with greater care as time went on. The immutability of territorial property was laid down in principle for the family. In default of male children it was admitted that daughters could inherit conquered lands.* Soon after this we find the possession of the land regarded as a gift made for ever by Iahveh, who endowed his own people by taking from others what they had planted and sown.† This is the eternal principle of conquest, which considers every kind of violence as legitimate, and which has the pretension of establishing for the future rights which it would be sacrilegious to attack. And the gods always appeared to consecrate the theft.

In those years of conquest a great deal of heroism was displayed. We are so accustomed to look upon Israel as a holy tribe that we have some difficulty in representing to ourselves the ancestors of Jeremiah, of Ezra, Jesus, and the holy Judah, like Achilles and Ajax, or even like so many Imrulkais and Antars. And yet Israel had its time of warlike enthusiasm. In its long struggles with Canaan there were incidents and adventures without number. These perilous campaigns, the ingenious means employed to capture towns, these stratagems which appear to us ill-contrived, but which were then considered extremely

* The five daughters of Zelophehad, Numbers, ch. xxvii., xxxvi.
† Deuteronomy, ch. vi., v. 10.

subtle, completed the epic poem commenced beyond Jordan. A thousand tales, for the most part legendary, celebrated the devices of Joshua, the daring of Caleb, the capture of Jericho, and the burning of Ai.

All this formed a veritable epic cycle, the branches of which were preserved in oral tradition during centuries. Each town, each province, had its legend. It was analogous to the *Fotouh*, or first victories of Islam, which afterwards became a pretext for all kinds of fables and exaggerations.* It was especially analogous to the ante-Islam Arab poetry. The custom of the Israelites, as of the ancient Arabs, was upon each solemn or characteristic occasion, especially where battles were concerned, to strike, metaphorically speaking, a medal by means of an ode which the people sung in chorus, and which remained more or less engraved in the memory of generations. Memory in those remote ages, before writing was known, was capable of miracles. These songs formed an unwritten record, resembling in every respect the Divans of the Arab tribes. In the tenth century B.C., the said songs were united and explained by little tales in prose. Hence a book like the *Kitâb-el-Aghâni* of the Arabs. It was called the book of the *Wars of Iahveh* † or the book of *Jasher*. Considerable portions of this old work have been preserved in more recent historical compilations.

These epic songs, while furnishing matter for a sacred book, visibly changed their character. The

* See the tales of the false Wokedi.
† See First Book of Samuel, ch. xviii., v. 17; ch. xxv., v. 28.

supernatural penetrated through the heroic history from beginning to end. The little song about the spring which the chiefs discovered with their wands gave rise to the miracle of Moses striking the rock with his rod. The rhetorical figure of the sun of Gibeon engendered the most hyperbolic of marvels. The passage of the Jordan, so easy to effect, was accomplished with the superfluous connivance of the river. The miraculous establishment of Israel in Canaan became a second pillar of the Jewish dogma. Joshua was the continuation of Moses. The cycle of sacred legends, commencing with the patriarchal paradise, and finishing with the partition of the land of Canaan between the tribes, was finished. But it took at least five hundred years, it required the action of a very fanatical religious party, before the necessary transformations for the establishment of such a historical system could be accomplished. I cannot do better than let the story follow its natural sequence.

CHAPTER V.

DEVELOPMENT OF MATERIALIST IAHVEHISM.

The Israelite conquest of Palestine was more radically affected by the rank accorded to Iahveh than by anything else. The adoption of this god by the Beni-Israel dated as we have seen from the most ancient teachings which Israel had received at Ur-Casdim, or rather in the Padan-Aram. But in the ancient patriarchal *elohism* such a name could never enjoy a great popularity. The author of the Book of Job, who endeavours to describe the theological ideal of that primitive age, avoids employing the name of Iahveh. One of the ancient biblical stories imitates this example up to the time of Moses.

We have seen how Israel's individual belief dawned upon the morrow of the coming out of Egypt. National individualism demands a special god. From that moment Iahveh became the protecting deity of Israel, bound to declare that they were right, even when they were wrong. A victory on the part of Israel was a victory gained by Iahveh; the wars of Israel were the wars of Iahveh.[*] The favours, thanks to which the people of Israel thought that they had crossed the desert,

[*] First Book of Samuel, ch. xviii., v. 17.

DEVELOPMENT OF MATERIALIST IAHVEHISM. 219

were the favours of Iahveh. Iahveh, in a word, was exactly to Israel what Camos was to Moab. Jephthah admits that Camos gave Moab to the Moabities, as Iahveh gave Canaan to the Israelites.*
He was a national god, identified with the nation, victorious with it, vanquished with it.† He was in some sort the *alter ego*, the genius of the nation personified, the *spirit* of the nation in the sense applied by savages to the word (*esprit*). It is easy to see how completely opposed such an idea is from Israel's point of departure. At the beginning, the *elohim*, with no individuality of their own, were kneaded more or less into one Elohim, sole master of the world, who, in due time, became the only God of the Christians, the Creator and Judge of the universe.

In the desert Iahveh was still but a god of nomads, a god without land, unable to dispose of an acre. Now he has conquered a country which he has bestowed on his servants. It is unnecessary to know if he be just or not; he favours Israel, that is sufficient. Israel is already almost a nation; it has all the defects of one. The essence of a nation is to believe that the entire world exists for it, that God thinks of nothing but it. As long as the old spirit of Elohism lasted that dangerous name of Iahveh was a matter of no consequence. El and Iahveh were two kinds of synonyms which were indifferently employed.‡ But everything

---

* Judges, ch. xi., v. 24, a slight confusion.
† Song of Deborah, essentially Iahvist (Judges, ch. v.). See below, pp. 255 and following.
‡ Schrader, *Die Keilinschr. und das A. T.*, pp. 23, 24.

was changed when Iahveh became a local, patriotic, national god. From that time he was ferocious. This new Iahveh was no longer the antique source of strength and life in the world. He was a political slaughterer, a god who showed favour to a little tribe *per fas et nefas*. All the crimes perpetrated were about to be ordered in the name of Iahveh.

Such an evolution is in the natural order of things, and we have seen one happen in our days. Germany, by the philosophy to which it has given birth, by the voice of its men of genius, had more successfully proclaimed than any other race the absolute, impersonal, and supreme nature of the Divinity. But, when she became a nation, she was led, according to the way of all flesh, to particularise God. The Emperor William has on several occasions spoken of *unser Gott*, and the god of the Germans. The fact is that nation and philosophy have little to do with each other. Patriotism, among other meannesses, has the pretension of having a god of its own. *Iahveh elohenu*, "Iahveh our god," said the Israelite. *Unser Gott* says the German. A nation is always egotistical. It desires that the God of heaven and earth should think of no other interests than its own. Under one name or under another it creates for itself tutelary divinities. Christianity offered some difficulties in this matter through the severity of its dogma; but the instincts of a nation always carry the day. Catholicism has escaped from the orthodox chains by means of the saints: St. George, St. Denis, St. James of Compostella, are really on a par with Camos and Iahveh. In our day we have seen the Sacred Heart employed in a similar manner. Protestantism, like Judaism, has no other resource, under similar circumstances, than the possessive pronoun, *unser Gott*. Strange contradiction, fearful blasphemy! God is the property of no nation, of no individual. As well say, *My absolute, my infinite, my supreme Being*.

Iahveh is simply the confiscation, sacrilegious assuredly, though to a certain extent logical, of the power of Elohim to the profit of Israel. The great Workman has only one care, that is to make the children of Israel triumph over their enemies. Henceforth God has a distinctive name in Israel as he has in Moab, which is a great decline from a religious point of view. A distinctive name is the negation itself of the divine essence, but a great progress in a national point of view!

If it had been the destiny of Israel to found a nation there would have been no reason to condemn this act of simple egoism which all nations have committed in their origin. But the national tendency, with its special god, was only a fugitive error on the part of Israel. Those terrible abolitionists, the prophets, the real depositaries of the instinct of the race, were destined to destroy in detail this cruel, partial, and rancorous Iahveh, and to return, by a series of more and more vigorous efforts, to the primitive *elohism*, to the patriarchal god, to the El of the large tent, to the true god. The history of Israel may be summed up in a word: it was an effort continued through long ages to shake off the false god Iahveh and to return to the primitive Elohim.

The revolution accomplished by the prophets did not go as far as a change of expressions. The word Iahveh was too deeply rooted in the nation to be removed. It was retained. The idea, universally accepted, that Iahveh was the most powerful of the gods, naturally led people to speak of Iahveh as they had formerly spoken of El or Elohim. Iahveh thus became the supreme being who made and governed the world. There was what the theologians call *communicatio idiomatum*. The words changed places, and in time the very name Iahveh was nearly lost. The utterance of it was forbidden, and it was replaced by the purely deist word "the Lord." The great Christian propaganda, as I have said,* knew only this word. The personal name did not come into use again until the seventeenth century, and even then it remained a scholarly affectation, which did not penetrate seriously into the religious conscience of Christian nations.

Gods may change their form, but they always retain the mark of their origin. Iahveh, through all his metamorphoses, remained essentially a god of Fire. The peal of thunder is his voice.† He never appears without storm and earthquake: ‡ —

Then the earth shook and trembled; the foundations also of the hills moved and were shaken, because he was wroth.
There went out smoke out of his nostrils, and fire out of his mouth devoured: coals were kindled by it.

---

* See above, p. 151.
† Exodus, ch. xix., v. 19; Psalm xxix., and following.
‡ Psalm xviii., 1-15.

DEVELOPMENT OF MATERIALIST IAHVEHISM. 223

He bowed the heavens also and came down; and darkness was under his feet.

* * * * *

And again*—

The voice of Iahveh is upon the waters: the God of glory thundereth: Iahveh is upon many waters.

* * * * *

Even the powerful associations which, at all events since the crossing of the desert, connected Iahveh with the mountains of Sinai were never destroyed. The principal dwelling of Iahveh was always there; his customary Olympus was in Sinai. There he resided in the midst of his thunderbolts; from there he emerged with terrible splendour when his people stood in need of him. His track, in such cases, was always the same. He came from the south, from the direction of Seir and Paran; he shone like an aurora borealis; the earth trembled; it was the signal for severe judgments about to be executed on the nations in order to revenge wrongs done to Israel.†

We have seen that the patriarchal age was not free from superstition, the *téraphim*, and the little gods in wood, in clay, and in metal. These *téraphim* represented special gods, not the only El, or the supreme Elohim. Iahveh retained the trace of his peculiar origin; being long represented in this manner. Our information on this subject is very incomplete, the puritans of a later age having suppressed whatever

---

* Psalm xxix.
† Song of Deborah and Psalm lxviii.

part of the text appeared to them too scandalous. But no doubt can exist that in ancient times Iahveh was the object of an idolatrous worship. He was often represented under the form which Egypt had rendered dear to the least enlightened Israelites,* that of a golden calf.† Sometimes he was given the attributes of the serpent;‡ at other times Iahveh was a plated image,§ or the winged disc flanked by the *uræus*, which is so common in Egypt, and which is never missing in a single Phœnician monument.‖ I am inclined to believe that the *urim*¶ of the symbols employed by the Israelites** was nothing but these two asps, †† which form an essential part in the great Egyptian symbol of the infinite. Both were called collectively *ha-Ourim* or *ha-Ouraïm*, the two *ourim ;* or else one was called *urim*, the other *thummim*, a word the meaning of which when thus employed completely escapes us.

These figurative images of Iahveh were called *ephods*,‡‡

* Exodus, ch. xxxii.; Deuteronomy, ch. ix., v. 21.

† First Book of Kings, ch. xii., v. 28, 29.

‡ The *nehustan*, or brazen serpent, Second Book of Kings, ch. xviii., v. 4.

§ Isaiah, ch. xxx., v. 22. Real meaning of אפוד and אפדה.

‖ *Mission de Phénicie*, index, words *globe ailé* and *uræus*. (asps).

¶ האורים. First Book of Samuel, ch. xxviii., v. 6; Numbers, ch. xxvii., v. 21.

** Hebrew seals, *vide* p. 126.

†† The word οὐραῖος is Greek and cannot be used in the argument. But the Egyptian word was ערת or עררת, which was probably pronounced *Oräit* or *Oraï*.

‡‡ Judges, ch. viii., v. 27 ; ch. xvii., v. 5 ; ch. xviii., v. 14, 17, 18, 20 ; First Book of Samuel, ch. xxiii., v. 6, 9; ch. xxx., v. 7 ; Hosea, ch. iii., v. 4 ; Isaiah, ch. xxx., v. 22. The passages in the Book of Samuel seemed too broad in the epoch of orthodox Judaism. They

like the robes of the Levites, surplices fastened round the waist by a belt, which the officiating priests wore during service. It is not known how this double signification arose. The idolatrous object, formerly known under the name of *ephod*, was of metal on a wooden frame.* The official ephod, if we may so term it, was in the ark, always at the service of the *levi*, or of the *cohen;* but it was sometimes taken out. It could not have been large, for it was easily carried in the hand.† Beside, private individuals who were sufficiently rich had ephods made for them and used them for their personal profit.‡

The ephod in fact, in addition to representing Iahveh, had a special use, that of being employed in divination and in oracles. In certain circles of Israelitish opinions Iahveh was a god to be consulted in order to know the future and to obtain useful indications. The patriarchal El was also consulted. He placed himself in communication with man by means of dreams and prophets.§ But the patriarchal age had nothing which resembled a direct consultation with God. Iahveh, on the contrary, was a god

were toned down in several copies, hence our present Hebrew text. The Greek translators have kept to the ancient version in all its simplicity.

* Judges, ch. viii., v. 27; ch. xviii., v. 18; Isaiah, ch. xxx., v. 22.

† Essential passages, First Book of Samuel, ch. xiv., v. 3 and following; ch. xxiii., v. 4 and following.

‡ Examples of Mikah and of Gideon.

§ First Book of Samuel. ch. xxviii., v. 6; Job, ch. xxxiii., v. 15

of lots, resembling the Temple of Fortune at Preneste, answering *yes* or *no* to the questions put to him.*

It is probable that the idea of the real presence of Iahveh on the ark, between the wings of two cherubim† forming a pedestal and serving for his throne, had been in existence since the days of the wandering in the desert. To this ark came those who wanted to consult him. ‡ The only form of process then known was the ordeal, and the judgments given took merely the form of answers to those who came to question God.§ Nothing important was done without the familiar genius of the tribe being consulted. But nevertheless matters were not left to chance. With the Israelites, as with the Greeks, the oracles were confided to the care of the wise men. What we should call imposture was then considered merely the faithful interpretation of the wishes of the tutelary deity.‖

When the tribes were formed Iahveh was above all the counsellor of the nation. The servants of Iahveh in those days of eclecticism were the persons who had an ephod and who knew how to turn it to account. The proper names into which that of Iahveh enters as a component part are to be found hardly anywhere else than among these strange persons. Thus

* First Book of Samuel, ch. x., v. 22.

† First Book of Samuel, ch. iv., v. 4; Second Book of Samuel, ch. vi., v. 2.

‡ Exodus, ch. xxiii., v. 7—11.

§ Exodus, ch. xviii., v. 15 and following; Numbers, ch. xxvii., v. 2, 5 and following; Judges, ch. i., v. 1.

‖ Even Mesa undertook nothing without having first spoken to Camos. *Inscr.*, lines 14, 32.

DEVELOPMENT OF MATERIALIST IAHVEHISM. 227

Gideon and his family appear to have been particularly attached to the practice of the ephod. The same may be said of Mikah or Mikaïahou.* Iahveh was the great oracle of Israel. Of a truth this powerful god was revered by all; but he had a special following of families more devoted to his worship than the rest of the nation. These first saints of Iahveh bore no reputation for moral purity or sober piety. They waited on the idol in whose name they returned answers, which were received with such profound respect. There is nothing to prove that they were in the least superior to the other Levites who wandered through the country.

* See pp. 266 and following, pp. 283 and following.

CHAPTER VI.

THE ORACLE OF IAHVEH.

How were these consultations of Iahveh, in which the most sagacious eye could certainly not yet have divined the least germ of the future, conducted? They were conducted often by lot, or by choice, which was rendered significative,* or by fortuitous indications, by signs which the priests interpreted as they liked.† In the event of *urim*‡ being employed there was sure to be some fraud in the affair on the part of the Levites, who placed themselves, owing to their subordinate situation, in the hands of the chiefs of the people. As in the *sortes prænestinæ*, some skilful trick was played.§ The motive power remained invisible, and the divine *tremolo* had all the appearance of spontaneous production.

It has never been ascertained by what mechanism the oracle was rendered. Some have supposed that a draught or a backgammon board was used, and that *urim* and *thummim* were dice. This theory is not inadmissible, firstly, because of the expression "cast lots"

* First Book of Samuel, ch. xiv., v. 10.

† First Book of Samuel, ch. x., v. 20 and following; ch. xiv., v. 36 and following.

‡ שאל במשפט האורים, Numbers, ch. xxvii., v. 21.

§ First Book of Samuel, ch. xiv., v. 20.

generally used for these kinds of oracles,* and secondly because of the manner of interrogating Iahveh: "in such a case give *urim*, in such another case give *thummim*,"† (which answered to the two technical expressions *iasa*, "gone out," and *nilkad*, "was kept in,"‡) to announce the result. Perhaps the two asps of the winged globe, meaning, one *yes*, the other *no*, were put in motion by means of a spring concealed behind the disc. It was naturally the priest who worked the instrument and who replied to the questions. It is remarkable that in all the cases of consultation, the answers of Iahveh were very brief.§ The question was asked in a sort of yea or nay manner, which hardly allowed for any hesitation.‖

An expression, however, which opens up another order of ideas is the following term employed: "The affair is before Iahveh," meaning that "the affair is accepted by Iahveh."¶ It would seem as if in this method of consultation Iahveh turned away or did not turn away his face from the object which was placed before him, and that it was concluded from the movement of the idol that the matter would or would not have a happy issue. Egypt, where these aberrations no doubt had their origin, did not act otherwise. The judgments of God by *yes* and *no* were,

* First Book of Samuel, ch. xiv., v. 41, 42.
† Same passage corrected by the Greek.
‡ Familiarly: "The affair is hung up before **Iahveh.**"
§ First Book of Samuel, ch. xiv., v. 37.
‖ First Book of Samuel, ch. xiv., v. 41.
¶ Judges, ch. xviii., v. 6.

at this epoch, the basis of Egyptian life.* The god who was consulted replied by moving his arms or head, and even by word of mouth.† These conjuring tricks were performed by means of complicated mechanism.‡

We see that nothing is more obscure than the apparatus by means of which Iahveh was consulted; nothing is more certain than the fact of this consultation itself. The *urim* and the *thummim* were considered as the property and as the title of honour of the family of Levi.§ In every difficulty which arose the authorities went and interrogated the oracle of the ark, and the oracle answered.‖ Political difficulties and civil prosecutions were terminated in this way. This was called "interrogate Iahveh," "come and search Iahveh," "present oneself before Iahveh," "draw near to Iahveh,"¶ expressions synonymous to "carry the affair before Iahveh." Some expressions seem to indicate that the reply of Iahveh was sometimes made by word of mouth ;** but the date of these expressions is uncertain.

* E. Naville, *Inscr. de Pinodjem*, iii. (Paris, 1883), p. 4.

† Maspero, *Recueil de travaux*, t. i., p. 157.

‡ Hero of Alexandria, *Pneumatica et Automata*, in the *Mathem. veteres* of Thevenot, pp. 167, 191, 192, 255, 266, 267, 273.

§ Deuteronomy, ch. xxxiii., v. 8.

‖ Numbers, ch. xxvii., v. 21; Judges, ch. i., v. 1; First Book of Samuel, ch. x., v. 20; ch. xiv., v. 36; ch. xxii., v. 10; ch. xxiii., v. 9; ch. xxviii., v. 6; ch. xxx., v. 7; Second Book of Samuel, ch. ii., v. 1.

¶ First Book of Samuel, ch. xiv., v. 36; Exodus, ch. xxi, v. 6; ch. xxii., v. 8.

** Joshua, ch. ix., v. 14.

It was the judgment of God,* with all its dangers; but it is doubtful whether the Israelites applied it, as was done in the Middle Ages, in criminal cases. Even limited to civil cases this superstition might have been terrible in its consequences had it not been confided to the chiefs and wise men of the nation, who dictated the reply of the priests, and consequently that of *urim* and *thummim*. In like manner the oracle of Delphi was always, so it appears, inspired in a way to favour the interests of Greece. What the material and sacerdotal oracle, which played heads or tails with the destinies of Israel, obviously threatened was prophecy. This was a most dangerous competition. The turnstile was about to annihilate intelligence, the *levi* was going to kill the *nabi*, the official oracle was going to stifle the free inspiration of Israel.

A serious abuse, in fact, was that private individuals who were rich enough to have an ephod and to pay for a Levite, had a domestic oracle of which they made use for their own profit. There were many instances of this abuse,† though the ark kept them within certain limits. The ephod of the ark overshadowed the other ephods. It lost a good deal of its own importance by the construction of the temple. It was out of the question to allow all those who wished to consult Iahveh to enter the holy of holies. At a later date the reform of Hezekiah did away with this barbarous custom. The victory of the spirit of pro-

---

* Exodus, ch. xxii., v. 8.
† Judges, ch. xvii., xviii.

phecy was complete. One of its effects was, without doubt, to throw into the shade this remnant of the ancient superstition of Israel.

However, did the ephod entirely disappear under Hezekiah, like the *nehustan*? That is not probable, for in the restored worship of the sixth century we find something which can only be considered as a transformation. The most characteristic sign of the rich and elaborate costume devised for the high priest, was a large breast-plate composed of twelve precious stones, on which were engraved the names of the twelve tribes of Israel. Without explaining matters as clearly as it might do, holy writ confounds this breast-plate with the ancient ephod, and places there, in a rather obscure manner, the *urim* and *thummim*. Perhaps the upper part of the breast-plate contained the winged disc and the *urœus*.* This is what was called the oracle.† The belief that Aaron wore the oracle of Israel on his heart gave general satisfaction.‡ This had no longer a practical meaning, and offered no danger. The old sacrament was nearly worn out, materialised, and converted into an ornament for the cope jewel. The priesthood had suppressed it by monopolising it.§ Religious imagination knows no bounds. This breast-plate oracle gave rise to the belief that the spirit of prophecy was

---

* See p. 229.

† Λόγιον or λογιεῖον of the Greek translators. See Gesenius as regards the expression חשן המשפט.

‡ Exodus, ch. xxviii., v. 29.

§ Numbers, ch. xxvii., v. 21.

plated, if we may so express it, on the breast of the high priest. Hence the popular idea that the high priest was a prophet once a year.*

Thus *urim* and *thummim* came to an obscure end. In the fifth century B.C. it was not clearly known what the *ephod*, *urim*, and *thummim* were.

In questions which could not be solved, the persons interested were put off until a priest could come to judge by *urim* and *thummim*.† There was a sort of irony in this, as if one were to say now, "That will not be clear until the judgment of God is known." The latest editors of the historical books effaced many traces of ancient materialism. The Alexandrian translators of the Bible, well acquainted with Egyptian customs, were very much struck with the little backgammon-board of precious stones which the chief judge in Egypt wore round his neck, hanging down his breast, and which in the era of the Ptolemies was called *Alethia*.‡ They rendered *urim* and *thummim* by Δήλωσις καὶ ἀλήθεια. They assumed them to have a kind of allegorical meaning. They confused the machine for delivering oracles with the backgammon-board of precious stones hung on the breast of the priest.

All analogy, it will be seen, leads us to look for the origin of *urim* and *thummim* to Egypt. But it is not necessary on this account to suppose that they were borrowed direct. The influence of Egypt was

---

* St. John, ch. xi., v. 49—51.
† Ezra, ch. ii., v. 63 ; Nehemiah, ch. vii., v. 65
‡ Diod. Sic., i., pp. 48, 75.

felt throughout the whole of Phœnicia. The ephod of Israel may have been copied from the divining utensils of the Phœnicians and the Philistines, who may themselves have copied them from Egypt. These superstitions are, unfortunately, only too easily handed down from one people to another. *Urim* and *thummim* were therefore to Israel what the Kaaba was to Islam. The Kaaba was a remnant of paganism which Mahomet did not dare to abolish. Nor did the Jewish monotheism dare to do away entirely with the old ephod; but it subordinated it and submerged it, so to speak, in the midst of the symbols of a triumphant monotheism.

The god-oracle was at the same time the god of vows and oaths,* especially of terrible oaths, where people swore extermination and vengeance as if to fortify themselves against any temptation to show pity. Every oath taken to Iahveh meant a kind of vow; Iahveh revenged himself, if he was called upon in vain; then his oracle was silent; and the silence of the ephod was regarded as a sign of wrath on the part of Iahveh;† the criterion of truth no longer existed. Iahveh was essentially a god of truth. He could not suffer his name to cloak the slightest inaccuracy. This redoubtable *Zeus Orkios* saw nothing but the material fact; degrees, extenuating circumstances, had no weight with him. He was ferocious when robbed

---

* Exodus, ch. xxii., v. 10.

† First Book of Samuel, ch. xiv., v. 36 and following, according to Greek.

of the quantity of blood which was due to him. Human sacrifices were much more common in Israel during the period of the judges and the first kings than during the age of the patriarchs. Old father Abraham, filled with justice, humanity, and kindness, was succeeded by a severe, inflexible god.

Morality, in its absolute sense as superior to gods and men, did not exist. The personal tie created between God and man by the vow and the oath replaced everything. It in some way resembled those conditions which children, in their games, make among themselves. Such and such things were forbidden, not because they were bad in themselves, but because they were tabooed in a way which removed them from the world below and surrounded them with an atmosphere of terror.* A deep feeling of rancour appeared to be the prevailing sentiment of this god, too capricious to be a just judge.

What was the popular conception, at this epoch, of the relation between these two divine names, Iahveh and Elohim? It would be difficult to say with certainty. It is probable that the use of the word Iahveh gained ground every day.† Elohim, however, was preferred in proverbs, in the maxims of parabolic philosophy, which doubtless existed already in a rudimentary fashion. The word Iahveh was never employed in this literature, because it related to an ideal anterior to Iahvehism. *Sabaoth* was seldom

---

* Joshua, ch. vi., v. 26, 27.
† The Song of Deborah, Judges, ch. v.

employed. Often the two words *Sabaoth* and *Elohim* were added to Iahveh, in this form: *Iahveh-Sabaoth*,* *Iahveh-Elohim*.† The expression *Adonaï-Iahveh*, "my lord Iahveh," was merely respectful. The expression *Iahveh élohé Israël*, "Iahveh god of Israel," expressed the truth. Elohim and Sabaoth were for the whole human race; Iahveh was for Israel only. To be sure on the other side of the Arnon they likewise said *Camos élohé Moab*, "Camos god of Moab."

The rude analogies upon which primitive theology was constructed naturally led to the formation of a celestial court of Iahveh. The sons of God were ascribed to him.‡ He had a general-in-chief of his armies,§ a *sar-saba*, a seraskier, who was sometimes met, a naked sword in his hand, and who was approached in trembling. Far more important still was the angel or messenger (*Maleak*) charged at first to carry the orders of Iahveh, and who soon became grand vizier, and shared the powers of Iahveh. From a very early age, in fact, Iahveh had at his side a sort of double-self, who was called *Maleak-Iahveh*; it was like his counterpart, his *alter ego*. The Phœnician religion presents ideas nearly similar. The visage of the god is distinct from the god himself.‖ What is more, the *Maleak-Iahveh* of the Hebrews may well have

---

* Second Book of Samuel, ch. vi., v. 2; ch. vii., v. 27.
† Second Book of Samuel, ch. vii., v. 22, 25.
‡ Job, ch. i., v. 6; ch. ii., v. 1.
§ Joshua, ch. v., v. 14.
‖ פן־בעל, so frequent in Carthage; the צלם of the Aramaic inscriptions.

THE ORACLE OF IAHVEH.

his counterpart in the *Maleak-Baal*, the *Maleak-Astoret* of the Phœnician epigraphy.* It is by no means sure that the Moloch or Milk of the Canaanite religion does not owe its origin to a similar source,† which appears to have in Egyptian theology its origin and its explanation. According to this theology, the influence of which was so great in the Canaanite region, the double of the god was the god himself. One finds at Thebes invocations to the double of Ammon. Elsewhere the double of Chons figures instead of Chons.‡

The *Maleak-Iahveh* is often only "a man of God"§ sent by Iahveh for some definite object. In most cases, however, the *Maleak* is not to be distinguished from Iahveh himself.|| At a more recent epoch this gave rise to a very singular abuse. Some pietists of Judah found fault with certain passages of the ancient books in which Iahveh acted as a man and compromised himself in vulgar adventures. They made a rule, in such cases, of substituting *Maleak-Iahveh* for *Iahveh*. The angel of Iahveh was the divine agent in all cases where Iahveh was brought into contact with man.

The Samaritans and the Jews of Alexandria, Josephus and the Judeo-Christians, exaggerated still more this theological mania. They managed in nearly

---

* *Corpus inscr. semit.*, part i., Nos. 8, 123, 147, 149, 195, 380.

† מלך perhaps for מלאך, as ملك in Arabic for ملاك, especially in the Koran.

‡ Champollion, *Monum.*, t. i., pl. lxxxiv.; Maspero in the *Recueil*, t. i., p. 156.

§ Vision of Manoah, Judges, ch. xiii., v. 2 and following.

|| Genesis, ch. xvi., v. 7, 13 and following.

all the old narratives to substitute for God this kind of second person of God. The "name" played a similar part. The name of the person was the person himself.* The word *shem* became thus an equivalent for Iahveh,† especially among the Samaritans.‡ One easily perceives how the theories of the Word and of the Trinity sprang from this sort of language. It was the commencement of that hypostatic theology into which Semitic monotheism plunged in quest of the variety and the life which were denied to it for want of a mythology.§

Sometimes these hypostatic divisions went still further : Iahveh appeared inseparable from his *haberim* or *maleakim*,‖ and as one of them. While travelling, especially, he liked to shake off his other self, allowing himself to be received, lodged, and fed. To those who found it strange that Iahveh should thus eat and drink, the answer was that it was not Iahveh but his *maleakim*. The real form of Iahveh, in fact, was never human. He was a kind of dragon, roaring thunder, vomiting flame, causing the tempest to howl;

---

* Exodus, ch. xxiii., v. 21 ; First Book of Kings, ch. iii., v. 2 ; ch. viii., v. 17, 20, 29 ; Second Book of Kings, ch. iii., v. 27 ; Isaiah, ch. xxx., v. 27 ; Psalm liv., and frequently in other Psalms.

† Gesenius, *Thes.*, p. 1433. Compare the name שמידע for יהוידע, perhaps ברשם for ברית.

‡ The Samaritans always substituted שימא for the word יהוה. The Jews also wrote חשם for יהוה.

§ See *Origines du Christianisme*, i., p. 257 and following; v., p. 415 ; vi., p. 64 and following.

‖ Genesis, ch., xix., v. 1.

he was the universal *rouah* under a globated form, a kind of condensed electric mass. Iahveh acted like a universal agent. He ate the sacrifice at the moment that the flame devoured it. In that case the flame was often spontaneous; it licked up the morsels of the victims stretched upon the rock and made them disappear. Sometimes two large nostrils were dilated over the smoke of the sacrifice in order to inhale it.* On other occasions the god was seen to ascend from the flame of the sacrifice; he disappeared in the tongues of fire which leaped from the altar.† Then man had in reality beheld Iahveh and was sure to die.‡

But it was not rare for Iahveh when he wished to reveal himself to men to employ disguises. He became Proteus or Vertumnus. Then he was peculiarly belligerent. He was to be met with in the deserted parts of the country which he preferred; he attempted to kill you, he thirsted after your blood.§ Or else one fancied that one was struggling with him in a nightmare. One perspired and exhausted oneself against an unknown force. This lasted all night long until dawn broke. Then one awoke enervated, having struggled against Iahveh or his *Maleak*.‖ This is what happened to Jacob, and hence no doubt the expression *Abir Jakob*,

---

* Genesis, ch. viii., v. 21.

† Judges, ch. xiii., v. 15 and following.

‡ Judges, ch. vi., v. 22 and following; ch. xiii., v. 22 and following.

§ Exodus, ch. iv., v. 21 and following.

‖ Genesis, ch. xxxii., xxxv.

"the strength of Jacob, or *Abir Israel*,* to indicate God. The *Maleak* was the fiction by which the shapeless or deformed being entered into the order of formed and visible beings. The general rule was, when the presence of *Maleak* was suspected, to furnish him with a copious repast.†

In general Iahveh was impalpable, invisible. It was difficult, under the caprices of this strange electriform agent to foresee that Iahveh would one day become a just God. The Iahveh of the time of the Judges had scarcely anything of the moral god about him. He chose certain people; he loved certain men; his preferences could not be explained. He was very inferior to the ancient *Elohim*. If we compare the religious condition of the nomad children of Jacob or of Isaac with that of the tribes of Israel at the epoch we have reached, the deterioration is great. It required centuries of progress for Iahveh to love good, to hate evil, and to become a universal god. Let us put our trust in the genius of Israel, in the persistent recollections of the age of the patriarchs, and the latent action of the pious examples of *Pater-Orchamus*. Let us put our trust above all in humanity, which always gains its end, has the power to transform what it loves, and eventually succeeds, by dint of beating the air, in extracting from the senseless *urim* and *thummim* some atom of justice and of truth.

---

* Genesis, ch. xlix., v. 24; Isaiah, ch. i., v. 44.
† Abraham, Gideon.

CHAPTER VII.

THE JUDGES.

If, upon their arrival on the banks of the Jordan, among the *Arboth-Moab*, at Jericho, the Israelites had been as dense in numbers as the Moabites and the Edomites, they would certainly have imitated those nations, who, having obtained fixed dwelling-places, chose kings for themselves. But the situation of Israel was quite different. The tribes made isolated efforts to gain a position in the midst of the Canaanites. The wars of Judah, of Ephraim, and Manasseh were undertaken without any unity of action. The want of a single chief was greatly felt. Religious centralisation did not exist. They still lived on what remained of the patriarchal elohism, greatly adulterated by the superstitions of the worship of Iahveh, especially by an abuse of the oracles of the ephod.

The ark had no fixed resting-place. From Gilgal it was carried to Bethel,* a town already holy and whose holiness it increased; then to Shiloh, where it appears to have remained a long time. Shiloh, owing to its central position, was nearly becoming a

* Judges, ch. x., v. 26 and following.

capital for Israel.* But there was no scruple felt in moving this sacred piece of furniture; it was like the *carroccio* of the Italian towns of the Middle Ages, the palladium of the nation. The ark was taken campaigning at the risk of losing it. Often it was placed under a tent; but after the end of their nomad life this mode of shelter appeared insufficient. It was generally lodged in the house of some person of rank, who thus became its guardian. The idea of constructing a special house for the ark ought to have occurred to the tribes, but they were so unsettled, so poor, so precariously established in the country, that no one mooted this idea. The establishment of the ark, with its ephod and its divining apparatus, nevertheless formed a kind of temple, which was called *bet ha-elohim*, "house of God."†

The ark, besides, in the olden time, did not play the exclusive part attributed to it. It gave notoriety to the place where it was, but it did not overshadow the opposition made by other places in the name of their private interests. We shall see Manasseh, Gilead, and Dan creating places where Iahveh could be consulted in duly established form. Private ephods were set up and obtained great success. It required, however, no great sagacity to see that the ark was the centre of the nation and the generating point of monotheism. The ark of Israel was a thing

* Frequently mentioned in Judges, Joshua, and First Book of Samuel.
† Judges, ch. xviii., v. 31.

THE JUDGES.

unique in its essence. It never occurred to anyone to create a second ark. Even when Jerusalem monopolised the ark, the kingdom of Israel made other sanctuaries, but never a private ark. The talisman which they called *nehustan* was unique and the most undoubted heritage of Moses; the ark, evidently, was supposed to date back to Moses. It consequently could have no double, which privilege was not shared by the ephod.

The persons in charge of the ark were limited to some Levites skilled in the manipulation of the ephod; the sacrifices continued to be made by the heads of families upon improvised altars* of stone or turf. These sacrifices were offered up no matter where, according to circumstances. The high places of the former inhabitants were preferred by the children of Israel.† The contagion especially of the Canaanite sanctuaries was strongly felt. Baal and Asera were adored in various places.‡ The evil Moabite worship of Baal-Phegor, a kind of priapism, seduced the least pure.§ The Baal-Berith of Sichem was almost as much respected by the Israelites as their own Iahveh.‖ The name of Baal, by which the Canaanites delighted to style their god, inspired no feeling of repulsion at this epoch. In the same

* Judges, ch. ii., v. 5; ch. xxi., v. 2 and following; Exodus, ch. xx., v. 24, 26.
† Deuteronomy, ch. xii., v. 29 and following.
‡ Judges, ch. ii., v. 13 and following.
§ Numbers, ch. xxv.
‖ Judges, ch. viii., v. 33; ch. ix., v. 27.

family are found Baal and Iahveh the one used as often as the other in the composition of proper names.*

The *nabis* in Israel, at that remote epoch, enjoyed no importance. The *urim* and *thummim* were too powerful rivals for them. The religious confusion may be said to have been as complete as possible. A few prophetic individualities appear to us, it is true, greatly attached to the worship of Iahveh. Deborah, if the text of her song has not been tampered with, was impressed with the idea that the misfortunes of the people, above all the wars, were the consequences of infidelity and the hankering after strange gods.† But the passage in question appears to have been altered.‡ The doings of Gideon, of Mikah, of the Gileadites, of the Danites of the north, show us how loose and how ill-regulated religion then was. Most of the tribes held Iahveh to be the tutelary deity of Israel; Iahveh was almost the only god from whom oracles were demanded; but they gave him for companions the gods of the country; they called upon Baal and Milik at the same time that they called upon him. They adored this god, already irritable and jealous, upon the open-air altars defiled by the natives; they associated him with impure rites. Did they even always know whether the sacrifices were addressed to Iahveh, to Baal, or to Milik? These words were almost synonymous. In all this, as one can see, there was nothing which foretold

* Families of Gideon and Saul: Iarebaal, Esbaal, Milkisua.
† Judges, ch. v., v. 8.
‡ See after, chapter ix., xi., xii.

THE JUDGES.

a religion of the spirit. The images, or rather the utensils of wood and of metal which were used for divination, became the object of a shameful traffic. The Levites who performed the service were persons of a very low order of morality.

There was as yet no centralisation in this rude worship.* Victims were offered to Iahveh and he was consulted at Bethel,† at Shiloh,‡ at Gibeah of Benjamin,§ at Gilgal,‖ at Mizpah of Benjamin,¶ at Mizpah of Gilead,** at Dan, and no doubt in the temples of Ebal and of Garizim beyond Sichem.†† Gibeah of Benjamin was a particularly mysterious place. The elohim dwelt there; it was called *Gibeahha-Elohim*,‡‡ "the hill of the gods." There was a high place there frequented especially by the prophets. It seems difficult to distinguish between the worship which was paid there to Iahveh and that which was paid to Elohim.

The festivals were rejoicings which bore reference to

* Judges, ch. xvii., v. 6; ch. xviii., v. 1; ch. xxi., v. 24.

† Judges, ch. xx., v. 18, 26 and following; ch. xxi., v. 2 and following; First Book of Samuel, ch. x., v. 3.

‡ Judges, ch. xxi., v. 12, 19, 21.

§ First Book of Samuel, ch. x., v. 5; ch. xxi., v. 6.

‖ First Book of Samuel, ch. vii., v. 16; ch. x., v. 8; ch. xi., v. 14 and following; ch. xv., v. 12, 21, 33; Hosea, ch. xii., v. 12.

¶ Judges, ch. xx., v. 1, 3; ch. xxi., v. 1, 5, 8; First Book of Maccabees, ch. iii., v. 46.

** Judges, ch. x., v. 29, 34; Hosea, ch. xii., v. 12.

†† Deuteronomy, ch. xxvii.; Joshua, ch. viii., v. 30—35.

‡‡ גבעת האלהים. First Book of Samuel, ch. x., v. 5 and following; Second Book of Samuel, ch. xxi., v. 6.

the various phases of agricultural life. The sowing in
spring, the harvest, the grape-gathering, the shearing
of sheep, furnished occasions for meeting and for
amusement,* in which religion, as throughout all
antiquity, had its place. The offerings were free, each
one brought what he could, beasts from his herds,
loaves of bread, skins of wine or of milk.† People
ordinarily went to the most revered sanctuaries to
celebrate these festivals, which resembled pilgrimages
without any established rules being observed.

Religion was, so to speak, personal. Each family
had its sacred anniversaries. The new moons were
accompanied by the ringing of bells and by feasting,
and the feast was always preceded by a sacrifice.‡
Nothing bore a greater resemblance to free worship,
such as it has been represented by the author of the
Book of Job.§ Each family had its household gods or
teraphim, which were like large wooden spatula, rudely
sculptured, and which, dressed out in woollen blankets,
had the appearance of men or rather of busts.‖ All
religions had nearly the same external forms and the
same rules, especially as regarded the state of *qods*, or
purity necessary for observing them. Several precepts, which were afterwards supposed to have been

---

* First Book of Samuel, ch. xxv., v. 2; Second Book of Samuel,
ch. xiii., v. 23 and following.

† First Book of Samuel, ch. x., v. 3.

‡ First Book of Samuel, ch. xx., v. 5, 18, 24.

§ Job, ch. i. See parallel passages First Book of Samuel, ch.
xx. and xxi.

‖ First Book of Samuel, ch. xix., v. 13.

THE JUDGES.

revealed to Moses, existed at that time. Nob, for instance, just to the north of Jerusalem, was the centre of a little Levite worship which greatly resembled that which was consecrated at Jerusalem. All this was anterior to the arrival of the Israelites in Canaan, and constituted that old religious stock in trade to a certain extent indigenous to the region, which survives all reforms, and which never changes.

Although definitively established on the soil Israel in reality continued to lead a nomad life. The family was the only group which existed. What distinguished the nomad tribes from those which had been nomad was their hatred for central government. Not alone did the Israelite nation, as a body, fail to recognise any federal authority, but each tribe lived in a sort of anarchy, very much resembling the condition of the Arab tribes of to-day, where the life and the property of the individual are sufficiently protected by the solidarity of the members of the tribe, although there was hardly anything to represent the public weal.

Judah had its chiefs. Ephraim had its chiefs. Every tribe had a principal or central point. The *sarsaba*, or chief of the army, the *sofer*,[*] or recruiter, had only temporary powers. The military organisation, so powerful at the time of the passage of the Arnon and of the Jordan, had evidently dwindled away. The armament was poor, the war-horse had not yet been

[*] Song of Deborah, Judges, ch. v., v. 14; Second Book of Kings, ch. xxv., v. 19.

imported from Egypt, the chariots of iron were wanting.

It was not that the activity of the race was not always intense. It spent itself in conquests by detail. Very prolific, the children of Israel spread like a drop of oil; they gained every day on the Canaanites by their power of procreation. But the military qualities which the people possessed, from the time they left Egypt until the end of the epoch which, rightly or wrongly, passes under the name of Joshua, had nearly entirely disappeared.

In presence of unfriendly neighbours a nation thus unprovided with institutions could not fail to experience reverses. The Philistines especially, a little warlike and feudal people, cantoned in five or six very strong places, Gaza, Asdod, Ascalon, Gath, Ekron, were very dangerous neighbours for peaceful Israel. When the tribes of Israel found themselves too hotly pressed they had recourse to temporary federations, which produced for the moment military unity. The transitory chief, designated by a kind of secret inspiration by Iahveh, was called *sofet*, "Judge." This was the name which the Canaanite towns, which had no royal race, gave to their consuls.* The Hebrew *sofet* resembled in every way the Roman dictator. Only the theocratic idea which is at the bottom of all the institutions of the Semitic people attributed a

---

* Suffetes (magistratis) of Carthage. See *Corpus inscr. semit.*, part i., t. i., Nos. 124, 132, 143, 165, 176, 199--228, 278, 367—371, especially 302.

religious character to this chief magistrate. The *sofet* was at once the chief elected by God and the inspired prophet. His authority was absolute, and, as always happens in the East, was shared by his family. But the necessity of centralisation was not sufficiently felt to lead to the creation of an hereditary power.*
Israel † retained this trace of its Bedouin origin in not tolerating any durable power. Family life, without any fixed government, was always its ideal.

Authority is generally regarded by the Arab as a vexatious tie upon his actions, and he desires to have the least possible of it, because he does not know how to moderate it, and because he does not see what good it does the community. Where such a state of mind exists powers are of short duration, but as long as they last they are cruel, terrible. The judge, during his magistracy, was a tyrant without a standing army or an organised government. Limited power, even in its principle, has never been understood in the East. The *sofet* was a very feeble sovereign, but the powers he possessed he could exercise in an absolute manner. A constitutional sovereign possesses more extensive powers, but cannot exercise them in an absolute manner.

These governors formed an almost uninterrupted

---

* It is remarkable that in the very ancient list of the kings of Edom contained in Genesis, ch. xxxvi., no king is the son of his predecessor.

† Especially Israel of the north, the true Israel.

chain,* they required only succession from father to son to form a real dynasty. One cannot understand this phenomenon of "spontaneous emergency" until one has studied the manner in which a man is elected among the Arabs to play the part of commander. This election is due neither to descent, nor to suffrage, nor to investiture derived from an overlord, nor to violence. It is accomplished by a kind of indication due to the superiority of the man— to his ascendency, to his strength, and to his courage in war. It was very rare for a man thus invested with a power due to peculiar circumstances to be deprived of it before his death.†

Writing was not yet common among the Israelites; there was no sort of order in their affairs or administration. Even the traditions are very indistinct. The memory of a nation as regards history is always very short. It is a general rule of criticism that there exists no history properly so called before writing. People remember only fables. The myth is the history of a time when people could not write. Endowed with little talent for inventing mythological creations, the Israelites made up for it, as the Hebrews in the age of the patriarchs, by *anepigraphical* monuments, heaps of witness, piles of stones, destined to serve as information for the future. The names

* The chronology, taken from the Book of Judges, is very doubtful, and is in contradiction with the First Book of Kings, ch. vi., v. 1.

† I do not, of course, speak of agitators like the Mahdis, who resemble prophets and not the *sofetim*.

THE JUDGES.

given to certain places, to certain long-lived trees, like the pine, were also *oth* (signs) or *monimenta* after their manner. Certain customs also had the reputation of aiding the memory and of keeping alive recollections. But all this was very vague, and led to confusion.

The popular songs constituted a much more substantial testimony. In the same degree, in fact, that a nation is incapable of retaining any precise facts like those which history loves, in like degree its memory was apt, before the age of writing,* to retain rhyme and song. It was thus that each Arab tribe, without the aid of writing, formerly preserved the whole Divan of its poetry; it is thus that the ante-Islamite Arab memory, appealed to in vain for any precise bit of historical information, preserved, until the men of letters arrived from Bagdad a hundred and fifty years after Mahomet, the enormous poetical treasures of the *Kitab el-Aghâni*, of the *Moallakât*, and other poems of the same kind. The Touareg tribes of the present day furnish phenomena of the same description.†

Israel thus possessed a very fine unwritten literature, as Greece retained, during three or four hundred years, the whole Homeric cycle in its memory. One may say, in fact, that the unwritten literature of each race is the best which it has produced. Studied compositions never equal spontaneous literary productions.

* Plato, *Phædo*, 59.
† Hanoteau, *Gramm. Tamachek*, Paris, 1860; *Poésies populaires de la Kabylie du Jurjura*, Paris, 1867.

At a later date these songs, committed to writing, proved the pearl of Hebrew poetry, as the old Arab songs formed the really original portion of Arab literature. The finest pages of the Bible came from the lips of women and children who, after each victory, received the conqueror with cries of joy and to the sound of the timbrel.

CHAPTER VIII.

DEBORAH.

EPIC tradition placed in these early times the invasion of the King of Mesopotamia, *Cusan Riseataïm*,[*] who subdued Israel. A certain Othoniel, nephew of the legendary Caleb,[†] is said to have delivered the people of Iahveh.[‡] All this episode is plunged in the region of fable.

The story of a very early collision between Israel and Moab appears to be much more authentic. Eglon, King of Moab, seems to have rendered Israel tributary. An enterprising man of the tribe of Benjamin, named Ehoud, of the warlike family of Gero, killed Eglon by surprise; then, at the head of the Benjamites and the Ephraimites, beat the Moabites at the ford of the Jordan, near Gilgal.[§]

A certain Samgar, son of Anat,[||] was *sofet* during a period disturbed by the Philistines. People attributed to him fabulous exploits resembling those of

---
[*] The meaning of these words is not clear.
[†] See p. 205.
[‡] Judges, ch. iii., v. 7—12.
[§] Judges, ch. iii., v. 12—80.
[||] Judges, ch. iii., v. 81; ch. v., v. 6.

the mythical Samson, exploits which perhaps had their origin in a popular song no longer extant.*

Jabin, the Canaanite King of Hazor, bitterly oppressed the Israelitish tribes of the north.† Hazor ‡ was the centre of a tolerably powerful Canaanite state, embracing all the southern portion of Lake Houlé, which then, as to-day, is dry during a portion of the year. These plains were propitious for the use of armour-clad chariots. It appears that Jabin had nine hundred of these formidable engines. His power extended over the plain of Jezrael, where the effect of these chariots was more terrible still. His *sar-saba*, or general-in-chief, Sisera, appears to have been a skilful man of war. He was the lord of a powerful fief which the Israelites called *Harosethaggoïm*. Perhaps even he became the successor of Jabin.§

Now there was a prophetess called Deborah who judged Israel in those days. The position of women in the patriarchal tribes was not at all what it afterwards became, when life in the harem, dating from Solomon, had entirely debased morality. An alleged sister of Moses, named Miriam, assumed at that period,

---

* Judges, ch. iii., v. 31. The words איש במלמד הבקר שש מאות appear to be the second part of a distich in which was hyperbolically related the triumph of a simple agriculturist over Philistine warriors.

† Judges, ch. iv., v. 2 and following; Joshua, ch. xi., v. 1 and following.

‡ The site of Hazor is uncertain.

§ There is no mention of Jabin in the Song of Deborah.

in the legend of the flight from Egypt, a part the nature of which it is difficult to gather from the Scriptures, as they now read.* Some women were their own mistresses, disposing of their property, choosing their husbands, performing all the acts of a virile existence, comprising prophecy and poetry. It was the same among the Arabs. The stories told concerning the existence of the tribes before Islam mention several Deborahs, uniting the functions of chief and of poet. The anecdotes relative to these heroines formed an essential part in the epic cycle of the nation.† Islamism itself crowned with a halo Hind, the daughter of Otbah, who sang, at the head of a choir of women, at the battle of Ohod, and greatly contributed towards the victory of the believers.

The inspired daughter of Israel usually sat under a palm-tree, which was called the palm-tree of Deborah, between Ramah and Bethel, and the Israelites went to her to learn the judgment of God. The prophetess, like all the patriotic women, was devoted to the worship of Iahveh, and considered, it is said, as criminal, all religious innovations, all the leaning of the people towards the worship of Canaan.‡ Deborah

* Remark Micah, ch. vi., v. 4.

† Amrah, daughter of Amir, Hind, daughter of Khouss, Hind, daughter of Otbah, Sedjah, the prophetess of Moseilama [Barbier de Meynard].

‡ Song, especially v. 8. The lesson is very doubtful. After all this idea does not much exceed that expressed by the King of Meza in his inscription, lines 5, 6 : כי האנף כמש בארצה.

took in hand the deliverance of her people. She sent an order, in the name of Iahveh, to a certain Barak, son of Abinoam, of Kadish in Naphtali, to assemble the Naphtalites and the Zabulunites at Kadish and then to march upon Tabor. She herself arrived, bringing with her the men of Ephraim, of Benjamin, and of Manasseh this side of Jordan. The tribes beyond Jordan, although summoned, the maritime tribes of Dan and of Asher, did not move. Judah and Simeon were perhaps occupied for their own part in struggling against the Philistines.* Besides at this epoch they almost always formed a separate band.†

This great muster of the forces of Israel at the foot of Mount Tabor alarmed the Canaanites of the Upper Jordan and the Plain of Jezrael. Sisera hurried there with the troops of the kingdom of Hazor. Tanach and Megiddo, which were Canaanite towns, also took up arms against Israel.‡ It is probable that the army of Israel marched from Tabor on the rear of their adversaries. Sisera came to their rescue. The battle, in fact, was fought near the brook Kishon, close to Megiddo. Sisera was totally defeated. It seems that the heavy rain,§ which may have hampered the chariots and which swelled the streams of which the

* They are not mentioned in the Song.

† Remark the omission of the feats of Judah in the Book of Judges, the name of *Israel* claimed by the kingdom of the north after the schism, the absence of Judah and of Jerusalem in the inscription of Meza, &c.

‡ Song, ch. v., v. 19.

§ Song of Deborah.

Kishon is formed, was prejudicial to the retreat of the Canaanites.

Sisera endeavoured, with the remains of his army, to reach the north. The Israelites pursued him. The men of Meroz,* ill disposed towards Israel, favoured his flight; but the Israelites found allies in the Kenites who were encamped in the vicinity of Kadish.

These nomad Kenites, who since the flight from Egypt had always been on good terms with Israel, were also at peace with Jabin. But the desire of pleasing Barak carried the day, and it was a Kenite woman who procured for Iahveh what was most dear to him, the death of one of his enemies.

Sisera, running on foot, arrived at the door of a Kenite tent. The husband was absent; the wife, named Jael, invited the fugitive to enter, and concealed him with a mantle. Sisera asked for a little water. Jael opened a skin of milk and gave him to drink. Sisera being weary fell asleep. Then Jael took one of those large pegs used for pitching a tent, seized a hammer, and smote the peg into the temple of Sisera so deeply that it went through the temples and fastened them to the ground. Shortly afterwards Barak arrived and was much pleased at the sight.

Upon that day Deborah and Barak the son of Abinoam sang thus.†

This noble song, written by the prophetess, was

* To-day Marous, between Safed and Lake Houlé.
† Here M. Renan quotes the entire Song of Deborah, frequently quoted from already. [TRANSLATOR.]

learned by heart, and became a model which was imitated in other songs of the same kind. It was afterwards written out and inserted in the *Kitab el-Aghâni* of Israel. No doubt it then underwent a good many alterations. Some pietist reflections may have been added; several passages became obscure owing to the faults of the copyists; but the originality of the old Hebrew *sir* shines out still, through all these mutilations, with unparalleled splendour.

CHAPTER IX.

FIRST ATTEMPTS AT ROYALTY.
GIDEON, ABIMELECH.*

OWING to the love of order and laborious habits of Israel, a great number of rich and powerful families were formed; but on all sides the nation, like an undefended town, was open to attack. It was impossible to found anything solid. Israel had not only to fight against the Canaanites, the Philistines, the Moabites, the Ammonites, "the dwellers in tents," as they were called, the nomad Midianites and Amalekites, but to repel the invasions of the Arabs of the great desert, known by the generic name of Beni-Quedem or Orientals (Saracens), who came with their camels, especially after seed time, encamped in the open, and destroyed the growing crops, like a plague of locusts. They advanced as far as Gaza, where the Philistines stopped them; then they returned to the desert, carrying away with them all the flocks and beasts of burden.

These annual invasions kept the people in terror. They did not dare to fight in the open ground. When the pillagers arrived the Israelites barricaded

* Judges, ch. vi.—ix.

themselves in caverns or improvised fortresses in the mountains. From this epoch were supposed to date the fortified caverns and the *masada*, or hill tops covered with stones, which are so common in Palestine, and which on many occasions served the people of the plain as refuges against sudden invasion.

A family of Manasseh, consequently of Joseph, that of Abiezer, which resided at Ophra, to the west of Sichem, near the lower slopes of Ephraim, assumed in this sad state of affairs a great importance, and nearly gave Israel that dynasty which would have realised its unity. These Abiezrites were very fine men, heroes, like unto the sons of a king. They were not exclusive servants of Iahveh. They raised altars to Baal and to Asera; they reserved their Iahvehism for what appertained to Iahveh, the oracles of the ephod. In acting thus they probably believed that they were doing him no more harm than the Latins or the Hernici thought that they were offending the Fortuna of Præneste in honouring Jupiter of Latium or Neptune of Antium.

But Iahveh was always a jealous god; he would tolerate no rival. There was a kind of struggle in this important Israelite family between the various tendencies into which the conscience of Israel was divided. Joas, the chief of the family, had an altar to Baal, surmounted by a large Asera in wood. Every day he sacrificed a bull upon the altar.* His eldest son, a superb and vigorous man, a regular *gibbor*, was called

* Judges, ch. vi., v. 25, 26.

FIRST ATTEMPTS AT ROYALTY. 261

Jerubaal (one who feared Baal), and was at first devoted to the worship of that divinity. It must be remembered that Ophra was in the midst of the Canaanite tribes of the coast. The great body of the population of that place worshipped Baal and Asera. The religious confusion was extreme. The Baal-Berith of Sichem still held its own in those parts against Iahveh.*

Motives of which we are ignorant induced Jarubaal to adopt the exclusive worship of Iahveh. This conversion was afterwards attributed to a vision, and it is quite possible that in the case of Jerubaal, as in that related by Moses, there was some tangible fact. Jerubaal appears to have seen one of those apparitions of flame in which it was believed that Iahveh revealed himself. One day while he was threshing his corn to save it from the Midianites who were ravaging the country he thought that he beheld Iahveh (or the angel of Iahveh). When an apparition of this kind took place, the best thing to do was to offer a repast to the *Maleak* in order to appease his hunger.† Jerubaal prepared a kid and some unleavened bread, and having placed the flesh in a basket and the broth in a pot he carried them under the pine-tree and offered them to *Maleak*, who said to him, "Take the flesh and the cakes and place them upon this rock, and as for the gravy pour it out." Iahveh touched the meat and the cakes with the end of the rod which he held in his hand. Then the fire issued from the rock, devoured the meat and the cakes,

* Judges, ch. viii., v. 33; ch. ix., v. 27.
† See Abraham and his three guests, Genesis, ch. xviii.

and Iahveh disappeared.* Jerubaal understood that he had seen Iahveh, and was much frightened, for he believed that he was going to die, as this god could not be looked upon face to face. Iahveh reassured him, and Jerubaal built him an altar which he called *Iahveh-Salom*, which existed a long time at Ophrah.

From that moment Jerubaal became a fervent worshipper of Iahveh. Now Iahveh, as we have said, was a jealous god. He liked not the other gods, even the most patient. One night Jerubaal took ten of his servants with him and demolished the altar of Baal and the Asera which was on it. The next day there was a tumult in the town, and in the house of his father. They demanded from Joas the life of the person guilty of this sacrilege. Joas seems to have replied that it was the duty of the god himself to avenge the insult. However that may be, Jerubaal went over to the worship of Iahveh, and thenceforward took the name of Gideon. He raised an altar to Iahveh in the acropolis of Ophrah, and offered up a holocaust with the wood of the Asera which he had overturned. It appears that the Abiezrites followed his example to a certain extent.†

The worship of Iahveh was in some measure synonymous to patriotism. Converted to the exclusive worship of Iahveh, Gideon became, like Deborah, an ardent champion of Israel. Later on we shall see the unity of Israel definitively accomplished by David in

* Judges, ch. xiii., v. 20.
† Judges, ch. vi., v. 34.

the name of Iahveh. Every action on the part of the central power was accomplished in the name of Iahveh, and it was not without reason that the book of the victories of Israel was called "the book of the wars of Iahveh." An opportunity soon presented itself to Gideon to serve his new god in the way which he liked.

The Midianites, the Amalekites, and the Saracens invaded the plain of Jazrael, under the leadership of the two chiefs Zebah and Zalmunna.* They found at Tabor some Israelites of good family, whom they killed, and who were related to the Abiezrites. Gideon assembled the Abiezrites, sent messengers throughout Manasseh, received the auxiliaries of Asher, Zabulon, and Naphtali, and, encouraged by divers signs, which assured him that Iahveh was with him, encamped in the mountains of Gilboa, near Ain-Harod. The Midianites were opposite to him, at the foot of the little chain of Moreh, called to-day *Dgebel-Dahi*. Gideon succeeded in putting them to flight to the cry of "For Iahveh and for Gideon."

The Midianites, instead of returning over the Jordan at the place where they had crossed it a few days before, diverged to the south-east, towards Bath-Sean, then towards the south, following the Ghor as far as Abel-Mehola. Gideon saw that he had not enough men with him to pursue them. He made another appeal to the tribes of the north, and asked the Ephraimites, whom he had up to that time neglected, to join him, in order to

* These may be imaginary names, like *Oreb* and *Zeeb*.

cut off the Midianites from the fords of the Jordan. The Ephraimites responded to this appeal on the part of Gideon. On leaving Abel-Mehola the Midianites split up into two bands. One passed the Jordan, under the command of Zebah and Zalmunna. The other continued to descend the Ghor in quest of the fords of the south. The Ephraimites, going across toward the east, came up with this band near the lower Jordan, and destroyed it in two places, which they called "the rock of *Oreb*," or of the crow, "the wine-press of *Zeeb*," or the wolf. The popular legend afterwards saw in the two names, *Oreb* and *Zeeb*, the names of two Midianite chiefs who had been slain at that place.

Gideon, however, with his vigorous Abiezrites, passed the Jordan on the heels of Zebah and Zalmunna, and plunged into the valley of Jabbok. The Gadites of Succoth and of Penuel ought to have aided him. They did nothing. They even refused to furnish the Abiezrites with bread. The Israelites beyond Jordan possessed little patriotism, or rather they were held in check by fear of the Bedouins. They refused to compromise themselves with dangerous neighbours against whom the tribes of the west could not always protect them. Gideon pursued the Bedouins as far as the road called "the dwellers of the tents," which passed to the east of Nobah and Jogbehah. He beat them at Qarqor, then he pursued them and captured the two kings, Zebah and Zalmunna. "What manner of men were those whom you killed at Tabor?" asked he of Zebah and Zalmunna. "Men like you," they replied; "all were fine men, like a king's sons." And Gideon said, "They were my brothers, the sons of my mother. As Jehovah liveth, if you had not slain them, I would not have killed you." And Gideon said to Jether, his first-born, "Arise and slay them!"

The young man hesitating to kill such heroes, Zebah and Zalmunna said to Gideon, "Rise thou and fall upon us, for as the man is, so is his strength." And Gideon arose and slew Zebah and Zalmunna, and he took the ornaments that were on their camels' necks. Returning by way of Penuel and Succoth, he cruelly punished the men of those two cities for their conduct when he had passed that way the first time.

The return of Gideon to this side of Jordan was a triumph. His height, his beauty, his strength proclaimed him a king. The raid he had made with the Abiezrites into the very heart of the Arab tribes of the east had procured treasures for him. All the Arab tribes known under the name of Ismaelim* had greatly enriched themselves by commerce. The plunder captured from them astonished the poor and laborious tribes of Israel. There were heaps of golden rings (*nezm*), collars and crescents for the necks of the camels, earrings formed of a single pearl, rich purple garments for their kings. Gideon took a large part of the booty for himself, the Abiezrites had the rest. The Ephraimites, on the contrary, displayed jealousy; Gideon had not called upon them until late. They were charged with the least advantageous duty of the

* Judges, ch. viii., v. 24.

campaign, that of pursuing the Midianite stragglers who had been unable to repass the Jordan. They took no part in the pillage of the great encampments of the East. Gideon soothed them with soft words and flattered their vanity. "The gleaning of the grapes of Ephraim," he said, "is worth more than the vintage of Abiezer."

This campaign of Gideon was one of extreme importance. The songs composed on this subject have not been preserved, but there was woven round it a legend which has come down to us and which can be compared with the finest episodes of the Greek *epos*.* A dream was related which was held to be symbolical. A cake of barley bread tumbled into the host of Midian, and came unto a tent, and smote it that it fell, and overturned it, that the tent lay along.† The cake of barley bread was the Israelite agriculturist, already settled on the soil, managing, in spite of his poverty, to destroy the nomads who invaded his land. The victory of Gideon was, in fact, a capital event in the history of Syrian Semitism. The Hebrew settler eventually subdued those of his race who had continued the same mode of life which he himself had long led. Midianites, Amalekites, Ishmaelites, and Beni-Quedem, were confined to their deserts to the east and to the south of Palestine. The sedentary tribes managed to defend themselves on their own soil, even when they had not, like the Israelites, any permanent central power.

Gideon appeared to be quite marked out to give to

* The chapters vi., vii., viii. of the Book of Judges have an epic character all their own.

† Judges, ch. vii., v. 13.

FIRST ATTEMPTS AT ROYALTY.

Israel what it required in this respect. He was tall, robust, courageous. The campaign against the Midianites of the eastern desert had made him rich, and had procured him royal garments. He possessed a numerous seraglio at Ophrah, and Canaanite concubines in several places, notably at Sichem.* It was reckoned that he had as many as seventy sons.

Gideon seemed therefore fated to achieve what David did afterwards; to create upon the one hand monarchical unity and a legitimate dynasty in Israel, and on the other hand to fuse the Canaanites and the Israelites into a single race. But the worship of Iahveh was at no epoch favourable to a royal form of government.† The system of the *sofetim*, taken from the crowd by popular designation equivalent to the choice of Iahveh, was much more in conformity with the spirit of that religion. Gideon replied to all the demands that he should accept the title of hereditary King of Israel, "It is Iahveh who reigns over you." He, perhaps, perceived in time the difficulties which afterwards revealed themselves to the unfortunate Saul. It appears that upon this point the text of the Book of Judges is intentionally obscure. The exalted idea of theocracy which it ascribes to Gideon scarcely corresponds with the extreme coarseness which he imported into his new religion. The Iahvehism of Gideon seems to have consisted for the most part in the superstitious practices of the ephod. Now these practices had little to do with the

* Judges, ch. viii., v. 31.
† First Book of Samuel, ch. viii.

principles of puritans and theocrats who had sworn hatred to royalty.

Gideon was neither above nor below the religious ideas of his time, and several of his acts which appeared scandalous afterwards were found quite natural in his epoch. He wished to employ in a pious work a portion of the money which he had gained during his expedition, and he had an ephod cast with the gold, that is to say an image of Iahveh, which could be used for delivering oracles. This ephod, set up at Ophrah, had a great vogue; all Israel flocked thither in pilgrimage and for consultation.

This was a crime in the eyes of the most recent Iahvehists, who held that Iahveh could be worshipped in one place alone, and that no material image should be made to represent him. But Gideon certainly did not believe that he was offending Iahveh when he cast in his honour a symbol of gold like that which was contained in the ark. There were many other ephods of this kind belonging to private individuals.*
The idea of unity of worship did not exist at that epoch. The ark was at Bethel or at Shiloh, that is to say, at a considerable distance from Ophrah and among rival tribes. Gideon was not, perhaps, so exempt from dynastic ambition as more modern historians wish to make out. He may have dreamed of creating round him a religious centre which would have been entirely under his control. We shall see

* The deed of Gideon is not in any way related as an isolated crime.

Jeroboam do the same thing, in an age when the ideas of centralisation were more advanced. The severity of the sacred historian comes from the fact that he had judged Gideon by the rules of another epoch. The Iahveh of Gideon, however, bore no resemblance to the Iahveh whose worship afterwards prevailed. It was a sacrament of gold, worked by a mechanical contrivance; it was above all a machine with which a great deal of money was made. The pilgrims, in fact, paid for an answer. It greatly increased the wealth of Gideon.

His contemporaries did not blame him for constructing his ephod. He lived happily, died at a very great age, and was buried in the tomb of his father Joash at Ophrah.

Gideon had so truly exercised, among the Josephites of Manasseh and Ephraim, an almost royal power, that his succession was disputed after his death as if he had been a king. His numerous family claimed to exercise, at Ophrah, the supremacy which the *sofet* of Manasseh had conquered. This soon produced opposition. A bastard named Abimelech, a son of Gideon by a Canaanite woman, who lived at Sichem, assumed a hostile attitude towards his brothers of Ophrah. A Canaanite and a Sichemite on his mother's side, he became the champion of the pretensions of Sichem and the tribe of Ephraim against the Abiezerites of Ophrah. The Sichemites gave him the money of the temple of Baal-Berith, whose rites he probably professed. With this money Abimelech raised a band of idle scamps, ready for anything, who swore to live or die in his service. The first crime which he caused them to commit was aimed at his half-brothers of Ophrah. It is said that they were all slain with the exception of Jotham, who succeeded in hiding himself.

Sichem was a mixed town, Israelite and Canaanite at the same time. Abimelech was, in a way, just the man to be popular there. His name indicated that he was devoted to the religion of Milik or Moloch, which shows at least a great amount of eclecticism. The two populations agreed to make him king. This royalty, which lasted for three years, remained almost exclusively Ephraimite, and was always disputed, even at Sichem. The survivors of the family of Gideon never ceased to proclaim the unworthiness of Abimelech, and to excite public opinion against this sham royalty. Here is the discourse which the old historian places in the mouth of Jotham:—"Harken unto me, ye men of Sichem, that God may harken to you. The trees went forth on a time to anoint a king over them: and they said unto the olive-tree, Reign thou over us. But the olive-tree said unto them, Should I leave my fatness, wherewith by me they honour God and man, and go to be promoted over the other trees? And the trees said to the fig-tree, Come thou and reign over us. But the fig-tree said unto them, Should I forsake my sweetness and my good fruit, and go to be promoted over the trees? Then said the trees unto the vine, Come thou and reign over us. And the vine said unto them, Should I leave my wine, which cheereth God and man, and go to be promoted over the trees? Then said all the trees unto the bramble, Come thou and reign over us. And the bramble said unto the trees, If in truth you anoint me king over you, then come and put your trust in my shadow; and if not let fire come out of the bramble, and devour the cedars of Lebanon."

This was equivalent to saying that really useful people avoid the task of governing men, and that those alone do not hesitate to undertake the burden who have nothing in them, and who believe that they can escape from all difficulty by vain boasting. The hostile allusion to Abimelech was transparent. As a matter of fact that wretched improvised royalty rapidly fell into disrepute. The bandits of Abimelech began to practise robbery in the mountains, nor could Abimelech hinder them. The Sichemites grew disaffected. In the feasts which took place at the temple of Baal-Berith, after the sacrifices they denounced Abimelech. He left the city in order to settle at Aruma, two leagues from there, to the south-west, leaving behind him as his lieutenant a man called Zeboul. A certain Gaal, son of Ebed, a stranger but of great influence, placed himself at the head of the opposition, and dared to do battle with Abimelech. Abimelech defeated him, and took the lower town of Sichem, upon which he revenged himself cruelly. The dwellers in the upper town, to the number of a thousand men and women, took refuge in the cellars of the temple of

Baal-Berith; Abimelech caused the cellars to be covered with green branches, set them on fire, and smothered all who were within.

He then marched against Thebez, four leagues from Sichem, towards the north. The inhabitants withdrew into the fortified place in the middle of the town. Huddled together on the roofs, they awaited their fate with anxiety. Abimelech approached the gate to set it on fire. A woman then flung the upper part of a millstone on his head and broke his skull. Abimelech called his armour-bearer and said, "Draw thy sword and slay me, that men say not of me, A woman slew him." So ended this first and not very well-sustained endeavour to create a stable power in Israel. The incapacity of Abimelech was the main cause of its failure. One hundred and fifty or two hundred years afterwards a man arose who combined the warlike heroism of Gideon and the boldness of his religious policy with the wickedness of Abimelech and his talent for surrounding himself with bandits. David was destined to prove a cleverer and more fortunate Abimelech. Jerusalem was to accomplish what Sichem could not do. Judah was to succeed where Joseph failed.

CHAPTER X.

GILEADITE LEGENDS.—JEPHTHAH.

THE tribes beyond Jordan, who were the first established, at an epoch when the idea of a common god for all Israel hardly existed, and who had, moreover, little to unite them with the rest of Israel, were more anxious than any of the others to have a special religion. The Iahvehists of the west accused them of not belonging to the religion of the rest of Israel.* The fact is that these tribes had, beyond Jordan,† an altar of their own which the puritans afterwards imputed to them as a crime. It was probably the old *Gilead* (heap of witness)‡ upon which they had offered up sacrifices, libations, and feasts of alliance from the most remote antiquity. This ancient holy place was probably that which was called *Mispa*, or *Mispé-Gilead*, or *Ramot Mispé*, or *Ramot Gilead*. There solemn oaths were taken. It was the religious capital of Trans-Jordan.§

* Joshua, ch. xxii.
† Joshua, ch. xxii., v. 10, 11.
‡ Joshua, ch. xxii., v. 34.
§ Judges, ch. x., v. 17; ch. xi., v. 11, 29, 34. See Hebrew dictionary, word *Ramoth*. Note specially Judges, ch. xi., v. 11:

The vast territory of the eastern half-tribe of Manasseh, that is to say of Bashan, was peopled slowly. This country possessed in reality no civilisation before the first century of our era.* Here the great coloniser was Jair, of the tribe of Manasseh, concerning whom tradition varies in a singular manner. Some make him out to be a contemporary of Moses, others give him rank among the Judges. What they called *Havvoth Iaïr*, "towns of Jair," corresponded to the Gaulonitide country east of Lake Genesareth.† It was a matter of doubt whether Jair was a real person or a geographical term. The legend or play upon words came in here. These cities, thirty in number (sometimes there were twenty-three and sometimes sixty), became thirty sons of Jair, possessing thirty towns (*aïárim* instead of the ordinary form árim). These thirty *aïárim* became thirty young asses (*aïárim*), and the legend spoke of thirty sons of Jair mounted on thirty asses. There were no war horses or riding horses in those days, and asses were looked upon as very fit animals to ride.

The most celebrated of the legendary heroes of Gilead was Jephthah. He was a bandit, and according to some the son of a prostitute, according to others of a concubine, and consequently not in a condition to

במצפה לפני יהוה. Ramoth-Gilead was situated near where we see the ruins of Gadare to-day.

* Waddington, *Inscr. grecques et lat. de Syrie*, No. 2329.

† First Book of Kings, ch. iv., v. 13; First Book of Chronicles, ch. ii., v. 21—23; Judges, ch. x., v. 3—5.

share the inheritance with the sons of his father. It will be remembered that such was also the case with Abimelech, and perhaps with David.* Solomon himself was a natural son. People had a tendency to suppose that there was some irregularity in the geneaology of great men;† this rendered their good fortune all the more striking. It has been the natural tendency of all ages to make out that their heroes were adventurers. Besides, Israel, even in its heroic legend, did not show itself imbued with a military feeling. The ideal warrior was not the regular head of the family, an eldest son destined to succeed his father; an illegitimate son was supposed to inherit more of the heroism of the race than the legitimate sons. The military hero was in general an outcast, forced to consort with vagabonds on account of being driven out of doors by his family. The antagonism which reigned between peace-loving Israel and the professional soldier began to show itself in this way.

Driven out by his brothers, Jephthah settled in the land of Tob, where he became the chief of a band of adventurers living on plunder. The land of Tob was the Ledja, that is to say that bed of lava of the mountain of Hor forming an almost equilateral triangle, thirteen leagues each side, the recesses of which have always served as a refuge for outlaws.‡ The bandit enjoys his revenge when he is appealed to for

* According to some he was descended from a poor Moabite, and to others from Rahab the harlot.
† See the clever remarks of St. Jerome on Matthew, ch. i., v. 5.
‡ It is the same in our day.

help in the hour of danger. The Ammonites unceasingly threatened the Israelites of Gideon and of Bashan. It even appears that the enemy often passed the Jordan and beat the tribes of the west. An unusually fierce attack compelled the Gileadites to appeal to Jephthah, who was leading the life of a brigand in Ledja. It is said that they promised him the sovereignty if he would deliver them from their enemies. Jephthah, in fact, gained the victory and drove the Ammonites out of all the cities of Manasseh, Gad, and Reuben, which they had occupied.

The popular songs of the time attributed to this war an episode which gained a great celebrity among the tribes, and gave rise to a good deal of poetry.* "And Jephthah vowed a vow unto the Lord and said, If thou shalt without fail deliver the children of Ammon into mine hands, then shall it be that whatsoever cometh forth of the doors of my house to meet me, when I return in peace from the children of Ammon, shall surely be the Lord's, and I will offer it up for a burnt offering." And after the victory Jephthah came back from Mispeh to his house, and his daughter came out to meet him with timbrels and with dances. Now she was an only daughter; an only child. When he saw her he rent his garments and said, "Alas! my daughter, canst thou be the cause of my sadness. I have opened my mouth to Iahveh and I cannot go back." And she said to him, "My father, if thou hast opened thy mouth to Iahveh,

---

* Judges, ch. xi., v. 30 and following.

GILEADITE LEGENDS.—JEPHTHAH.

do with me according to that which has proceeded out of thy mouth; forasmuch as Iahveh has taken vengeance for thee of thine enemies, even of the children of Ammon." And she added, "Grant me this: let me alone two months that I may go up and down upon the mountains and bewail my virginity, I and my fellows." And he said, Go; and he sent her away for two months, and she went with her companions and bewailed her virginity upon the mountains. And it came to pass that at the end of two months that she returned unto her father who did with her according to his vow which he had vowed: and she knew no man. And it was a custom in Israel that the daughters of Israel went yearly to lament the daughter of Jephthah the Gileadite, four days in the year.

These ballads, annually renewed, celebrated the traditional incident on every occasion with new rites more and more dramatic.* The narrative which has been handed down to us by the Book of Judges is one of the best arranged versions. The truth probably is that Jephthah, before undertaking a difficult war, sacrificed one of his daughters according to the barbarous custom put in practice on solemn occasions when the country was in danger.† Patriarchal deism had condemned these immolations: Iahvehism, with its exclusively national principle, was rather favourable to them. Not many human sacrifices were

---

* Compare the annual *agadas* upon the Passover among the Jews and the Persian *Téaziés*, &c.

† Second Book of Kings, ch. iii., v. 27.

offered to God nor to the *elohim*. The gods whom they thought to propitiate by means of human sacrifices were the patriot gods, Camos of the Moabites, Iahveh of the Israelites, Moloch of the Canaanites, Melqarth of Carthage.

> Tantum gentis amor potuit suadere malorum.

The daughter of Jephthah was probably not the only victim offered up to Iahveh before he became more lenient in the eighth century. Besides, it would be impossible to say, at this distance of time, to what extent Iahveh reigned in the hidden recesses of Israel. The narrative of the Book of Judges represents Jephthah as a servant of Iahveh. Possibly this was so, but if it had been otherwise the writer would not have held different language, his preconceived system being that no victory could have been gained by Israel without the aid of Iahveh. In fact, these distinctions, so capital for us, were then rather frivolous. If we could ask Jephthah whether he had sacrificed his daughter to Iahveh, to Baal, or to Milik, he would perhaps have found it difficult to answer.

Iahveh, indeed, became more and more synonymous with Israel. It was a maxim that the national god should not be distinguished from the nation.* What each nation possessed was what had been given to it by its god. The narrator of Judges makes Jephthah thus speak to the King of Ammon, " Wilt thou not possess

* Inscr. de Mesa, line 12.

that which Camos, thy god,* giveth thee to possess?†
Whomsoever Iahveh shall drive out before us, them
will we possess." This phrase rightly expresses the
low idea which the national spirit of those little
tribes had led them to form of the divinity. To
despoil the original occupants who had cultivated the
soil, in order to hand over the land to new-comers,
objects of an undeserved preference, appeared fair
play. In this donation of the god they saw a
definitive title. How much greater, more just, and
better was the god of the nomad who possessed no
land!

The success of Jephthah excited the jealousy of the
Ephraimites, as that of Gideon had already done.
They complained that they had not been called to the
war against the Ammonites, while it appears that it
was they themselves who held aloof in the hour of
danger. The Ephraimites invaded Gilead, probably
close to Mispeh, and wished to burn the house of
Jephthah; but Jephthah completely routed them.
The Gileadites occupied the fords of the Jordan, and
when an Ephraimite presented himself to pass made
him pronounce the word *Shibboleth*. The Ephraimites
in fact pronounced the *chuintante* like a common "s"
just as the Arabs do. Those who said *Sibboleth* were
slain without pity.

Jephthah after this victory exercised a certain

* Slight inadvertence of the writer, Camos being the god of Moab.
† Judges, ch. xi., v. 24.

amount of authority over Israel. But he was only a soldier; he had no family or posterity. He did nothing to make his power last after him.

The ancient lists of the Judges had been formed by placing one after the other the names of the oldest and most eminent men who were remembered.* After Jephthah came Ibsan of Bethlehem.† "He had thirty sons and thirty daughters, whom he sent abroad, and he took in thirty daughters for his sons." ‡ Abdon, the son of Hillel, had forty sons and thirty grandsons, and they rode upon seventy asses.§ He was buried at Pirathon, in Ephraim, in the mount of the Amalekites. These lists, full of repetitions, have all the appearance of having been learnt by heart, while to aid the memory no scruple was made about resorting to the childish device of alliteration and punning.‖

* Judges, ch. xii. The sub-titles of tribes, such as Jaïr, Tola, &c., were sometimes used.

† There can be no connection between this and the greater Bethlehem, Judah being scarcely mentioned in the Book of Judges.

‡ Judges, ch. xii., v. 8 and following.

§ See above, p. 274.

‖ For instance, אילון buried at אילון, &c.

CHAPTER XI.

THE DANITES.—MYTH OF SAMSON.

THE combats against the Canaanites of Hazor, against the Ammonites, against the Midianites were sharp but short. The struggle with the Philistines was continuous. That energetic little band of Pelasgians in all probability* came from Crete, and was a redoubtable neighbour for Dan and for Judah.

Dan especially bore the wounds of this sword driven into the flesh of Israel with astonishing courage. Entrenched in a few strong places situated between Jerusalem and the sea, the Danites were merely encamped in the country. It was the least solidly established of all the tribes. It had hardly shaken off its nomad existence. Its chief resort was the *mahané* or camp situated generally between Zorah and Estaol, but sometimes elsewhere. A *mahané* of this kind was to be seen to the west of Kirjath-Jearim.† The Danites appear to have been accomplished brigands; war was their habitual occupation. The land round Zorah and Estaol was a kind of battlefield for the Philistines and the Israelites; the two races were brought into

* Genesis, ch. x., v. 14 ; Amos, ch. ix., v. 7 and following.
† Judges, ch. xiii., v. 25 ; ch. xviii., v. 11 and following.

such close contact at this point that sanguinary conflicts between them were inevitable.

This really epic state of affairs, which lasted several centuries, produced a cycle of stories a portion of which alone has come down to us singularly transformed.* A fable was woven round the exploits of a certain man called Samson, the son of Manoah, of Zorah, a warrior of the tribe of Dan, of extraordinary strength. He took the gates of a city on his back and carried them several miles. He threw down a building by laying hold of two pillars and shaking them. He passed his life in fighting against the Philistines of his district, in performing feats of strength, in riddles, in stratagems. There were episodes to excite astonishment and episodes to excite shouts of laughter. His strength lay in the hair which covered his head. He was weak where women were concerned, and each act of treachery on their part found him defenceless. A Philistine woman put him to sleep on her knees and cut off his hair. Made a slave and the sport of the Philistines, he ended by killing them and himself with them.

All this was related with numerous details which charmed the listener. Samson was for centuries the Antar of the Israelites. Afterwards when it became a question of inserting the story in Holy Writ, a story in many respects little edifying, it was touched up in an extraordinary way. The burlesque hero of Dan was transformed into a respectable judge

* Judges, ch. xiv., xv., xvi.

THE DANITES—MYTH OF SAMSON.

of Israel. It was announced that Samson like all providential men was born of a barren woman. The fact, originally of a naturalist order, as to his strength lying in his hair was explained by a vow. Samson was supposed to have been *nazir*. According to the vow no razor was to shave his head. Through the devices of Dalilah the vow was broken, and the compact between Iahveh and his Hercules came to an end.

The scene of the whole epic of Samson is laid in the vicinity of a small place called Beth-Semes, or Ir-Semes,* or Har-Heres, about six leagues from Jerusalem.† The worship of the sun, *Semes*, which was the local worship of that country, together with the name of Samson (diminutive, like *soliculus*, sun), gave birth to surmises which must be taken into account, though too much importance may easily be attached to them.‡ The ancient Hebrews had no taste for pure mythology. But they were not above transforming figurative creations ill understood into heroic anecdotes. Let us suppose in the temple of Beth-Semes the picture of the sun in the shape of a head surrounded by rays: this picture may well have been considered as the head of a warrior, whose strength lay in his locks (his rays);§ all the more so as the

---

* Equivalent to Heliopolis.

† See Robinson, ii., pp. 324, 325.

‡ The name שמשון can very well come from the root שמם
ὁ ἰσχυρός (*Josephus*).

§ See curious heads of hair drawn by Doughty, *Doc. épigr. recueillis dans l'Arabie du Nord*, pl. xli.

sun was often compared to a warrior.* The Philistines (Carian and Pelasgian) may well have introduced the solar myths and those of Heracles; but in order to establish a parallel between the arid legends of Israel and the mythological creations *à priori* of the Aryans, it would be necessary to have some more striking resemblance.

The neighbourhood of the Philistines made the situation of the tribe of Dan intolerable.† The Phœnicians of Jaffa, on the other side, prevented them from possessing the fertile plain along the sea-coast. The people of Zorah and Estaol decided upon emigrating. They sent spies to study the general situation of the country of Canaan, and to find some weak tribe whose territory it would be possible to seize upon. The Danite spies found what they were looking for at Laish,‡ situated on the slopes of Mount Hermon, in the midst of streams descending from the Panium. They there discovered a peaceable population living like the Sidonians,§ that is to say, by their labour, and not dreaming of war. There was no king in the neighbourhood to lend them aid,‖ and the Sidonians, their congeners and their allies, could not defend them. The distance from Laish to Sidon in a straight line was not great, but the almost impassable region of the

* Psalm xix., v. 6.

† Judges, ch. i., v. 34, and following; ch. xviii., v. 1; Joshua, ch. xviii., v. 8, 47 and following.

‡ To-day, Tell-el-Kadi.

§ Judges, ch. xviii., v. 7.

‖ I thus understand the altered passage, v. 7: עצר for עזר. Remark the form of the ע in the inscription of Siloah.

THE DANITES—MYTH OF SAMSON.

Litani lay between the two cities. The spies at once considered the fertile land of Laish as belonging to their fellow-countrymen. An oracle of Iahveh which they went to consult confirmed them in this opinion. The details of this curious consultation are recounted at length in a page which may be considered as the most precious sketch of the morality of that distant epoch.*

There dwelt in the mountains of Ephraim a man named Micah, a name which indicates a special devotion to Iahveh.† The Iahvehism of Micah appears to have resembled that of Gideon. Like Gideon, Micah had in his house an oracle of Iahveh which brought a good deal of custom. His enemies, either then or later, spread the report that the images were made with money which had been stolen, and, what is worse, with money stolen by a son from his mother, with silver labouring under the maternal curse. However that may be, Micah had in his house an ephod and a teraphim ‡ in wood and in metal, that is to say, a complete "house of God" like that of Shiloh.

It was necessary to have a priest for this temple. For this Micah first ordained one of his sons, but he soon conceived scruples. It was, in fact, understood that divine service could be performed only by one of those persons, belonging to no tribe, who wandered among the Israelites, and who were called Levites.

* Judges, ch. xviii., v. 13 and following.

† If this name be not altered, the meaning is "Who is like Iahveh?" Remark also the Iahvehist theophore names in the family of Gideon.

‡ This word is used in the singular, First Book of Samuel, ch. xix., v. 13, 16.

One day one of these Levites passed through the village where Micah dwelt. He was a young man of Bethlehem of Judah. Like all the Levites, he was attached to a tribe, but he was almost a stranger to it.* He left Bethlehem, where he had no means of existence, in quest of a place where he would be paid to act as priest and soothsayer. Micah received him, hailed him father and priest, gave him ten shekels a day besides food and raiment, and took him to live in his house. Then Micah said, "Now know I that the Lord will do me good seeing that I have a Levite for my priest." The oracle acquired great notoriety and was very profitable to Micah.

Now it happened that the spies of Dan, crossing the mountains of Ephraim, heard of the oracle of Micah and wished to consult it as to the good or evil issue of their undertaking. The Levite set the machine in motion and came out, saying, "The thing is before Iahveh." The spies returned quickly and told this to their fellow-countrymen. An emigration was decided upon. Six hundred men set out from Zorah and Estaol with their arms, their families, and their flocks. They halted at Kirjath-Jearim, and perhaps sojourned there. The emigrants afterwards ascended the mountains of Ephraim and arrived at the house of Micah. The spies who had consulted the oracle then gave them a curious piece of advice; it was to steal the instruments of worship, the *ephod*, the *teraphim*, the *fesel*, the *masseka*, and to carry them away, seeing that in

* Judges, ch. xvii., v. 7; ch. xviii., v. 30.

the new settlement they were about to found they would have no sacred vessels. The Levite made some objections at first, but they pointed out to him that it would be better to be the father and priest of a tribe of Israel than of one man. He carried off the *ephod*, the *teraphim*, the *fesel*, the *masseka*, and took his place in the middle of the band.

The children, the cattle, and the baggage were placed in front, for they expected to be attacked in the rear. In fact, when Micah and his neighbours who worshipped Iahveh at his religious establishment saw that the image had been stolen, they set out in pursuit of the Danites with great cries. "What aileth thee that thou comest with such a company?" asked the Danites. And Micah said, "Ye have taken away my gods which I made, and the priest, and ye are gone away: and what have I more? and what is this that ye say unto me, What aileth thee? And the children of Dan said unto him, Let not thy voice be heard among us lest angry fellows run upon thee and thou lose thy life with the lives of thy household. And the children of Dan went their way; and when Micah saw that they were too strong for him he turned and went back unto his house."

The march of the children of Dan through the tribes of Israel was accomplished without difficulty, and it was the same with the conquest of Laish. The Canaanites of these countries were peaceful and confiding people; they had little to say to the kings and Bedouin tribes by whom they were surrounded, and

Sidon was too far. They were all massacred and their city was burned. This was odious in the extreme. But there is not a race whose ancestors have behaved better.

It appears that the Danites had first of all the intention of recommencing their nomad life, but the beauty and richness of the country made them change their minds. They gave up robbery, rebuilt the city and called it Dan. They installed there the ephod and the images which they had taken from Micah. A Levite priesthood was established there for the service of the ephod, and, by dint of imposture, they succeeded in gaining over Gershom, a pretended son of Moses.* This lasted as long as the kingdom of Israel. The other Israelites abhorred the worship of the Danites of the north. They called the sacred image of Dan "the *fesel* which Micah had made." They opposed to it, with all the pride of orthodoxy, the ark which was then at Shiloh.†

Laish was no doubt not the only point of the region round Lake Huleh occupied by the Danites.‡ As for the Danites of the south they almost entirely disappeared. All the energetic portion of the tribe went north; what remained ended by becoming absorbed in the tribe of Judah.

* Judges, ch. xvii., v. 7; ch. xviii., v. 30. On the addition of נ in משה, see Bertheau or any other commentator.

† Judges, ch. xviii., v. 31.

‡ The name of the Danite city *Saalbin* is to be found again in a striking manner in the present village of Schalaboun (see *Mission de Phénicie*, pp. 677 and following).

CHAPTER XII.

THE CIVIL WARS OF THE TRIBES.

It will be seen that not one of the wars of which we have spoken was general; not one chieftainship established by war extended to the whole of Israel. The children of Joseph often joined the tribes of the north; Gilead formed a distinct division; Judah hardly ever ranged itself with the tribes, and is rarely mentioned in the Book of Judges. Judah was scarcely comprised in the generic denomination of Israel.

The existence of the tribe of Benjamin was also very peculiar. Its territory was small and almost entirely occupied by the Canaanites, either allies like the Gibeonites or enemies like the Jebusites. The Benjamites were little else than a special military corps, of a high cast as regards the use of the sling, their young men being accustomed to use the left hand instead of the right. Their strong place was Gibeah, to the north of Jerusalem. They were not liked, and their morality was said to be very low. The following adventure was related with horror:*

A Levite of Ephraim, overtaken by nightfall when near Gibeah, left the road with his concubine to pass

* Judges, ch. xix., xx., xxi.

into the city, and sat down in the street. No one
invited them in until an old man, who was a stranger
to the city, took them to his house. What happened
then was monstrous and resembled the infamies of
Sodom. It became necessary to hand over the concubine to the Benjamites. After having satisfied their
lust during a night of debauch, the unfortunate woman
fell dead at the threshold of the house where her
husband had received hospitality. The Levite on
opening the door in the morning found the dead body,
placed it on his ass, and on reaching home cut it into
twelve pieces, which he sent to the twelve tribes of
Israel.

It was very general in ancient times for great wars to
be attributed to trivial causes, and sometimes these
details, which appear surprising to us, were true. The
affair of the Levite of Ephraim was, we are assured, the
occasion of a general assembly of the nation at Mispeh,
near Jerusalem, and of a sort of federal war against
Benjamin. It is probable that there was some more
serious cause for this attack. Nearly all the tribes
hated Benjamin. It is said that a great many Israelites swore at Mispeh never to give their daughters to
a Benjamite. The oracle of the ark,* several times
consulted, recommended a war of extermination.

The rock of Gibeah resisted heroically. The sallies
made by the Benjamites were very deadly, and
the Israelites only succeeded in taking the place by

* According to Judges, ch. xx., v. 26, 27, the ark was then at
Bethel. It was probably at Shiloh.

THE CIVIL WARS OF THE TRIBES. 291

surprise. They placed men in ambush near the city; then by a pretended flight they drew the besieged away from the place. The men in ambush then took the city, and massacred every one in it and set it on fire. The Benjamites who were disseminated in the plain, turning round, saw the smoke going up to heaven. In their despair they fled into the desert. The confederates pursued them and killed them by thousands.*

At Sela-Rimmon† the fugitives defended themselves for four months. At the end of that time the wrath of the tribes was appeased and the Benjamites were allowed to escape. It was supposed that all the women of Benjamin had been exterminated. In order to procure wives for the survivors of Sela-Rimmon, and not leave a void among the tribes, the Israelites resorted to the most primitive devices.‡ The legend had certainly exaggerated the extermination of Gibeah. Benjamin, far from disappearing, was soon to give Israel its first king; Gibeah was destined to become the city of Saul, and within its walls was to be exercised for the first time a central power in Israel.

A federal execution, similar to that which punished Benjamin, is said to have fallen upon the city of Gabesh-Gilead. According to the legend, the inhabitants of that city alone were absent from the sort of diet held at Mispeh; they were all slain with the

---

* The exaggeration of this account will be remarked.

† To-day Rummon, two leagues N.N.E. of Toleil-el-Foul.

‡ Judges, ch. xxi.

exception of the virgins, who were reserved to perpetuate the race of Benjamin. What is true in this story is that Gilead, or perhaps Jabesh in particular, lived apart, and entered for very little into the common work of Israel.

Thus continued during two or three centuries the distinct life of a dozen families notoriously of the same race, fully aware of their relationship, but rarely united in a common action. The children of Joseph always maintained their superiority. The signs of the future supremacy of Judah were still very obscure.* Genealogies had been established at a very early date, destined to show the unity of origin of the different families. The ancient names of tribes, Isaac, Jacob, Israel, Joseph, allowed of ingenious combinations, at the head of which always figured the High Father, the *Ab-ram*, identical with the *Père-Orcham*, brought from Chaldæa. The very old name of Isaac furnished a son and immediate successor to the *Ab-ram*. The ancient names of Jacob and Israel were considered as one. All the tribes descended from supposed sons of Jacob or Israel. It is true that there was something arbitrary in this choice. The powerful groups of Jair, of Machir, of Abiezer had quite as much right as Gad or Dan to figure in this list.†

If not too critical, we can make up the sacramental number of "twelve." Joseph was counted

* Judges, ch. xx., v. 18; Genesis, ch. xlix., v. 8 and following.
† Machir figures as a tribe in the Song of Deborah.

double in the persons of his two sons, Ephraim and Manasseh. Two divisions were formed, it appears, irrespective of relationship, the division of Levites and the warrior division, known by the name of Benjamin. The Levites had greatly multiplied in various tribes. People became accustomed to believe that they were descended from a son of Jacob named Levi; they were called a tribe but they dwelt with other tribes and at their expense. The *Beni-Jemini*, skilful archers and slingers, were placed on the tops of the lofty hills to the north of Jerusalem.

Thus Benjamin and Levi became two sons of Jacob, although the different Levites who wandered through the country were not bound by any parental tie. As the use and skill in handling certain weapons afterwards became, in antiquity, the appanage of special families, who handed them down from father to son, it cannot be asserted that the *Beni-Jemini* did not originally form a family in the ordinary sense of the word. At all events it was admitted that a tribe could exist without territory. Levi had none, and the territory of Benjamin was confined almost exclusively to the hill of Gibeah.

Reuben and Simeon, whom it was soon difficult to discern from Moab, Edom, and the Arabs of the desert, disappeared at an early period as tribes. They were considered, like that of Levi, as sporadic tribes dispersed through the rest of Israel. There were thus tribes in some measure ideal alongside of tribes totally disinherited, like Dan. The chief thing was to ally oneself by tongue, by race, or by some link more or less authentic to the venerable Jacob of antiquity.

Jacob was supposed to have had two wives and two concubines. Each tribe naturally endeavoured to trace its descent from the common father in the manner the most honourable. Then a kind of classification was made, favourable to some, unfavourable to others, in which the opinion of the powerful tribe of Joseph preponderated. Joseph and Benjamin, of the oldest aristocracy of Israel, were born of the dearly-beloved wife Rachel, under circumstances which made them privileged and favourites. Dan, Naphthali, Gad, and Asher were sacrificed and made to descend from the concubines. As there was a great deal of rivalry between the members of this family, anecdotes, often ill-natured, were circulated with regard to the true or supposed sons of the patriarch, and greatly afflicted their descendants. In the same way, in those country places where people are still simple-minded, they annoy one another by abusing the saints of one another's parishes. But it was chiefly among the Arab tribes, before Mahomet, in the *Kitáb-el-Aghâni*, in the divans of the tribes, that one must look for the intelligence of this age, in appearance so contradictory, in Israel. The Arab tribes, although of the same race, hate each other cordially, and spread abroad the most odious calumnies about one another. A collection has been made[*]

---

[*] The *Raïhan-el-albâb* in the *Journal asiatique*, June, 1853.

THE CIVIL WARS OF THE TRIBES.

in which these inventions, sometimes obscene, are compared, embittered and commented on.

The love and the hatred of the tribes were also expressed in Israel in burning and passionate epigrams. Sayings sometimes flattering, sometimes satirical, were circulated concerning each tribe. These sayings have been handed down to us in the shape of blessings pronounced by Jacob* or by Moses.† They are full of originality, although obscure, tampered with, often unintelligible, based upon untranslateable puns.

Zebulun shall dwell at the haven of the sea; and he shall be for an haven for ships; and his border shall be unto Zidon.
Issachar is a strong ass couching down between two burdens.

* * * * *

That age of gold which became for Israel a kind of second ideal was never forgotten—the patriarchal ideal belonging to the pastoral life; the ideal of the times of the Judges belonging to an agricultural and settled life. Those days were represented as an epoch of gaiety, of intermittent happiness, of pure morality often, of liberty always, when the individual, master of his land, not exposed to the abuses of a monarchy, lived in the state nearest to perfection, which was the primitive nomad state. As Israel never had any real love of royalty, this recollection of an era of

---

* Genesis, ch. xlix.
† Deuteronomy, ch. xxxiii. Compare with the Song of Deborah.

the absence of government and of supposed theocracy always enchanted his imagination. A cycle of delicious pastorals was embroidered on this pleasant and tranquil canvass. The book of the *Wars of Iahveh* and the *Jasher* afterwards absorbed nearly all those anecdotes, to which a happy mixture of idyllism and heroism gave a charm that the epic poems of the Greeks and the *Kitáb-el-Aghâni* of the Arabs alone have equalled.

The Book of Judges inherited that flowery style of poetry which the pietist proclivities of later ages did not destroy. This portion of the ancient historiography was very little touched up. The episodes of Gideon, of Jephthah, of Samson, of Micah, of the Levite of Ephraim are admirable pictures, simple and grand, of remote antiquity, quite equal to the finest Homeric productions. A number of episodes of the same kind relating to Caleb and to the heroes of the south are lost. Others were manufactured at a later period and appended at Bethlehem to the family of David.* Upon reaching a more advanced state of organisation, Israel represented to itself that age as one when it was happy, when at least it was young and free. This gave rise to an exquisite romantic vein.

Romance requires, in order to locate its dreams, a country and an epoch which lend themselves to fiction and furnish it with a luminous background which floods the picture in a kind of mirage. As among

* Book of Ruth.

the Arabs every anecdote was ascribed to the time of Haroun-al-Raschid, and as in the Middle Ages every tale which related to the time of King John was allowed a peculiar licence; even so it was sufficient to write at the head of a story, "Now it happened in the days when the Judges judged Israel," or, "It was an ancient custom in Israel in the days of the Judges," to create for it a poetic halo, and for the mind to be prepared for idyls and for tales untrammeled by pietism. Every licence was atoned for if the passages which shocked modern piety were terminated by this formula: "And in those days there was no king over Israel, and every one did as seemed good in his own eyes." The time of the Judges thus became a continuation, as it were, of that of the patriarchs. The Book of Ruth is one of those rare pearls of literature where the simple expression of the reality suffices to shed over the whole story a flood of soft and glowing light.

It is here that the Homer of the Greeks and that the Arab cycle is surpassed. Not a shadow of literary effort; one grain of the most innocent fiction being sufficient for the ideal. No law but that dictated by the vague *elohim*. Ruth and Boaz are immortalised alongside of Nausicaa and Alcinous. The further humanity recedes from primitive life the more pleasure it finds in these charming contrasts of modesty and artlessness, in manners at once simple and refined, when man, without obeying any superior authority, or law, or city, or king, or emperor, or religion, or priest, lived nobler, greater, stronger, than when fettered by a thousand conventions, and when moulded by successive centuries of discipline.

Thanks to the Homeric poems, we have the picture of the life of the Greek tribes at an epoch parallel to that of the Judges. The analogy is striking. Although separated by a gulf in all that relates to ethnography and geography, the Grecian and the Israelite tribes bore stamped on their foreheads the same marks of poetic childhood. The Greek believed in a greater number of divinities more entirely distinct than the Israelite. But their moral condition differed little. The divine intervention in matters human and natural was continuous. Their ideas concerning sacrifice were nearly the same. The Greek God, however, identified himself more with his *hiereus* than the God of Israel with his *cohen*. The idea of a tutelary deity, again, was stronger among the Greeks than among the Israelites. The God of Israel was capable of becoming a universal God, and this cannot be said of the Grecian gods, even of Jupiter. One feels that Jupiter will never be able to kill his fellows, while Iahveh was destined soon to have no rival.

The ideas concerning oracles were the same with both races. The oath, especially that of extermination, the *herem*, was more terrible among the Israelites; and therein lay a very dangerous germ of fanaticism. Human sacrifices were, with both, the sporadic remnant of an anterior evil. There was little difference

THE CIVIL WARS OF THE TRIBES.

of religion; no temple,* hardly any vessels of worship, the sacrifice was not separated from the religious feast; the share of the gods was set apart in a set form.

The morality of the Hebrew in the days of the Judges, and of the Achean in the Homeric days, was much the same. The state of society was brigandage, and the hand of every tribe against his neighbour. Internally, the tie which bound each tribe within itself was very strong. A Danite would never slay a Danite, he would always revenge him; but a Danite would ill-treat a Zebulonite. However, two Israelites would begin by recognising a bond of fraternity between them. As for a person who was not an Israelite, every member of the family of Israel would see in him an enemy. It was the same with the Greek tribes. The innate gentleness and humanity to be found in noble races already inspired some rules which the gods laid to heart. The gods were not very earnest in their efforts to make good prevail, but still they did so in a way, and there were crimes which they punished with penalties inflicted in this life. The souls of the dead were underground, in gloomy places, leading a life which greatly resembled nothingness. Sometimes they were successfully summoned up from there by giving them blood to drink. Was there any difference in their lot according to their

* The temple among the Greeks was still only the high place, τέμενος and βωμός (bama, Hebrew and Phœnician). Cf. especially Iliad, viii., 48; xxiii., 148; Odyssey, vii., 363. See fine reflection of Socrates, Xenophon, Mem., III., viii., 10.

more or less guilt or innocence? The tendency to believe in reward and punishment beyond the tomb was much deeper with the Greeks than with the Israelites. One feels that, the idea of justice once awakened, the Israelite would like to see that justice rendered in this world, and that the Greek would more easily console himself for the iniquities committed here below with the dreams of the *Phædo.*

CHAPTER XIII.

PROGRESS OF THE RELIGIOUS AND POLITICAL ORGANISATION OF SAMUEL.

THE period of the history of Israel which we have just studied has no precise chronology. It is about 1100 B.C. that we commence to catch a glimpse of a series of facts which henceforward unrolled themselves without interruption. Through a thousand hesitations a real progress began to appear. Israel commenced to organise itself and to unite. Mispeh, the culminating point of the tribe of Benjamin, became the meeting place of the tribes, the Washington of the Israelite federation.* This mountain, which rises nearly 4,000 feet above the level of the sea, on the horizon of Jerusalem, was not made to serve as the site of a great city.† On the contrary, it was an excellent spot for those federal diets which were soon to assume a sacred character. The ark was never established there; but the *sofet* was induced to make it his habitual residence, and no doubt the political importance of Mispeh had some weight in the providential selection of Jerusalem for such brilliant destinies. Jerusalem is only a league

---

* Judges, ch. xx., 1, 8; ch. xxi., v. 1, 5, 8.
† Robinson, i., p. 457 and following.

from Mispeh and from the top of the mountain the little acropolis (*millo*) of the Jebusites on the hill of Sion must have been visible.

The power of the Judges increased every day. The relations of the tribes between each other were more closely cemented; the idea of the unity of Israel gathered shape. Iahvehism became more and more the national religion. It is probable that the broad lines of sacred history were already traced in the Israelite mind without being written. The Israelites said to themselves that Iahveh had saved them from Egypt and had promised them the full possession of the land of Canaan. The art of writing began to spread; no books were composed, but many things, for which the old mnemonic system had till then sufficed, were henceforth traced in the clear and simple characters which the Sidonians found so useful.

Shiloh became, at the same time, a kind of religious capital for the nation.* Iahveh alone appears to have been worshipped there. The ark, after a long sojourn at Bethel, had been removed there, and every one went thither to consult the oracle. There were annual festivals, a kind of pilgrimage. People flocked to Shiloh as to a holy city from all parts of Israel. This was an immense step in advance. In Israel the ark was the centre of all movement, the initial cell of the organisation of the future, which in *embryogeny* is the first development of life. It was at Shiloh that the importance which this chest would have on the unity

* First Book of Samuel, ch. i., ii., iii., especially ch. iii., v. 21.

of the nation first became apparent. It was, in short, the essential factor, for if there were numerous *ephods* and numerous places of sacrifice, there was never more than one ark; and this was why there was afterwards but one temple. The presence of the ark at Shiloh did not, however, prevent Iahveh from being consulted at Mispeh and at Gilgal.*

It is not probable that the ark was as richly decorated then as in the days of Solomon. No doubt the wood of which it was constructed was several times renewed. The sphinxes, or hawks with folded wings, never ceased to adorn the lid. If gold had been used with the profusion described by modern writers the little sanctuary would have been in great danger at an epoch when the land of Israel was so ill protected against robbers. Nor do we find that the tent in which the portable *naos* was deposited ever received any remarkable ornaments. But the priesthood assumed importance. Eli, priest of Shiloh, was for forty years a kind of judge. His two sons, Phineas and Hophni, began the era of imposition. Long did Israel remember the three-pronged flesh-hooks which they plunged into the cauldrons and pots of the poor people who went there to sacrifice. It was also related that Hophni and Phineas profaned the sacred tent with the women who served there. The result was that for the moment the pilgrimage to Shiloh fell into discredit.†

---

* Judges, ch. xx. and xxi.; First Book of Samuel, ch. vii., v. 5 and following.

† First Book of Samuel, ch. ii., v. 12 and following.

The new ideas, however, made their way in spite of everything, with the childlike logic of primitive ages. It was imagined that by taking the ark into battle against the Philistines victory would declare itself for Israel, and in a war they removed it from Shiloh to the camp near Afeq. Contrary to their anticipation, the Israelites were beaten; the ark was captured and taken to Asdod. According to custom* the Philistines placed it as a trophy in the temple of their god Dagon. Then, again, the superstition common to all the people of antiquity made them believe that certain maladies were caused by the presence of this piece of sacred furniture among them. They sent it to Beth-Semes, in the land of Israel, placing it in the field of a man called Joshua. Iahveh was then rather an object of terror than of love. Joshua was seized with fear, and proposed to the men of Kirjath-Jearim to receive this terrible guest. The men of Kirjath-Jearim came and took the ark and brought it into the house of Abinadab, who dwelt on a hill, and who sanctified Eleazar his son to keep it. It appears to have remained at that place for twenty years.†

The priesthood of Shiloh had a certain tendency to become hereditary. In thirty years' time we shall find the ephod in the hands of the great-grandson of Eli. The *ephod*, that is to say the divining machine,

* Inscr. de Mesa, lines 12, 13, 18.
† First Book of Samuel, ch. iv., v. 1 and following; ch. xiv., v. 18. The text of this passage must have been altered. Compare Greek.

THE ORGANISATION OF SAMUEL.

being a small portable object, the people became more and more accustomed to carry it with them during their expeditions, in order to consult Iahveh at any moment. But the rival power of the ephod, the spirit of prophecy, assumed much greater proportions. It was towards the end of the period of the Judges that the *nabi*, without attaining the importance he acquired in the ninth century B.C., commenced to show himself with that originality which was to make him the very axis and the pivot of the history of Israel.

Along with the *nabi*, a simple sorcerer, who was consulted as to the weather, in order to find lost property, and who was always approached with a present or small piece of money in the hand,* there was the *nabi* who busied himself with politics, and who was mixed up in all the affairs and all the intrigues of the country. The prophets of old lived isolated, without any common doctrine. At the epoch we have reached they had a discipline and were formed into groups. They even managed to form themselves into schools round Ramah and Gibeah, establishing what we may term seminaries.† The secrets by which they procured an *orgiastic* intoxication converted them, as it were, into priests of Cybele (*corybantes*). They paraded the country in companies, "in string," ‡ with the choirs of dances to the sound of the tabret and dulcimer.

* First Book of Samuel, ch. ix., v. 6—14.

† First Book of Samuel, ch. xix., v. 18 ; Second Book of Kings, ch. vi., v. 1.

‡ *Hébel nebiim*, a cord of prophets, First Book of Samuel, ch. x., v. 5, 10.

It was something resembling the howling dervishes and the *khouan* of Mussulman countries. They might be seen descending from the high places preceded by pipes and timbrels, and flutes and harps, singing, shouting, gesticulating, and answering each other in chorus. It was enough to join the company of the prophets, or to meet it, to be seized with the same enthusiasm, followed by prostration and a cataleptic sleep. During days and nights the convulsionists rolled on the ground entirely naked.* These fits of divine fury were attributed to the spirit of God, which working on the people carried them away and led them to commit acts bordering on madness.† The individual possessed by the spirit was no longer responsible for his acts; he became another man. The spirit acting in him, he had nothing to do but to let matters take their course, and everything he did was supposed to be of God.‡

This new type of prophet was essentially the "man of God." He was a divine agent, and it is easy to understand the superiority that this character gave him over the Levite and the *cohen*, even armed with the *urim* and *thummim*. He was also *hozé* or *roé*, "seer;"§ he saw what others could not see. He divined the

* First Book of Samuel, ch. xix., v. 24.

† התנבא, "play the prophet, act as a prophet, go mad."

‡ First Book of Samuel, ch. x., v. 6 and following; ch. xix., v. 18 and following.

§ According to the *scolie* (or explanation), First Book of Samuel, ch. ix., v. 9, the word *nabi* was posterior to *roé*. This is very doubtful.

most secret thoughts.* He had raptures and visions of God. In this state he expressed himself in parabolic verses, in lyric stophes, of which we have the type in the oracles attributed to Balaam.†

The parallelism, which was the rhyme of the Hebrews, came into existence and produced its first miracles. Their charming melody intoxicated the audience, and the *masal*, imitating the clashing of cymbals, seemed to come from heaven. Primitive man was much more moved than we are by harmony. The cadence worked on his nerves, creating a kind of responsive vibration which in some cases upset the whole system.

The prophet based his authority on *signs*, that is to say upon predictions which it was easy to verify, the accomplishment of which proved the divine character of his inspirations.‡ The skilful use of coincidences was the most essential part of the prophet's art, and this was made all the easier for him by a boundless credulity of which we can hardly form an idea. "Now therefore stand and see this great thing which the Lord will do before your eyes. Is it not wheat harvest to-day? I will call upon Iahveh and he will send thunder and rain. . . . ." So Samuel called unto Iahveh, and Iahveh sent thunder and rain that day, and the people greatly feared Iahveh and Samuel.

This Samuel, who was the most celebrated of the

* First Book of Samuel, ch. ix., v. 19; ch. x., v. 2 and following.

† Numbers, ch. xxiv., v. 3—4, 15 and following.

‡ First Book of Samuel, ch. ix., v. 19 and following; ch. x., v. 2 and following.

prophets of the new type, took a prominent part, if one can believe the history of the time, in the triumph of Iahveh and the organisation of Israel. As in the case of Moses, a great allowance must be made for the mania of antedating ideas, which seems to be a general rule in religious history. The life of Samuel is known to us by little else than legendary documents. It appears, however, that his influence in the slow growth of the dogma of Israel made itself felt, although it could not be compared to that of the prophets of the ninth century B.C. He came from the village of Ramah or Ramataim-Sophim, near Gibeah of Benjamin.* He played the part of both judge and prophet. The cause of his power was the influence which he exercised over the assemblies at Mispeh. Each year he went the round of Bethel, Gilgal, and Mispeh. He held assizes there, and decided the affairs of the country as if he were a sovereign. His activity was especially displayed in Benjamin and the south of Ephraim. His house in Ramah was the business centre of those places. As for Sichem, Gilead, and the tribes of the north, they do not appear to have recognised the authority of Samuel.

The Philistines continued to beat Israel in nearly every encounter. Samuel succeeded in persuading a portion of the people that their disasters were caused by their infidelity to Iahveh.† It was agreed that the Baals and the Astaroths should be put away. There

---

* To-day, *Er-Ram*, a league north of Jerusalem.
† The Song of Deborah.

THE ORGANISATION OF SAMUEL. 309

appears to have been a solemn reconciliation at Mispeh. The people drew water and poured it out before Iahveh, then fasted, and Samuel offered up sacrifices.*

During the next engagement with the Philistines it thundered. The Israelites were encouraged by this manifestation of Iahveh. The Philistines, who knew that Iahveh was a god of lightning, trembled and fled beyond Beth Car. Samuel raised a monument to this battle between Mispeh and Shen, and called it "the Stone of Help." It was near the spot where some years previously the unfortunate battle of Afeq had been fought.

Samuel played a still more important part in the development of Israel if it be true that he established in the ark, or near the ark,† the *sefer*, that is to say the open register, in which were inscribed the first records of Israel. The ark in this case would assume a loftier signification, if it be possible, than that of having founded monotheism, since it would have been the cradle of the Bible, the first *archivium* of the history of humanity. But the grounds for this opinion are very slight.‡ There is no proof that Samuel himself ever wrote.§ What may be true is that in his time Israel made a certain progress in the art of writing.

---

* First Book of Samuel, ch. vii.; Judges, ch. xx., v. 21.

† לפני יהוה, First Book of Samuel, ch. x., v. 25.

‡ The manner in which the erection of Ebenezer is related (First Book of Samuel, ch. vii., v. 12) leads one to suppose that the art of writing was rare.

§ First Book of Samuel, ch. x., v. 25, has little value. It belongs to the most feeble part of the history of Samuel. The expression משפט המלכה (First Book of Samuel, ch. x., v. 25) does not

Up to that time writing had not been in common use either among the Israelites or the Canaanites. I say in common use, for a distinction is here necessary. The question of the origin of writing among a people is not so simple as one may believe. It is one thing to know the alphabet, and another to use it consecutively in written documents. A people may have known writing for centuries without having turned it to any literary use. Is there any more striking example than that of the Latins and of the Italian populations, whose alphabet is more ancient than that of the Greeks, and yet who did not commence to have a literature until about 200 B.C.? This depends in a great measure on the substances used for writing, on the cost of those substances, and on the facilities of procuring them. People do not gossip upon stone or metal as they did when papyrus became cheap. The Greeks, before writing their great compositions, often prolix, had an age of "graphic parsimony," during which they counted their letters as it were,* and confided all that was possible to memory. The Sidonians, the Canaanites, and the Israelites were for centuries acquainted with

---

indicate a constitution or rule of royalty. It is rather a transcript of the verse, ch. viii., v. 9 and following, which Samuel is supposed to have wished to preserve so as to be able to show one day how right he was in his predictions against the royalty. The meaning of משפט המלך is, "the character of a king, the type of a king." Compare Judges, ch. xiii., v. 12; ch. xviii., v. 7; Second Book of Kings, ch. i., v. 7, and the frequent expression כמשפט.

* *Traité des Eléens et des Héréens. Corpus inscr. gr.*, No. 11.

THE ORGANISATION OF SAMUEL. 311

the Cadmean alphabet without employing it for literary or sacred purposes.

It is certain that people wrote under David. We may even suppose that long before David lists* of men, of objects and genealogies, all kinds of details difficult to remember, were recorded in alphabetical characters. Poetry, which the memory, on the contrary, easily retains, was not written until a relatively recent epoch. The inscription of Mesa, the original stone of which is in the Louvre, is hardly 200 years later than Samuel. Now the country of Moab does not appear to have been in any way in advance of the neighbouring countries. The movement which commenced in Israel about 1100 B.C., and which prepared the age of David and Solomon, was too deep, too rich in consequences, to have been the work of a listless people unable to write.

Besides, we do not learn that Samuel introduced the slightest change into the state of religious affairs which he found established. Iahveh was no doubt exclusively his personal god; but he did not object to the names of Baal and Milik being made use of.† He never thought of unity for a place of worship, for he raised an altar to Iahveh in his house of Ramah.‡ He sacrificed no matter where;§ without the least scruple he honoured

---

* This is the exact meaning of the word *sefer*.
† Family of Saul; names composed of Baal and Milik.
‡ First Book of Samuel, ch. viii., v. 17.
§ First Book of Samuel, ch. xvi., v. 2 and following.

Iahveh on the heights of Baal. Saul and his companions were witnesses of this free worship in the open air. They sought the seer to consult him respecting the loss of a she-ass.* "They went to a city where there was a man of God. As they went up the hill to the city† they found two maidens going to draw water, and said to them, Is the seer here? And they answered them, He is; behold, he is before you. Make haste now, for he came to-day to the city, for there is a sacrifice of the people to-day in the high place. As soon as ye be come into the city ye shall straightway find him, before he go up to the high place to eat; for the people will not eat until he come, because he doth bless the sacrifice, and afterwards they eat that be bidden. Now therefore get you up; for about this time ye shall find him. They went up to the city, and at the very moment they entered it, behold Samuel, who came out before them to go to the high place. Then Saul drew near to Samuel in the gate and said, Tell me, I pray thee, where the seer's house is. And Samuel answered Saul and said, I am the seer. Go up before me into the high place, for ye shall eat with me to day. . . . . And Samuel took Saul and his servants and brought them into the parlour, and made them sit in the chiefest place among them that were bidden, which were about thirty persons. . . . . Then they descended from the high place into the city." ‡

* First Book of Samuel, ch. ix., v. 10 and following.
† No doubt Ramah.
‡ Compare with the strange story of sacrifices of Bethel, First Book of Samuel, ch. x., v. 3 and following.

THE ORGANISATION OF SAMUEL.

Samuel left the ark at Kirjath-Jearim; his religious horizon did not extend beyond Bethel;[*] he appears to have taken no account of Shiloh, whose religious reign had nearly expired. We perceive that Israel's centre of gravity descended towards the south; at the epoch of Samuel it was in Benjamin at Mispeh, Ramah, and Gibeah. Samuel was *cohen*[†] in a general sense after the manner of the patriarchs, not according to a special rite. He certainly was *nabi*, exercising authority in virtue of direct inspiration. Like all the *nabis* he had to oppose the superstition of the *urim* and *thummim* and the manufacture of ephods of plated silver. Without doubt he was not free from fanaticism. If one of the stories told of him be true, his mind was not without a certain amount of flexibility; in it we see him, in fact, playing a part which is most honourable because it is rare in politics. According to this story Samuel founded in Israel a *régime* against which he had the strongest objections, almost an antipathy; he sacrificed his own interests and those of his family to the will of the nation which he believed to have been led astray. But we are about to see that this way of representing matters is quite fictitious, and that it was due to the philosophy of history which, after the victory of the spirit of prophecy, was taken by the most advanced of the theocrats, or, in other words, by the sincere Iahvehists.

[*] First Book of Samuel, ch. x., v. 3.
[†] Afterwards it was said that he had been nazir. The Chronicles make a Levite of him.

CHAPTER XIV.

INSTITUTION OF ROYALTY.

ROYALTY became an absolute necessity for Israel. All the Semitic tribes in passing from a nomad to a sedentary condition had adopted this institution. Israel alone struggled during two or three centuries against a fatality which was unavoidable. The old patriarchal *régime*, to which had been tacked on the unsatisfactory religious institutions of Gilgal, of Bethel, of Shiloh, of Mispeh, the ark, the ephod, the oracle of Iahveh, the *nebim*, the *softim*, had become an impossibility. It placed Israel in a state of inferiority as regarded their neighbours, especially the Philistines, whose territory was not a twentieth part that of Israel, but whose military and political institutions were far superior. To all the objections raised by the wise men, partisans of old ideas, the people replied, "No; we must have a king, so that we may be like other nations, and that our king may judge us, and go out before us and fight our battles."[*]

The king, or *mêlek*, so ardently desired, evidently because the condition of the age demanded one, is, as we perceive, the *basileus* of the Greeks of Homer.

[*] First Book of Samuel, ch. viii., v. 5, 6, 19, 20.

INSTITUTION OF ROYALTY.

The *basileus*, as his name indicates,* marched at the head of his people, led them to battle, with a staff in his hand; this was his part and lot. He was the German war-lord. Great transformations must take place before a royalty born under such auspices could become a kind of sacrament. At the period at which we have arrived the problem was both profane and military: Israel was resolved to exist as a nation. Each step that it took towards national unity was a step towards the monarchy. The work which Gideon, Abimelech, and Jephthah had attempted in vain was about to be accomplished by a Benjamite, of no great talent, but brave and strong, whom the necessities of the time were about to raise above what his merits and his ambition seemed to warrant.

"So Saul took the kingdom over Israel," says the most ancient writ concerning these events.† It cannot be denied, however, that Samuel played a decisive part, not in opposing the establishment of the monarchy, as the later versions adopted by the theocratic historians have it, but on the contrary in aiding it, as the most ancient authorities say.‡ According to the Scriptures, Samuel, listening to the voice of Iahveh, indicated the king and anointed him. It is impossible to say how these things happened, seeing their great antiquity. Independently of having been

---

* Compare *Agesilaus*.

† First Book of Samuel, ch. xiv., v. 47. The word לכד means to take like a prey, like plunder.

‡ First Book of Samuel, ch. ix., x., xi., xiii., xiv.

designated by prophetic utterance, Saul possessed the royal qualities of the time. In those simple days, when bodily strength was considered as the greatest of gifts, he was looked upon as an accomplished person.

He was a hero of antiquity; a tall and handsome man, very brave and robust, from Gibeah in Benjamin. The tribe of the Benjamites still formed the military portion of Israel. The men were powerful, skilful, and accustomed to bodily exercise. When Saul stood among the Benjamites he was head and shoulders taller than any of them. · Circumstances, which have since served as a groundwork for fable, brought him into intercourse with Samuel.* Saul appears to have remained for a long time among the prophets dancing and singing with them.† He there contracted habits of frenzy, which, after having been of service to him, worked his ruin. The men of Gibeah, his fellow-countrymen, seeing him thus moved by the spirit of the Lord, said, "Is Saul also among the prophets?" and this became a proverb. Saul observed a certain amount of reserve at first in his relations with Samuel. He waited until some signal occasion should point him out to the choice of the tribes.

This was not long in coming. The city of Jabesh in Gilead, sorely pressed by Nahash the Ammonite, sent message after message to the tribes to come to its aid. Gibeah, which was a great military centre, was

---

* Ramah and Gilead were only half a league from each other.

† See two accounts difficult to understand: First Book of Samuel, ch. x., v. 10 and following; ch. xix., v. 18 and following.

thrown into a fever of excitement; Saul was moved by the spirit of God, and his anger was kindled greatly. He took a yoke of oxen and hewed them in pieces and sent them through all the coasts of Israel by the hands of messengers, saying, Whosoever cometh not forth after Saul and after Samuel, so shall it be done unto his oxen. And the fear of the Lord fell on the people, and they came up with one consent. The affair was promptly executed, and in the course of a few days the siege of Jabesh-Gilead was raised.

This was certainly a proof of the great progress accomplished in the work of the unification of Israel. The sight of Benjamin rising and flying to the aid of a city so far away as Jabesh was quite a novel one. The Benjamite hero who had brought this about had a right to be king of Israel. There were signs of opposition which Samuel appears to have calmed.* The prophet had fixed upon Gilgal † as the place where the establishment of the monarchy was to be proclaimed. His wishes were complied with. At Gilgal, the people being assembled, Saul was anointed king of Israel in presence of Iahveh. And the people made sacrifices of peace-offerings, and Saul and all the men of Israel greatly rejoiced.

According to this account, by far the most authentic, the monarchy was a good institution. It was God who gave it to the people, without having been

* First Book of Samuel, ch. x., v. 26, 27; ch. xi., v. 12 and following.

† Great doubts exist as to which Gilgal this was.

asked for it, as a protection. Everything was done with the connivance of Samuel. Afterwards this event was related in quite another manner. It was stated that Samuel, having grown old, established his two sons, Joel and Abiah, judges over Israel,* but that they, far from imitating their father, allowed themselves to be corrupted, received presents, and brought justice into disrepute. Then all the elders of Israel went to Samuel at Ramah and demanded a king to reign over them, " like all the other nations." Not without raising many objections, and after having painted in gloomy colours the abuses of the royalty, did Samuel give an unwilling consent.

These were, in fact, the sentiments of the prophets at a much more modern epoch. They were retrospectively attributed to Samuel. The men of God, the prophets whose ideal ever was to return to the old patriarchal life, and who generally found in the monarchy an obstacle to their utopian ideas, regarded this transformation, which made Israel like to any other country, as a sacrilege. Iahveh was the real king of the people in the theocratic system. To substitute for him a profane king was a piece of impiety, an act of ingratitude, an apostasy.† It was a mark of distrust; it was as much as to say to Iahveh that

* According to the First Book of Samuel, ch. viii., v. 1, they both judged at Beersheba. This is hardly probable. I suppose that the real text was מדן ועד באר־שבע, as in the First Book of Samuel, ch. iii., v. 20, in conformity with the false idea that all the *sofet* judged throughout all Israel.

† First Book of Samuel, ch. viii., v. 7.

he was unable to defend his people, and that it would be better to have a king. Theocracy thus assumed the appearance of democracy. The king, representative of a lay and profane society, appeared like a degradation of religious society.

This was assuredly not the opinion of Samuel. The satire which he is supposed to have aimed at the monarchy was directed against the reign of Solomon, which he could not have foreseen sixty years in advance. But, speaking in an ideal sense, the clever and artless passages in which are summed the policy of the Israelite theocracy* contain nothing but truth. The duality was already established. Israel sought after two contradictory things: it wished to be like other nations and to be a nation apart. It wished to enjoy at the same time a real and tangible existence and an idealistic and impracticable dream. Prophetism and the monarchy, from their very existence, were placed in opposition to each other. A lay nation obeying all the necessities of lay nations, and a theocratic democracy perpetually undermining the bases of civil order, this was the struggle which in its development filled up the whole history of Israel, and stamped it with so much originality. In selecting the very conscience of Samuel as the theatre of this struggle, the theocratic historian set an example to Dionysius of Halicarnassus, who attributes the most profound reasoning to the policy of Romulus.

* First Book of Samuel, ch. viii.; ch. x., v. 17 and following; ch. xii., v. 1 and following; ch. xv.

The institution of the monarchy in Israel was quite a profane affair: there was no religious idea about it. Although very ancient accounts describe Saul as acting in concert with the *nabis*, it seems that he had nothing to do with *cohenism*. The phial of oil which Samuel is supposed to have poured on his head* is a legend, but not irreconcilable with the more trustworthy evidence which pictures for us the monarchy of Israel owing its existence to a kind of *champ de mai*. The sacrifices which are said to have been offered up at Gilgal were obligatory festivities, such as were common on all solemn occasions. The biblical writer means, no doubt, that these sacrifices were offered to Iahveh. That may be the case. Let me remark, however, that Saul was, like Gideon and Jephthah, an intermittent worshipper of Iahveh. His sons were called Jonathan, Meribaal, Isbaal,† Milkisua;‡ which proves that he wavered between the words Baal, Milik, Moloch, and Iahveh as signifying the divinity. The fact that during the whole course of his reign he found it impossible to agree with the prophets and the priests, clearly shows the lay origin of his power, and this was the character which the monarchy maintained in Israel up to the end. "And the king was proclaimed in Israel when

---

* First Book of Samuel, ch. x., v. 1 and following, little agrees with what follows. Saul was anointed before there was any question of a monarchy.

† One of his grandsons was called Meribaal.

‡ Compare with Elisha, son of David.

the heads of the people and the tribes were gathered together;" here is one of those rare historical generalities to be found in the old Hebrew writings, and the curious place in which this maxim* is to be found is by no means the least significant proof of the important constitutional meaning attached to it.

* Deuteronomy, ch. xxxiii., v 5: prologue of the Blessing of Moses, composed of phrases bearing no relation to the maxim, which they wished to insert somewhere.

CHAPTER XV.

REIGN OF SAUL.

SAUL appears to have reigned twenty years over Israel. His legitimate wife was Ahinoam, daughter of Ahimaas. She bore him four sons,[*] only one of whom distinguished himself. He had besides several concubines, who created at Gibeah numerous collateral branches of the house of Saul.

Saul had no capital properly so called. He usually dwelt in Gibeah of Benjamin, the place of his birth, named Gibeah of Saul after him. He there led a family life, without any show or ceremony, the simple life of a peasant noble, cultivating his fields when he was not at war, and holding aloof from all business. His house was large. At each new moon sacrifices and feasts were celebrated there, at which all the officers had their places marked out. The king sat with his back to the wall.[†] To execute his orders he had couriers,[‡] similar to the Eastern *schaousch*

---

[*] First Book of Samuel, ch. xiv., v. 49 ; ch. xxxi., v. 2; Second Book of Samuel, ch. ii., v. 8 ; First Book of Chronicles, ch. viii., v. 33.

[†] First Book of Samuel, ch. xx., v. 25.

[‡] First Book of Samuel, ch. xxii., v. 17.

REIGN OF SAUL.

of the present day. There was nothing which resembled a court. His proud neighbours, who were more or less his relations, like Abner, kept him company. This was a nobility at once rustic and military, a solid corner-stone, such as we find at the base of durable monarchies. But the incapacity of the man rendered everything useless. The monarchy was founded, but the dynasty was not discovered; the Israelites had not yet escaped from the period of experiments.

At a more modern epoch the reign of Saul was represented as having been perpetually disturbed by Samuel. The old prophet, who was supposed to have established the monarchy in spite of himself, had endeavoured to recover bit by bit what he had been obliged to concede. This, we repeat, is an account conceived from a theocratic point of view at a later age. Nothing in the really historic writings proves that Samuel wished to injure Saul. What could have caused this opposition? Saul never endeavoured to trespass on the prophetic part played by Samuel; his power was exclusively military; in religion he innovated nothing. His Iahvehism does not appear to have been very strict, but was that of Samuel more so? Theocratic eclecticism was very elastic in those days. There were priests of Iahveh who called themselves Ahimilik, and it is a question whether the same priest who called himself Ahiah in one place, was not Ahimilik at another.* Like Samuel,

* First Book of Samuel, ch. xiv., v. 3, 8; ch. xxi., xxii.

Saul sacrificed in places already consecrated,* raised altars of unhewn stone, and displayed no repugnance for the names under which the Almighty was worshipped in the high places. David and his wife Mikal, the daughter of Saul, had in their house, as we shall see, carved *teraphim*, which played the part of household gods and were the object of religious worship.†

The fits of inspired *corybanticism* to which Saul was subject had no more to do with Iahvehism than with any other form of worship. These fits were considered as produced by the spirit of God blowing whither it listed. This was pure *elohism*. The brain of Saul appears to have been turned by these odd tricks which seem to have been practised in the schools of the prophets. His intelligence, which was subject to all the credulity of the age, became impaired. He went as far as necromancy, and, as it appears, became disgusted with it, for a law against necromancers and sorcerers is attributed to him.‡ Hardly any progress in religion was made during his reign. Never was there a greater abuse of *urim* and *thummim*.§ The gravest questions were decided by dice with a confidence showing the blindest faith in the adepts, and a really unheard-of audacity among the priests, guardians of the sacred machine.

It is as a war-lord that Saul stands out so promi-

---

* First Book of Samuel, ch. xiii., v. 8—14.
† First Book of Samuel, ch. xix., v. 13.
‡ First Book of Samuel, ch. xxviii., v. 3, 9.
§ First Book of Samuel, ch. xiv., v. 3, 18, 20, 36 and following.

nently in the history of Israel. He was powerfully seconded in this task by his son, the brave and faithful Jonathan. When Saul assumed the royal title the situation was deplorable. The Philistines occupied posts in the heart of the country, at Geba,* for example. Saul and Jonathan almost alone were armed. It seems that the conquering Philistines had so sternly prohibited the manufacture and even the repair of objects of iron in Israel, that in order to sharpen their agricultural implements the Israelites were obliged to apply to the Philistines.† The military disorganisation produced by the exclusive importance of men like Samuel, strangers to the art of war, was complete. Saul and Jonathan performed prodigies of valour and activity to improve the position. Up to that time the army of Israel had been merely a militia, commanded during its period of training by a temporary chief. From Saul's time there was a permanent army; at all events there were skeleton corps, a *sar-saba* or commander, a soldier by profession, and officers having their men in hand. Such an one notably was a certain Abner or Abiner, who appears to have been a first-cousin of Saul,‡ and who was evidently a captain of great capacity.

In his first campaign Saul selected Michmash, Bethel, and Gibeah as his points of support. Saul and Jonathan established themselves firmly in those

* First Book of Samuel, ch. x., v. 4; ch. xiii., v. 8. Not to be mistaken for Gibeah.

† First Book of Samuel, ch. xiii., v. 19 and following.

‡ Compare First Book of Samuel, ch. xiv., v. 51, and ch. ix., v. 1.

regions, and Jonathan beat the small Philistine garrison at Geba. This partial success led to an offensive movement on the part of all the Philistine forces. The country was entirely occupied; the inhabitants had to hide themselves in caverns, in cisterns, among rocks, and in thickets. A great many crossed the Jordan and took refuge in Gad and in Gilead. A powerful cavalry and numerous chariots of war swept the whole region north of Jerusalem over an area of many miles.

This number was a source of weakness to the invaders. They had with them a numerous body of camp followers, most of them Israelites, who, seeing the stand made by Saul and Jonathan, made common cause with their former fellow-countrymen.* The battle took place between Michmash and Ajalon. The pursuit was deadly for the enemy, who left behind a considerable amount of plunder. The Israelites, half starved, took sheep and oxen and calves, and slew them, "and did eat them with the blood." This circumstance terrified Saul. The fact of eating flesh that had not been bled was considered a crime.† Saul caused a large stone to be brought; upon this stone each one brought his sheep or his ox and slew it there; then they recommenced their banquet, which lasted all night. The great stone was considered an altar, "the first which Saul built to Iahveh."

* First Book of Samuel, ch. xiv., v. 21. Read ועבדים with Greek translators.

† First Book of Samuel, ch. xiv., v. 31 and following.

The priest of Shiloh, Ahiah, the great-grandson of Eli, followed the army with his ephod, which was consulted whenever a difficulty arose. At a given moment the ephod refused to answer, and this indicated a serious perturbation. Iahveh was no longer in communication with his people. It was suspected that a great crime was the cause of this momentary ill-humour on the part of Iahveh. The *herem*, that is to say the anathema, carrying death with it, was to be visited on the person designated by Iahveh. The proceedings were commenced as usual by division; on one side stood the whole army, on the other side Saul and Jonathan. "If the fault be with me and with Jonathan," said Saul, "give *urim*. If the fault be with the people, give *thummim*." It was *urim* which came out. The question was then between Saul and and his son, and Jonathan was taken. It happened that Jonathan had, without knowing it, incurred the penalty of death sworn by his father. The Israelitish mind loved these legends, which illustrated the strict character of an oath. The case of Jephthah will be remembered. But in the case of Jonathan the people protested, and he was saved.

Heroic accounts were soon circulated concerning these wars, in which individual adventure held the first place. The Philistines were supposed to possess in their ranks many remnants of the ancient race of the Anakims, almost all from Gath. As the Israelites were of middle height, these giants astonished and frightened them. A very ordinary type of the military legend was to bring one of these giants and an Israelitish warrior into contact, the victory being naturally gained by the latter. At least four of these stories are known.* The most modern and the most detailed is that in which the youthful David kills Goliath with a sling;† but this legendary name had already been made use of, for the sword of Goliath was handed to David by the priests of Nob as a trophy which had been long consecrated.‡ The feeble weapons of the Israelite, compared to the terrible arms of the enemy, formed the most amusing part of these adventures, which always terminated by the pleasant spectacle of the foreigner killed in spite of his helmet and his breastplate by the most childish means.§

Saul kept as it were a school of war, of which the tribe of Benjamin formed the sinews. The Carian and Pelasgian bands of Gath and Ekron found themselves opposed to an organisation capable of resisting them. There was perpetual war, a kind of duel only interrupted by the seasons. The general result was favourable to the Israelites; the Philistines were driven back into the plains on the coast and the mountains were almost freed from their depredations.

The campaigns of Saul against the Moabites, the Ammonites, and the Aram of Soba are little known.

* Second Book of Samuel, ch. xxi., v. 15—22; ch. xxiii., v. 21.
† First Book of Samuel, ch. xvii.
‡ First Book of Samuel, ch. xxi., v. 9. The words בעמק האלה אשר הכית must surely have been added by the last editor.
§ Second Book of Samuel, ch. xxiii., v. 21. Story of Benaiah similar to that of David. Opposition of שבט and חנית.

What is related of his war against the Amalekites and their king Agag belongs to modern story, distorted with the intention of lowering the monarchy for the benefit of the prophets.* It is certain, however, that Saul employed a good deal of his time in putting down the Bedouins of the East who pillaged the peaceful children of Israel.†

It is less easy to understand the bitterness displayed by Saul against the Canaanites, especially against the Gibeonites, who had obtained a charter when the country was conquered. It would have been better policy to make an effort for the assimilation of these tribes, from which little danger was to be apprehended seeing their disorganised condition. Saul on the contrary tried to exterminate them, and in this circumstance displayed great cruelty. The result was that his family afterwards suffered terrible reprisals.‡

A royalty of this description founded on all the rules of history, on heroism, and the greatest services rendered to national unity, deserved to enjoy peace and tranquillity and to serve as the basis of a dynasty. Such was not the case. The reign of Saul, although very advantageous for Israel, was for the son of Kish and for his family full of adversity and trouble. A man of great courage and an excellent soldier, Saul was not a man of sagacity. He made an abuse of the ephod, and sought in the *urim* and *thummim* what he

---

* First Book of Samuel, ch. xv., v. 1 and following.
† First Book of Samuel, ch. xiv., v. 48.
‡ Second Book of Samuel, ch. xxi.

ought to have sought from common sense. One seldom reads of any one more superstitious than him. The constant terror of some unknown and capricious force paralysed his judgment. His long connection with the school of the prophets had given him a nervous debility which verged upon epilepsy. This added to a melancholy temperament and the responsibility of a position new to Israel, was the ruin of poor Saul. He fell into a kind of madness, and it was said that he was troubled with an evil spirit from the Lord.* Bereft of his senses, he indulged in the wildest gesticulations, like the prophets in their fits.† He could be tranquillised only by music similar to that of the *nabis*. More than all else, the solemn sounds of the harp calmed him. In his moments of despondency he called for the cleverest harpers to soothe his troubled mind.‡

Among the excitable and ambitious people of the East a man has no right to commit a fault. There is always some one ready to take advantage of it. The intermittent attacks of madness from which Saul suffered would have been of little consequence if fate had not placed at his side a man who was endowed with all the talents of which he was deficient. The etymological myth of Jacob, "the supplanter," often became a reality in the ancient history of Israel.

---

* First Book of Samuel, ch. xvi., v. 14; ch. xviii., v. 10.
† חרתנבא, First Book of Samuel, ch. xviii., v. 10, wickedly.
‡ First Book of Samuel, ch. xvi., v. 14—23.

CHAPTER XVI.

DAVID'S EARLY LIFE.—DEATH OF SAUL.

"AND there was sore war against the Philistines all the days of Saul; and when Saul saw any strong man or any valiant man, he took him unto him."* These words appear to have been the opening of a chapter concerning David in the book of the *Wars of Iahveh*. They form the finest eulogy of Saul and a clear narrative of the historical part which he played. Saul was the organiser of the Israelite army, which up to his time had not existed. But in history, as a rule, man is punished for the good he does and is recompensed for the evil. The open-hearted nature of Saul was destined to bring into notice the man who was to undermine him, his family, and his house. The fate of those who labour at a work is often to see it pass into hands more capable of causing it to succeed and find what they had created completed more perfectly by others. History is quite the contrary of virtue rewarded. The family of the real founder of the force of Israel was exterminated. The unscrupulous soldier of fortune who followed was the king "after God's heart," the supposed ancestor of Jesus, of him whom

* First Book of Samuel, ch. xiv., v. 52.

the opinion of humanity has crowned with every kind of halo. Such was the justice of Iahveh; the world belonged to those who pleased him.

In the campaigns against the Philistines, the theatre of which was in the neighbourhood of Shochoh and Ephes-Dammim, in Judah,* a Bethlehemite of the name of David, the son of Jesse,† commenced to distinguish himself. At that time the heroism of a certain Eleazar, the son of Dodo, the Ahohite,‡ who, almost alone, stopped the conquering Philistines, was much admired. David was at his side the whole time, fighting desperately. The reputation of this youthful warrior rapidly increased. He was brave, enterprising, skilful, and, like the Benjamites, an excellent slinger. But more extraordinary still were his civil and social qualities. In the Semitic countries of the East, whose ordinary features are so stern and grim, there are sometimes developed prodigies of grace, elegance, and wit. David was one of these charmers. Capable of the greatest crimes when circumstances required, he was also capable of the most delicate sentiments. He knew how to make himself popular : no one could know him without becoming attached to him.§ His type of

* Second Book of Samuel, ch. xxiii., v. 9 and following, corrected by First Book of Chronicles, ch. xi., v. 12 and following; ch. xxvii., v. 4. Compare First Book of Samuel, ch. xvii., v. 1.

† Mem. on the *Noms théophores apocopés*, in the *Revue des études juives*, October and December, 1882, pp. 168, 169. *Journal des savants*, 1st March, 1887.

‡ Ahoh was a subdivision of Benjamin.

§ First Book of Samuel, ch. xvi., v. 21, 22.

DAVID'S EARLY LIFE.—DEATH OF SAUL.

face contrasted with the tanned countenances of his fellow-tribesmen. His complexion was ruddy, his features well-formed and blooming,* his voice soft and fluent.† Very ancient writings represent him as skilled on the harp and an accomplished poet.‡

He appeared to have been born to succeed. He was the first man of Judah who acquired notoriety, being helped by the obscure efforts of those who preceded him. A circumstance which does great honour to Jonathan is the lively friendship which he conceived for this young man, till then unknown, who was as brave as and more intelligent than himself, and who was one day to prove so fatal to his family. He clothed him and armed him, and the two young men swore an eternal friendship.

David was soon ordered upon a raid, which proved a complete success. He was much liked by all the tribe of Benjamin. On returning from an expedition with Saul the women of the villages through which they passed came out before the victors with timbrels, dancing and singing. The burden of their song upon that day was, "Saul hath slain his thousands and David his ten thousands."

---

* First Book of Samuel, ch. xvi., v. 12, 18.

† Ibid.

‡ Amos, ch. vi., v. 5. The *Jasher* comprised the poems attributed to him (Second Book of Samuel, ch. i., v. 17 and following; ch. iii., v. 33 and following). The part he is made to play as harpist to Saul is legendary; still more his *rôle* of psalmist. All this reposed on the poetic character which he gained by the *Jasher*.

Saul was by nature jealous, and it must be admitted that it would have taken less to make most people jealous. Popularity goes out to meet some men, almost without being sought; public opinion, as it were, takes them by the hand, exacts from them the commission of crimes as part of the programme which it imposes on them. Such a man was Bonaparte; such a man was David. The culprit in such cases is the crowd, the Lady Macbeth, which, as soon as it has chosen its favourite, intoxicates him with these magic words, "Thou shalt be king." Jonathan himself with exquisite modesty bowed before David. The latter did not act outwardly as a pretender; but he looked upon himself as a kind of destined heir, in the event of the king dying. The situation between Saul and David became daily more strained.

According to a version contained in those parts of the biography of David which are not very trustworthy,* Saul once or twice tried to kill him with his javelin. What we know is that the unfortunate king was wroth within himself, and that he did what he could to drive David away. He is accused of having entrusted him with perilous missions in order to get rid of him. He is said to have exclaimed, "Let him die by the hands of the Philistines!" But all these little expeditions, of which so many wonderful stories are told, only made David more popular. The people doted on him, and poor Saul may well have pronounced in his heart the

* First Book of Samuel, ch. xviii., v. 10, 11; ch. xix., v. 8 and following.

words attributed to him, "What can he have more but the kingdom?" If what is related of the misunderstanding between Samuel and Saul possesses any historical truth,* it might be said that the Iahvehist party, discontented with Saul, passed over to the side of David. We have not sufficient information to enable us to make so precise a statement. David, however, was what may well be called, taking the difference of the time into account, the chief of the clerical party. The schools for prophets at Ramah, the priests of Iahveh at Nob, conspired openly in his favour. The clerical party, under the most different circumstances, has always the knack of aggravating its enemies. It is easy to imagine how all those trivial worries, aggravated by the susceptibility of Saul, must have acted upon a sickly imagination and over-excited nerves.

Pretending to share the enthusiasm of the crowd, but in reality with a view to the ruin of his rival, by entrusting him with dangerous missions, Saul next gave him his daughter Mikal † in marriage. But everything goes wrong with those who are jealous. Mikal dearly loved the young hero and sided with him against her father. Jonathan two or three times turned aside the homicidal projects of Saul, and Mikal, having heard that a plot had been formed to slay her husband, got him to escape, and placed

* It is doubtful if Samuel was still alive. There is nothing to show positively when he died.
† First Book of Samuel, ch. xviii., v. 20, 21.

in his bed the *teraphim* of the house,* covering it with cloth and putting a pillow of goat's hair for a bolster, in order to deceive the assassins. Thus we see that these large wooden *penates* entered even into the houses of persons supposed to be the most devoted to Iahvehism. No one was blamed for this, and no one considered these graven images as an insult to Iahveh.†

David was thus obliged to lead a wandering life, during which he found numerous opportunities for the exercise of those expedients in which he was so skilled. This period of his existence was filled with adventures which were turned to good account by the tale-bearers. They loved above all to bring into bold relief the services rendered by Jonathan to the disgraced man, and the trials to which the fidelity of the two friends was exposed. Many of these episodes may have been written from the tales told by David‡ himself, who probably found pleasure when he was old in relating certain deeds of valour which he alone could have known: how, for example, he had been saved by Mikal his wife; how in the cave of Engeddi he had had the life of Saul in his hands, and had contented himself with cutting off the skirt of his cloak when he was asleep; how he fled to Achish, the

---

* First Book of Samuel, ch. xix., v. 18

† The word *teraphim*, like all those signifying the deity, is used in the singular (as *Elohim*).

‡ It is remarkable that all these anecdotes are related as David would have wished.

king of Gath, and feigned madness, a piece of deceit very common among Orientals.

The life of a banished man did not in antiquity differ materially from that of a brigand. David, without any place of safety, hid himself in a cave near Adullam. His brothers and several of his relations joined him, and the cave soon became a lair for brigands. "And every one that was in distress, and every one that was in debt, and every one that was discontented gathered themselves unto him; and he became captain over them, and there were with him about four hundred men." This was the nucleus of the *Gibborim* or strong men of David. These warriors lived by plunder; they lived in that epic period when the hero pillaged the country which he was afterwards to protect.

The greater portion of the family of David had remained at Bethlehem; they were in the power of Saul, and David feared that they would be subject to the most sanguinary reprisals. He found means to take them into the land of Moab and placed them under the protection of the king of that country. Then he returned to his cave at Adullam, where he fortified himself, but the prophet Gad persuaded him not to remain there, on the ground that Adullam was too near the country where Saul reigned supreme. In the midst of the tribe of Judah, however, the authority of Saul was hardly recognised, and Gad advised him to fly thither. In fact, David went and hid himself, with his brigands, in the forest of Heret.

A cruel incident which occurred soon after this still further embittered the struggle and led to all kinds of atrocities. One of the places in which there was a tendency towards religious centralisation was Nob, to the north of Jerusalem. Nob possessed a sacred tent, with an altar upon which were spread the unleavened loaves, an ephod, a treasury of consecrated vessels, and above all a numerous priesthood which took care of the sanctuary and lived there. David, in a raid which he made with his people in that direction, applied to the chief priest, called Ahimilik,* and asked him for bread for his men. Ahimilik, having no ordinary bread to give him, thought that he might set aside the rules of the liturgy, and offered David and his men hallowed loaves which were before the altar if the young men have kept themselves from women.† David then asked Ahimilik if he had any arms, and the priest answered, "The sword of Goliath the Philistine, whom thou slewest, is here wrapped in a cloth behind the ephod; if thou shalt take that take it, for there is no other here." David said, "There is none like that, give it me." Ahimilik, in addition, consulted his ephod for David; in a word, the greatest sympathy reigned between David and the priests of Nob.

* This name, into which enters that of the god Milik, is a proof of the eclecticism of the times. Two generations afterwards we find the same name in the same family (Second Book of Samuel, ch. viii., v. 17). Our Ahimilik is called further on (First Book of Samuel, ch. xxii., v. 9) son of Ahitoub.

† First Book of Samuel, ch. xxi., v. 1 and following; ch. xxii., v. 9 and following.

All this was told to Saul by Doeg the Edomite, a jealous and wicked man. The king sent for Ahimilik and his family. Ahimilik defended David with much moderation. All was useless: Saul ordered the priests of Nob to be put to death. His Israelite *racim* refused to do the deed. He had to fall back upon Doeg for the execution. According to the legend all the priests were slain and Nob was destroyed. A single son of Ahimilik,* Abiathar, escaped and fled after David. What is probable is that Abiathar remained at Nob, and on hearing of the massacre of his father and his brothers went to David. He took the ephod with him, since it is not probable that the priests would have taken the sacred image with them when they went to Saul after being denounced by Doeg.

The oracle of Iahveh thus fell into the hands of David, and rendered him signal service. The rumour having spread abroad that the Philistines had attacked Keilah and were pillaging the threshing floors, David consulted Iahveh, saying, "Shall I go and smite these Philistines?" The answer was favourable. David marched, in spite of the advice of his companions, and completely succeeded. He, however, committed an imprudence in entering a walled city with a handful of men. This is a fault which the Bedouin brigands avoid, knowing that they lose all their advantages in the cities. Saul saw the blunder, and resolved by a rapid march to capture David. The question was

* Evident exaggeration.

whether the men of Keilah would hand him over to Saul. The oracle left David no illusion on this subject. He hastened therefore to leave Keilah with six hundred men, and remained in a mountain in the wilderness of Ziph, near Hebron, where he lived an adventurous life, hiding himself in caverns and strong places.*

Hebron is nearly at the summit of the mountain range of Judah, which runs several leagues to the south. Upon this continuation of the line of separation between the Mediterranean and the Dead Sea stood, and still stand, the towns or villages of Zip, Carmel, and Maon.† To the west of these places the country is rich and fertile; but to the east, on the side of the Dead Sea, is the fearful wilderness of Judah. It was there that David fixed the head-quarters of his band. Saul could do nothing against him. The Hebronites seemed favourable to him. To the south were the Jerahmelites and the Kenites, always friendly to Israel.

Zip and Maon were the real centres of the kingdom of David. The difference between him and Saul became every day more violent. The power of Saul was hardly owned anywhere but in Benjamin. Judah, in reality, was for David. However, the Ziphites betrayed their guest. They went to Gibeon and denounced him to Saul, who arrived with a strong force to seize him.

* See *Scenery of David's Outlaw Life*, in *Survey of Western Palestine*, special papers, pp. 208 and following

† The names of these localities still exist.

DAVID'S EARLY LIFE.—DEATH OF SAUL.

David was at that moment in the desert on the rock of Slips, near Maon, and Saul was pressing him closely when he heard that the Philistines had invaded the land, and he was obliged to return. It was afterwards thought that the rock derived its name from this event, as David had there slipped like an eel between the fingers of his enemy.

David, fearing that Saul after having defeated the Philistines would turn back upon him, left the region of Zip and descended towards the Dead Sea, where he established himself in the strongholds above Engeddi. These mountains seem only accessible to the chamois. Saul, however, went there with two thousand picked men commanded by Abner. According to a pretty story, cleverly invented if it be not true, David, hiding in a cave, at one moment had his enemy in his hand, but was satisfied with cutting off the skirt of his raiment. According to another anecdote, still more artistically arranged and worthy of the romance of *Antar*, David found means to steal from Saul his lance and his pitcher of water, which furnished him with a good opportunity for laughing at Abner. David, if one excepts the consequences which are inseparable from brigandage, behaved with relative moderation. His conduct towards the Maonite Nabal, a wealthy man who owned many flocks in the neighbourhood, is related as a prodigy of wisdom. With the ordinary feeling of a Bedouin who thinks that he ought to be paid for what he does not steal, and who looks upon himself as the protector of the people he does not plunder, David's men observed one day to Nabal that not one of his sheep was missing, which on the part of half-starved neighbours was very meritorious. Nabal was churlish; his wife Abigail made it up by hospitality. Nabal died a few days afterwards, and David married Abigail. He also married another woman of those parts, called Ahinoam. Mikal had not followed David in his exile. As a woman, according to the ideas of those days, should never remain without a husband, her father had given her to one of his officers of the tribe of Benjamin.

An incident in the wandering life of David, far more difficult to justify, was his sojourn among the most bitter enemies of his country, the Philistines. There can, however, be no doubt about it. David spent six months, accompanied by six hundred men and his two wives, with the son of the king of Gath, Achish, who gave him Ziklag, in the country of the Philistines, which from that time belonged to the kings of Judah. This became a complete Israelitish colony. Abiathar with his ephod represented the worship of Iahveh in its chief functions, which consisted in giving advice with regard to the future.

From Ziklag David sent out expeditions which pillaged and massacred the nomad tribes of the desert of Paran, especially the Amalekites. These tribes were the friends of the Philistines and the enemies of Israel. David therefore considered it patriotic to do them all the harm he could. Fearing, on the other hand, that these massacres would displease the Phi-

DAVID'S EARLY LIFE.—DEATH OF SAUL.

listines, he took the precaution of killing men, women, and children. He brought back to Gath, in the way of booty, nothing but the flocks and goods stolen. When Achish asked him against whom he had directed his last raid, he replied, " On the side of the Negeb [*] of Judah," or "against the Jerhamelites," or "against the Kenites," tribes friendly to Israel. Achish was delighted, for he shared the booty, and said to himself that by such exploits David rendered himself odious to his fellow-countrymen; and this would oblige him to remain in his service for ever.

The situation became still more embarrassing when Achish informed David of his intention to undertake an expedition against the Israelites, and to appoint him upon his own body-guard. David replied in an evasive manner. It was now question of a real war and not of a simple raid, the army of the Philistines marching towards the plain of Jezreel with the intention of establishing itself there in a durable manner, as also at Bethsean and in the valley of the Jordan.[†] David and his men marched in the rear with Achish. That good fortune which had so often stood by him favoured him on this occasion, backed it is true by his own superlative cunning, and extricated him from this most dangerous position. The lords of the Philistines, very justly it must be said, pointed out to Achish how much it was to be feared

---

[*] *Negeb* means the south, and signified the southern or hot part of Judah.

[†] First Book of Samuel, ch. xxxi., v. 7, 10.

that David would turn round upon them in the battle and reconcile himself to his old master at the expense of his new allies. David was sent away and returned to Ziklag in three days.

A terrible surprise awaited David and his men. Taking advantage of their absence the Amalekites had invaded the Negeb, pillaging equally the Judahites, the Calebites, and the Philistines. They had seized upon Ziklag and had burned it. The women and all that was there had fallen into their hands, and they had gone into the desert. Great was the desolation. The two wives of David, Ahinoam and Abigail, were captives. The people had lost their sons and their daughters. There were symptoms of indiscipline, and there was a talk of stoning David, who resolved, after consulting the oracle, to go in pursuit of the Amalekites. He made Abiathar bring forth the ephod, and he inquired of Iahveh, "Shall I pursue after this troop? Shall I overtake them?" And Iahveh replied, "Pursue, for thou shalt surely overtake them and without fail recover all." David set out with six hundred men. At the brook of Besor two hundred could go no farther. He continued his march with the four hundred who remained.

An Egyptian, the slave of an Amalekite, whom they found in the fields half dead with hunger, led them to the camp of the Amalekites. They found them eating and drinking and dancing, and rejoicing over the great spoil they had taken out of the land of the Philistines and out of the land of Judah. David slew

DAVID'S EARLY LIFE.—DEATH OF SAUL.

the whole band, save some young men who seized upon the camels and fled. The comrades of David recovered all that they had lost, and David recovered his two wives. They carried back with them immense flocks and herds.

An idea worthy of the scamps who composed the troop of David then occurred to these victorious bandits; it was that the Philistines, the Judahites, and the Calebites would come and reclaim their property, and that it would be necessary at least to share the plunder with the stragglers who had remained behind at the brook of Besor. At the head of the column they cried, "This is David's spoil," to show that those who had not taken part in the expedition had lost their rights to what was formerly their property; in other terms, that everything had become the property of the Amalekites, and then that of the small expeditionary force. When they met the stragglers of Besor, the dispute was sharp. The scamps who had taken part in the expedition would only restore to the stragglers their wives and their children. David considered that the former proprietors of the stolen goods had lost all right to them; but "he made it a statute and an ordinance," that those who remained with the baggage should have their part in the spoil, and this principle became an absolute rule in Israel.

David took a large share for himself, out of which he sent handsome presents to his friends in Judah, to the elders of the cities, especially to those of Hebron, Eshtemoa, and Hormah. The Kenites and the Jerahmelites were not forgotten, and the holy city of Bethel received its share. This successful raid had serious consequences. Up to that time David had been poor. The spoil taken from the Amalekites had placed great riches in his hands. Ambitious as he was he saw in this wealth merely a way to increase his influence. Judah was soon gained over. The elders of the cities had all become his friends. How was it possible not to recognise that a man who succeeded so well must be, as his name indicated, the "favourite of Iahveh"?

What above all is extraordinary in this run of good fortune is that his adversaries died just at the moment necessary for his welfare. Saul and Jonathan disappeared at the same moment, and at the very hour that the adherents of David would have wished. On hearing of the bold advance made by the Philistines in the direction of Jezreel, Saul went from Gibeah with his son, and marched bravely to the north. The two armies met beyond Jezreel. The moral condition of Saul was deplorable. The effects of prolonged religious error exhibited themselves in a pitiful manner. By dint of constantly seeking to discern the opinion of Iahveh in the replies of the *urim* and *thummim*, and by other frivolous means, he had become incapable of acting with decision. Samuel, who while he lived was always his dreaded prophet, had died at Ramah, without leaving any heir to his spiritual authority. Samuel had on several occasions found rivals who disputed with him the feeble mind of Saul; necro-

DAVID'S EARLY LIFE.—DEATH OF SAUL.

mancers, sorcerers, ventriloquists. These puerile illusions were in vogue among simple-minded people. The hollow and distant voice of the ventriloquist, appearing to come from the other world, was considered as the voice of the *refaim*, leading a miserable existence under ground. Like all simple-minded people, dominated by vulgar illusions, the Israelites believed in ghosts, in voices, and in spirits. They attributed to certain persons, especially to women, the power of holding communication with the dead, and of making them speak. The *nabis*, whose art was often not much more serious, were naturally jealous of the authors of these tricks. Samuel had them banished by Saul.[*] But the fact of prohibiting chimeras is a proof that they are believed in, and merely lends them importance in the minds of credulous people.

Saul was with his army on the slopes of Gilboa, and nearly in the position formerly occupied by Gideon.[†] The Philistines were encamped opposite to him, at Shunem, on the ground afterwards occupied by Kléber in 1799. Saul was afraid and hesitated. He inquired of Iahveh, who answered him neither by dreams nor by *urim* nor by the prophets. Samuel failed him. Samuel had been his good genius. Saul had been accustomed to act only on the advice of the seer of Ramah; deprived of him he could no longer live. He wished to see him again, at no matter what price. It was then that the unfortunate king heard of

---
[*] First Book of Samuel, ch. xxviii., v. 8, 9.
[†] See p. 263.

a witch who practised her art not far from there, at Endor. He disguised himself and went to Endor with two men. The witch at first suspected a snare. She asked Saul whom she should bring up. The king replied, "Samuel." "Why hast thou deceived me," said the woman, "for thou art Saul?" "Be not afraid, what sawest thou?" "I saw gods ascending out of the earth." "What form is he of?" "An old man cometh up, and he is covered with a mantle."

Saul did not doubt that this was Samuel. "Why," said the spirit, "hast thou disquieted me, to make me come up?" "I am sore distressed," said Saul, "for the Philistines make war on me; God is departed from me and answereth me no more, neither by prophets nor by dreams; therefore I have called thee that thou mayest make known unto me what I shall do." This story has been handed down to us by the theocratic narrator, who naturally makes Samuel speak in a manner corresponding to his own ideas concerning the downfall of Saul.

Facts agreed only too well with these forebodings. The Philistines gained a complete victory. Three sons of Saul, Jonathan, Abinadab, and Melchishua, fell. Saul himself was pierced through with an arrow, and fearing to be abused by the enemy called upon his armour-bearer to run him through. The armour-bearer refused, and so Saul flung himself upon his sword.

The mountains of Gilboa were strewn with the dead. Among the corpses found by the conquerors were

DAVID'S EARLY LIFE.—DEATH OF SAUL.

those of Saul and his three sons. They cut off their heads, took their armour and set it up in the house of Astaroth, fastening their bodies to the wall of Beth-shan. But the men of Jabesh-Gilead, whom Saul had formerly saved, went by night and took away the bodies and brought them to Jabesh.* They burned them there, and buried their bones under a tree; then they fasted for seven days. Afterwards David removed the remains from Jabesh to Selah, to the tomb of the family of the sons of Kish.

David, who was at Ziklag, on hearing of the death of Saul and of Jonathan, made a great display of grief. The most ancient collection of songs contains one attributed to him, on the death of the two heroes —a song which opened with a vivid apostrophe to the mountain which witnessed the disaster:—

The beauty of Israel is slain upon thy high places; how are the mighty fallen.†

*   *   *   *   *

---

* First Book of Samuel, ch. xxxi.; compare with First Book of Chronicles, ch. x., inferior as regards text.

† Second Book of Samuel, ch. i., v. 17 and following.

CHAPTER XVII.

ISH-BOSHETH SUCCEEDS SAUL.—DAVID KING OF HEBRON.

In addition to Jonathan and his two brothers, killed in the battle on the mountains of Gilboa, Saul had a fourth son, named Ish-bosheth, upon whom the party opposed to David kept their eyes fixed, especially as Jonathan had almost abdicated, openly declaring (as the adherents of David asserted) that on the death of his father it was David who should reign. After the battle of Gilboa, Abner, who had probably passed the Jordan with the remains of the army,[*] proclaimed Ish-bosheth at Mahanaim, in Gilead. Ish-bosheth was recognised by all Israel with the exception of the tribe of Judah. Then arose the distinction between the words *Israel* and *Judah*,[†] which eighty years afterwards may be said to have become, as it were, two hostile standards. Judah, as regards the nation of the Beni-Jacob, became a separate unity. The division, for a moment suppressed by the bravery of Saul, re-

---

[*] First Book of Samuel, ch. xxxi., v. 7.
[†] See Second Book of Samuel, ch. i., v. 9 ; First Book of Kings, ch. i., v. 35.

appeared; so little did unity enter into the spirit of the ancient populations still mainly engaged in tribal rivalities and in contests regarding chiefs!

While Ish-bosheth was being proclaimed beyond the Jordan, David did not move from his retreat at Ziklag. Though mourning for Saul, he was taking steps to succeed him. By his gifts he had won over nearly all the tribe of Judah. To give to one what has been stolen from another is a device which, so selfish is man, nearly always succeeds. Besides, David had formed with his brigands the nucleus of a solid army. Three Bethlehemites, all three belonging to his family, had become in his school very bold soldiers; they were Joab, Asahel, and Abishai, all three sons of Zeruiah, the sister or sister-in-law of David. The brigands of Ziklag determined on seizing Hebron, the chief town in those parts. David, according to custom, consulted the ephod of Abiathar. He asked, "Shall I go up into any of the cities of Judah?" Iahveh replied, "Go up." And David asked again, "Whither shall I go up?" and he said, "To Hebron." So David went up thither with his two wives, Ahinoam and Abigail, and his band, and they encamped in the neighbourhood of Hebron. The tribe of Judah joined them, and David was unanimously proclaimed King of Judah (about 1050 B.C.). He was then thirty years of age.

Henceforwards his views extended to the whole of Israel. He announced his election as King of Judah to the different cities, in particular to Jabesh-Gilead, which he thanked for the manner in which it had buried the ashes of Saul. He behaved in all respects as the heir and partner of Saul, making it plain that he had at heart the interests of all Israel.[*] To the bravery, the flexibility, the talent, which he had exhibited up to then, he was about to join the skill of the consummate politician, the subtleties of the most refined casuist, the doubtful art of taking advantage of every crime without ever directly committing one.

The gratitude which he owed to the family of Saul did not stand much in his way. He contented himself with speaking with compunction of Saul and Jonathan; he did not consider that he owed anything to Ishbosheth. This latter appears to have been a man of very limited parts, who was governed by Abner. From Mahanaim, Abner took him to the country of Benjamin, where the house of Saul was deeply rooted. The first encounter between his adherents and those of David took place at Gibeon. Joab and Abner, the chiefs of the two armies, met on either side of the reservoir, which is still visible. They began by a combat of twelve against twelve; then a battle took place which ended in favour of David.

The three sons of Zeruiah performed prodigies of valour that day. Asahel, who was a swift runner, determined to kill Abner. It was Abner who killed him, but not without regret, for he knew that his blood would stand between him and Joab. Joab and

[*] Second Book of Samuel, ch. ii., v. 5 and following.

DAVID KING OF HEBRON.

Abishai pursued Abner in the direction of the Jordan, but the Benjamites retired in good order, and formed up again in battle array on the top of a hill. Negotiations were opened. The men of Abner succeeded in recrossing the Jordan and in reaching Mahanaim. Joab and his army marched all night, and came to Hebron. Asahel was buried in the tomb of his family at Bethlehem.

This war of skirmishes between the two kingdoms continued for a long time. The power of David increased day by day, while that of Ish-bosheth diminished. A harem quarrel sowed dissension between Ish-bosheth and Abner. The latter began to find that there was much to say in favour of having a single king from Dan to Beersheba. Concessions were made on both sides. David insisted as a preliminary condition that his wife, Mikal, the daughter of Saul, should be restored to him. This was accorded, in spite of the remonstrances of her new husband. Abner now laboured with a will at the reconciliation of the two parties. Nearly all the generals of Ish-bosheth were won over. Abner came to Hebron with twenty men. David received him with apparent cordiality. Abner took upon himself the task of effecting a prompt pacification.

They had not taken into account the honour of Joab, absolutely pledged according to Hebrew-Arab ideas to avenge the death of Asahel. Joab was absent from Hebron on a raid when Abner came. On his arrival he learned that Abner was leisurely returning to the land of Benjamin. He reproached David for having allowed such a man to escape, took means to induce Abner to return to Hebron, and drew him aside between two gates and slew him.

David protested that he was not responsible for the death of Abner, of which Joab alone was guilty; and he cursed Joab in a most terrible manner, knowing that his malediction would have no effect. He made his people go into mourning, and he buried Abner in pomp at Hebron. He himself followed the bier and wept aloud on the tomb, and he composed an elegy for Abner as he had composed one for Jonathan. Only one verse has been preserved, which appears to imply a little irony: "Died Abner as a fool dieth? Thy hands were not bound nor thy feet put into fetters. As a man falleth before wicked men so fellest thou."*

David pretended to be inconsolable. It was necessary to force him to take food. Some persons may find it strange that in spite of his despair he left Joab unpunished. David made the remark that although he was king he had no great power and that these men (the sons of Zeruiah) were stronger than he was, and he called upon Iahveh to chastise them. The people believed, or pretended to believe, in his sincerity, and entirely approved of his conduct. In reality, he reaped the fruit of the assassination. Abner would have greatly hampered his policy, and

* Second Book of Samuel, ch. iii., v. 88 and following.

moreover the death of that chief was a severe blow to the party of Ish-bosheth.

That unfortunate sovereign was abandoned by every one at Mahanaim. He was assassinated in his bed by two Benjamites, who carried his head to Hebron. David, as usual, expressed his indignation, and ordered that the hands and feet of the assassins should be cut off and that they should be crucified near the pool of Hebron. The head of Ish-bosheth was put in the tomb of Abner. His unstable reign had lasted about two years.

Thanks to this second murder, the responsibility for which David warmly repudiated, the monarchy of Israel was definitively established. The son of Jesse had succeeded; his throne was founded for five hundred years. All the tribes came to Hebron and tendered their submission, saying, "Behold, we are thy bone and thy flesh. In time past, when Saul was king, thou leddest Israel to battle. It was to thee that Iahveh said, Thou shalt feed my people Israel and shalt be a prince over Israel." The league was concluded between them; David was anointed with oil, and from that moment became inviolable and sacred.

Thus what neither Ephraim, nor Gilead, nor Benjamin had been able to do, Judah fully realised. Hebron became the capital of Israel, and David continued to reside there for five years and a half. His family began to establish themselves there. He contracted alliances, in particular with Talmai, king of

Geser,* whose daughter, Maaka, he married. Ahinoam gave birth to his eldest son, Amnon; Abigail gave birth to Kileab (or Delaïa);† Maaka gave birth to Absolom; Haggit gave birth to Adoniah; Abital gave birth to Sefatiah; Eglon gave birth to Itream.

David had no longer any rival. Of the family of Saul there remained but one child who was a cripple, Merribaal,‡ the son of Jonathan. He was five years old when the news of the death of Saul and of Jonathan arrived. The slave to whom he had been confided fled with so much haste that she allowed him to fall, and this made him lame in both legs.§ We shall see amid what vicissitudes the agitated existence of this unfortunate youth was passed.

* No doubt Geser in the south-west desert. Joshua, ch. xiii., v. 2; First Book of Samuel, ch. xxvii., v. 8.

† Name altered.

‡ Or *Mephibaal*. But there is no theophoric name in *Miph* or *Miphi*. Compare First Book of Chronicles, ch. viii., v. 34. See above, p. 169.

§ First Book of Samuel, ch. iv., v. 4.

CHAPTER XVIII.

DAVID KING OF JERUSALEM.

HEBRON was a Hittite city, the centre of an ancient civilisation, which to some extent had been inherited by the tribe of Judah.* It was undoubtedly the capital of Judah, a city of the highest religious character, full of recollections and traditions. It could boast of fine public buildings, good water, and a vast and well-kept pool. The unification of Israel had just been accomplished there. It was only natural that Hebron should become the capital of the new kingdom. Though at a considerable distance from the tribes of the north, its situation was not an undesirable one. Paris is not in the centre of France, nor is Berlin in the centre of unified Germany.

It is not easy to say what induced David to leave a city which had such ancient and evident claims for a hamlet like Jebus, which did not yet belong to him. It is probable that he found Hebron too exclusively Judahite. It was necessary not to wound the susceptibilities of the various tribes, more particularly those of Benjamin. Better a neutral city without any past.

* Hittites were still to be found in the time of David. First Book of Samuel, xxvi., v. 6.

This, no doubt, it was which hindered David from dreaming of Bethlehem as the capital of his country. The hill occupied by the Jebusites was just on the limits of Judah and of Benjamin, and was close to Bethlehem.

The position was very advantageous. A small spring within the walls allowed it to stand a siege.* A great capital would certainly have been hampered on such a site; but great cities were neither to the taste nor among the habits of these tribes. They preferred citadels easy of defence. The Jerusalem of the Jebusites fulfilled these conditions. The Jebusites pretended that their city was impregnable. They said to David, "Thou shalt not come in hither. The blind and the lame will suffice to defeat thee." After that people were accustomed, by way of fun, to call the Jebusites the lame and the blind. And it was a proverb at Jerusalem, "The blind and the lame shall not come into the house." †

The Jebusite city was composed of the fortress of Sion, which must have been situated where the mosque of El Akasa‡ now stands, and of a lower town (Ophel)

* Now called the Well of the Virgin.

† Second Book of Samuel, ch. v., v. 8. I read ציון instead of צנור. Acts, ch. iii., v. 2 ; John, ch. ix., v. 1.

‡ The true position of Sion has been definitively fixed on the eastern hill of Jerusalem by the works of Messrs. Schick, Guthe, and Klaiber. See the *Zeitschrift der deutschen Palæstina-Verein*, t. iii., iv., v. (1880, 1881, 1882). The pretended Mount Moriah should be eliminated from a serious topography of Jerusalem. The name of Mount Moriah is symbolic, and it is by a supposition without value that the author of the Chronicles (Second Book of Chronicles,

DAVID KING OF JERUSALEM.

which runs down from there to the well which they called *Gihon*. David took the fortress of Sion, and gave the greater portion of the neighbouring lands to Joab,* and probably left the lower town to the Jebusites.† That population, reduced to an inferior situation, lost all energy, thanks to the new Israelitish influx, and played no important part in the history of Jerusalem.

David rebuilt the upper town of Sion, the citadel or *millo*, and all the neighbouring quarters. This is what they called the city of David. The money which David had gained with his bands of Adullam and Ziklag allowed him to undertake important constructions. Tyre was then the centre of civilisation in southern Syria. The arts, especially architecture, were highly developed there. This Syrian, or, it may rather be said, this Phœnician art, was Egyptian art modified according to the materials of the coast of Syria. Syria has neither marble nor granite to be compared with that of Egypt, but the timber furnished by Lebanon was the finest in the world. From Tyre to Jerusalem came a regular army of architects, stone-cutters, carpenters, and wood-carvers, as well as loads of materials such as Judah did not produce, especially

---

ch. iii., v. 1) identifies this imaginary place with the hill where Solomon built a temple. The name of Moriah is not mentioned in the really historical books.

* First Book of Chronicles, ch. xi., v. 6, 8, passage of little value surely and in contradiction with Second Book of Samuel, ch. v., but which must be founded upon some tradition respecting Joab.

† Judges, ch. i., v. 21 ; Zechariah, ch. ix. (very old), v. 7.

cedar. The Tyrian architects built David a palace near the Millo, in the upper town of Sion, near the south-east angle of the present Haram. Art, properly so called, had up to that time been unknown in those countries. The prestige acquired by David was extraordinary. The land of Canaan had never enjoyed anything like so much splendour and power.

As for Israel, David gave it what it had quite lacked up to that day, a capital. There will be schisms and protests; it will take some time for this capital to be loved and adopted by all Israel. But the corner-stone is laid, and, as all the sympathies and antipathies of Israel have been shared by the whole world, Jerusalem will one day be the beloved capital of humanity. This little hill of Sion will become the magnetic pole of the love and poetry of the religious world. Who accomplished this? It was David. David in reality created Jerusalem. Out of an ancient citadel, which remained standing as a memorial of an inferior order of things, he made a capital, feeble at first, but which was soon to occupy an important place in the history of humanity. *Gloriosa dicta sunt de te, civitas Dei.* For centuries the world will dispute the possession of Jerusalem. An irresistible attraction will draw thither people of various races. This rocky hill, without a horizon, without trees, almost without water, will cause hearts to leap with joy thousands of miles away. Every one will exclaim with the pious Israelite, "*Lætatus sum in his quæ dicta sunt mihi: In domum Domini ibimus.*"

DAVID KING OF JERUSALEM.

Every aggrandisement on the part of Israel was an aggrandisement on the part of Iahveh. Iahvehism, up to that time so ill organised, is now to have a metropolis and soon a temple. Not for another four hundred years will this metropolis become exclusive among all other places of worship; but the spot is fixed upon. Among so many other hills which Iahveh might have preferred, the choice is made.* The religious battle-field is marked out.

David was the unconscious agent of these great humanitarian designs. Few people appear to have been less religious : few of the adorers of Iahveh had less understanding of the sentiment which was destined to uphold Iahvehism—justice. David was Iahvehist, as Mesa, that king of Moab whose confession is still extant, was Camosist. Iahveh was his tutelary deity, and Iahveh was a god who caused his favourites to prosper.† Besides, Iahveh was very useful; he spoke valuable oracles through the ephod of Abiathar. This was all, for David and his companions had no aversion to Baal.‡ David had no more idea than had Gideon, Abimelech, and Jephthah what the religion of Iahveh would become in the hands of the great prophets of the eighth century.

But he was the founder of Jerusalem and the father

---

* Psalm lxviii., v. 16 and following.
† First Book of Samuel, ch. xviii., v. 14.
‡ One of the sons of David was called indifferently *Eliada* or *Baaliada*, Second Book of Samuel, ch. v., v. 16 ; First Book of Chronicles, ch. xiv., v. 7.

of a dynasty intimately associated with the work of Israel. That marked him out as a subject for future legends. One never can handle with impunity, even indirectly, those great problems which are being worked out in the hidden depths of humanity.

We shall witness these transformations century after century. We shall find the outlaw of Adullam and of Ziklag assuming little by little the airs of a saint, becoming the author of the Psalms, the sacred *chorège*,* the type of the future Saviour. Jesus will be called the Son of David! The evangelical biography will be distorted in a number of instances, in order to make the life of the Messiah reproduce the features of that of David! Pious souls delighting over the sentiments so full of resignation and tender melancholy contained in the finest of liturgical books will fancy themselves in communion with this bandit; humanity will believe in a future state on the testimony of David, who never dreamed of it himself, and of the Sibyl, who never existed. *Teste David cum Sibylla!* O divine comedy!

[* The χορηγός (*choregus*) among the Greeks was the person who found money for spectacles. — Note by TRANSLATOR.]

www.ingramcontent.com/pod-product-compliance
Lightning Source LLC
Chambersburg PA
CBHW022007300426
44117CB00005B/73